PRAISE FOR DAN BUCHANAN AND *THE WRECK OF HMS SPEEDY*

"*The Wreck of HMS Speedy: The Tragedy That Shook Upper Canada* is a terrific page-turner—a vivid recreation of a story that rocked 1804 Upper Canada. More than a story of a shipwreck, Dan Buchanan captures the swirl of events from a murder to an arrest, and the political decision that led to twenty people drowning on Lake Ontario."

> —*David Raymont, Past President,*
> *York Pioneer and Historical Society, Toronto*

"HMS *Speedy* had one stop along the way on its last journey of the season, to discharge passengers destined to attend a murder trial, including an accused prisoner chained in its hold. But the *Speedy* never reached its destination; the trial didn't take place; and it was almost two hundred years before a dedicated local diver sighted what he believed to be the wreck of the vessel in shallow water off Presqu'ile Provincial Park near the small community of Brighton. How did this marine tragedy change history? And is the discovered wreck really the remains of the HMS *Speedy*? You need to read this book to find out."

> —*Peter Lockyer, Owner/operator of History Lives Here, Picton,*
> *Prince Edward County*

"Dan's knack for pinning all relevant information to the personal lives of the characters that he is researching lends a human warmth to the book, and his meticulous research lends authenticity to his theories. In short, Dan presents local history as your stories, the way your favourite aunt or uncle would recount a fascinating family legend that you enjoyed hearing over and over."

> —*Phil Spencer was a member of the H.M.S. Speedy*
> *Foundation and lives on the north shore of*
> *Presqu'ile Bay directly north of the Speedy site.*

"Dan has a way with history. His combination of diligent research and finely crafted writing deliver an enjoyable journey for the reader. Whether it is a personal historic story (*Murder in the Family*) or averting a national crisis (*38 Hours to Montreal*), Dan takes the reader along for the ride. Historical accuracy and a gifted writing style make Dan's books informative and a pleasure to read. They are a welcome addition to any bookcase."

—*Catherine Stutt, Editor,* County & Quinte Living *magazine,*
and active member of the Brighton Digital Archives

"It's not often we can put the words history and page-turner in the same sentence. Dan Buchanan's history books make it possible. He puts the story in history. Dan's assiduous research and witty writing make every one of his books a treat."

—*Lindi Pierce is an active blogger on*
www.ancestralroofs.blogspot.com

THE WRECK OF
HMS
SPEEDY

Other books by Dan Buchanan

Murder in the Family: The Dr. King Story

*38 Hours to Montreal: William Weller and the Governor
General's Race of 1840*

THE WRECK OF
HMS
SPEEDY

The Tragedy That
Shook Upper Canada

DAN BUCHANAN

MILNER &
ASSOCIATES INC
· EDITING · PUBLISHING · COMMUNICATIONS · CONSULTING ·

ISBNs: 978-1-988344-24-9 (print)
       978-1-988344-25-6 (e-book)

Production Credits
Front cover, painting: *Last Fight of the Speedy* by Pete Rindlisbacher,
     www.rindlisbachermarineart.com
Publishing consultant: Beth Bruder
Developmental editor: Sylvia Barrett
Copy editor: Lindsay Humphreys
Cover design: Adrian So, AdrianSoDesign.com
Interior design and typesetting: Adrian So, AdrianSoDesign.com
Publisher: Milner & Associates Inc.
Printer: Friesens

Published by Milner & Associates Inc.
www.milnerassociates.ca

Printed in Canada
10 9 8 7 6 5 4 3 2 1

DEDICATION

My dad used to ask me when I was going to write a book. For him, a genealogy website with tens of thousands of names was no substitute for a nice, solid, paper book. Charles Buchanan passed away in 2012, a few years before I published my first book, so he did not get to see the tangible product he had envisioned. Now I am publishing my third book, and I expect Dad would be pleased.

Charles Buchanan grew up in Colborne and was an excellent student. In fact, he liked school. However, when he was fourteen, his father said that was enough education and arranged a job as hired man on the farm of an uncle. Charles loved his dad, and so he followed the path set out, learning to be a good farmer. After he married Mary Ames in Codrington in 1949, he combined the role of husband and father with that of lifelong student.

It started with Sunday school and the school board. Then it escalated to helping the local minister and having deep involvement in the Masonic lodge. He learned how to prepare a message and deliver it in an effective way. People looked forward to hearing him speak. My father grew into the role of layman minister, travelling around the countryside, filling in where ministers were ill or on holidays. As his oldest boy, I sometimes went with him, mostly in the winter, when an extra pair of hands might be needed for snow shovelling or an extra push required to negotiate a slippery slope.

By the time Charles Buchanan reached age fifty, he was a renowned layman and decided to follow his dream. With support from his second wife, Shirley, and others, he pursued a degree in theology at Queen's University in Kingston. In 1973, Reverend Charles Buchanan began the career that he really wanted, as a full-time United Church minister. Until retirement in 1985, he improved attendance as well as the financial foundation of the churches where he was minister, and he got people to work together.

After retirement, my dad was as busy as ever in a freelance role. He was asked to fill in for ministers who were away, or at churches where a permanent minister was being sought. There was constant travelling to perform weddings, funerals, and christenings, often for people who recalled him performing similar rites for earlier generations of their family. Rev. Buchanan was in demand.

When people see me at events and realize I am the son of Reverend Charles Buchanan, I often hear stories of how my dad, in his role as a volunteer chaplain at Belleville General Hospital, helped to make the worst day of their lives a little less bad. Rev. Buchanan seemed to have a skill for comforting people in stressful situations, knowing the right thing to say in order to help them keep their faith.

Sometimes, people say that I remind them of my dad.

A fellow could do worse.

CONTENTS

Preface   xi

Map of *Speedy* Places   xii

Part I   1

Chapter 1   Death at the Trading Post   3

Chapter 2   Over the Scugog Carrying Place   9

Chapter 3   Along the Shore to York   17

Chapter 4   Muddy Little York   25

Chapter 5   A Critical Question   43

Chapter 6   The Survey   51

Chapter 7   Planning for a Trial   61

Chapter 8   The Ship and the Captain   69

Chapter 9   The Accused and the Law   79

Chapter 10   Preparations at Newcastle   87

Chapter 11   All Aboard!   93

Chapter 12   On the Way to Newcastle   101

Chapter 13   Beacon Fire   111

Chapter 14   A Stop to All Business at York   117

Chapter 15   Widow Paxton   127

Chapter 16   Life Goes On   133

Chapter 17   No Poem for Ogetonicut   143

Part II   151

Chapter 18   Searching for HMS *Speedy*   153

Chapter 19   99.99% Sure   167

Epilogue   The Mystery of HMS *Speedy*   177

Acknowledgements   181

Appendix A   Details of the *Speedy* Project   185

Appendix B   "Loss of the Speedy"   195

Appendix C   "Elegy"   199

Appendix D   Recollections of Mary Warren Breckenridge   205

Appendix E   Newcastle Town Status: Petition and Legislation   209

Appendix F   *Statutes of Upper Canada*   215

Appendix G   More Information   217

Notes   218

Bibliography   245

Illustration Credits   249

Index   251

About the Author   260

PREFACE

My phone rang one day in September 2018, a year after the death of underwater explorer Ed Burtt. It was his long-time companion, Kirsten, on the other end. She said she had documents from Ed's search for the remains of HMS *Speedy*. Was I interested in seeing them? Absolutely!

A few hours later, Kirsten arrived at my door with a large plastic bin overflowing with file folders and three-ring binders. I stammered about how long it would take to go through everything before I could return all those documents, and she replied, "Oh, you keep them."

Ed and I had talked about writing a book, but we'd had different approaches, so it went nowhere. Now, with all his original records, the road was wide open for a new publication on HMS *Speedy*. I knew I was stepping into a minefield. Most of my history work had to this point been benign, mainly because that's my nature. However, after reading this cache of new information, I knew the *Speedy* story deserved a fresh airing.

There have been more than forty-five accounts of what happened in 1804. Most provide a similar basic story, but the peripheral details are often different. The following version is told from original documents and, where there are multiple records, is based on the earliest available accounts.

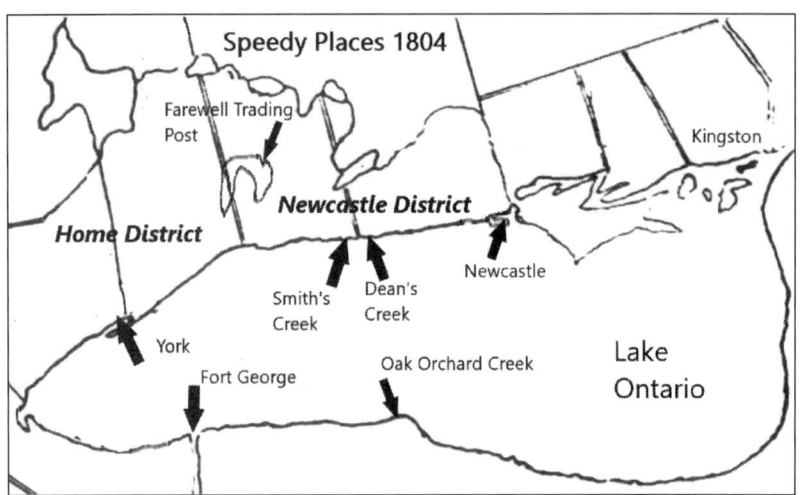

Lake Ontario was the highway in 1804 and all the events related to HMS *Speedy* happened around its shores or on its waters. This sketch of Lake Ontario illustrates the locations of events from the murder of John Sharp on Lake Scugog to the sailing of HMS *Speedy* to Newcastle. We even see where Moody Farewell was camped, at Dean's Creek, the last person to see HMS *Speedy* before it was lost. Across the lake on the US side, is Oak Orchard where Captain Paxton's binnacle washed ashore.

PART I

CHAPTER 1

DEATH AT THE TRADING POST

A birchbark canoe eased onto Lake Scugog's sandy beach with a slight crunch from the underlying gravel. The young man jumped into the shallow water and pulled the heavily loaded craft farther up onto the shore. On this sunny day in early May 1804, Moody Farewell was glad to be back at the trading post. Earlier that day, he had paddled down the Scugog River, then crossed the open water at the eastern end of the lake, finally arriving at the south end of a peninsula that jutted down from the mainland, where the trading post was located.[1] Moody did not see his brother's canoe on the beach, which meant that William was still on his way from the northwest, hopefully laden with furs. He stretched his legs as he gazed across the calm waters, but there was no canoe in sight.

Lake Scugog is about thirty kilometres north of Oshawa, which is sixty kilometres east of Toronto. In 1804, there were only three towns on Lake Ontario: York, which would later be Toronto; Newark at the Niagara River; and Kingston at the far-east end of the lake. York had been the capital of Upper Canada for a decade and Kingston was the supply depot for the whole area, with the army base, the naval base, and the Point Frederick shipyards.

Lake Ontario was the water highway for the province. Roads were few and far between, though ancient trails were available for trips into the interior. A small number of settlers had established themselves close to the lakeshore, but the lands to the north were still largely unknown to the newcomers.

The Farewell brothers were agents for the North West Company under the leadership of Lawrence and Jacob Herkimer, who had trading posts on Rice Lake and at Smith's Creek,[2] which would later be called Port Hope. Only two years before, the Herkimers had set up the small trading post on Lake Scugog, in order to direct more furs from the area into the company's stores in Montreal. The Farewell brothers were put in charge of the new post. They were new to the fur trade but had taken to the life with enthusiasm.

As Moody Farewell pulled his pack of clothes and personal items from the canoe, he could not help but think of his new wife, Elizabeth, who was living with her parents, Charles and Sarah Annis, near the mouth of Annis Creek, which later would be known as Oshawa Creek. The Annis family had settled near the shore of Lake Ontario in Whitby Township in 1796.[3] Moody and Elizabeth had been married just a month ago,[4] and the young husband was very anxious to see his bride.

He strode across the sandy beach and into the woods, toward the small, rough log cabin that housed the trading post. He had expected John Sharp to meet him on the shore, since the plan was for the brothers to return on this day. Sharp had been left in charge while the brothers travelled north for furs.[5] Retired from the British Army, he had hired on with the Farewells in order to make some money. Many fellows who missed the excitement and comradeship of the army chose to work in the fur trade rather than farming.

A few paces from the cabin, Moody stopped in his tracks and immediately crouched beside a bush. He didn't like what he saw. The cabin door was swinging open and there was no smoke coming from the chimney. Slowly, he edged back through the woods to the canoe and took a minute to think as he pulled out his musket and loaded it with shot and powder. With a loaded gun, Moody stood on the beach for a moment, planning his next steps.

Before he could continue, he heard William hailing him from his canoe as it neared the shore. As Moody helped his brother disembark, William asked why he had loaded the musket, and the two men had a quick discussion. They needed to survey the area to determine where Sharp might be and if there was anyone else there.

William headed south, down the shoreline, then went east through the trees, toward the creek that ran past the cabin and emptied into Lake Scugog along the southern shoreline. Moody went north a bit, then east to the cabin. If they found something, they would yell to warn the other, then join forces to deal with whatever it was.

Within a few minutes, Moody was standing in front of the cabin, when he heard a loud shout from his brother. Moody raced through the woods, toward the sound. As he neared the creek, William stepped around a bush in front of him, bent over with his hand to his mouth. He mumbled something unintelligible as he stumbled past, then fell to his knees, retching.

Glancing around the bush where William had emerged, Moody saw two legs, with no boots on the feet, no sock at all on one foot, and a woollen sock dangling in the breeze from the other. Preparing himself, Moody moved around the thicket and was met with the most horrible scene he could imagine. John Sharp was lying on his back with his arms flung out wide from his body. Pools of blood surrounded his torso, and his battered head was covered with feasting flies and bugs. Suppressing the urge to run away, Moody composed himself and tried to understand what had happened.

Immediately, one overwhelming thought came to mind: this was not a robbery. Sharp's skull had been so brutally bashed in with a club that the remaining mass of bone and flesh did not resemble a human being at all. Sure, the man's boots had been taken and probably goods from the cabin, but this act of extreme violence spoke of a more profound anger and hatred than one would expect with a robbery.

Moody considered several events of the past year, when members of the local Mississauga camps came to the trading post demanding liquor and threatening the traders. He knew there were some hot-headed young fellows who were angry at being refused, and things could grow very tense at times. Up to now, they had been able to avoid any real violence.

He also thought about a much-discussed incident the previous winter, when a young Mississauga man named Whistling Duck had been killed by a settler, Samuel Cozens, in Clarke Township.[6] The authorities had told the dead man's family that justice would be done, but after evidence suggested self-defence, no legal action was taken against Cozens. In recent weeks, word had circulated that Whistling Duck's relatives were angry, especially his brother, Ogetonicut, who was threatening to impose his own style of justice. Moody Farewell did not know if John Sharp's death was connected to Whistling Duck, but as he gazed at Sharp's lifeless body, he feared for the future.

At twenty-five years of age, William Farewell[7] was three years older than Moody[8] but shorter by a few inches and more heavily built. He insisted on being his own man but usually deferred to his younger brother when it came to figuring out what to do next. Moody suggested they complete the search they had started before finding the body. They walked together through the trees and bushes, following the creek south to the beach where visitors most often landed. There they could see evidence of several canoes and maybe half a dozen people. The tracks were fading, so they might be a couple of days old by now. The brothers began to think that this event had occurred not long after they had left on their northern trips.

They completed a sweep to the north and east, confirming there was nobody else near the trading post. Back at the cabin, they came across several broken rum bottles outside the door. Stepping carefully inside, they found empty shelves behind the counter where they kept items like tobacco, salt, and sugar. The door to the cellar, where the rum was kept, was broken and tossed on the floor. Not one bottle of rum remained.

After securing the area, the most important task was to bury their associate. They collected a blanket and two shovels from the cabin, selected an appropriate spot, and set to digging. The ground was mostly sand, so the task was not difficult. Soon they had cleared a hole about three feet deep and long enough for John Sharp's body. They rolled the body over onto the blanket, wrapped it around as best they could, then lifted the bundle into the grave. After shovelling dirt back into the space, they pounded it hard, then cut branches from nearby bushes and placed them on top to hide it from view. The brothers intended that it would remain undisturbed by man or beast.

The two men stood silently for a few minutes over their friend's fresh grave, then Moody felt it was necessary to say a few words about the deceased. They had not known him long, but he had been a reliable employee during their time together. Like the Farewell brothers, Sharp had joked about setting himself up in a tavern with the money he made in the fur trade. Sadly, he did not have a chance to realize his dream. The ceremony seemed inadequate, but it was the best they could do at the time. Solemnly, they walked back to the cabin, deep in their own thoughts.

They struck a fire, did a general cleanup, and prepared a meal, using some salt pork and potatoes that still remained in the cabin. After eating, they pulled out the last bottle of rum in their possession, one that had been stowed safely in Moody's canoe. It would provide yeoman's service on this night.

A candle flickered on the rough kitchen table and the brothers talked long after darkness fell. They were disturbed by the events of the day. As they discussed the situation, they could see that the impact of the death of John Sharp would reach far outside their own trading enterprise. A death like this could easily inflame the existing conflict between the Mississauga people across the region and the British authorities in York. In their own area, the young traders had worked hard to develop good relations with the people who provided them with furs, but, after only two years, this incident could destroy the business.

The Farewell brothers made a plan of action that night and then, after finishing the last dregs of the rum bottle, slept fitfully. In the morning, they would take both canoes south across Lake Scugog and portage over the high ground to the headwaters of Annis Creek. They wanted to continue with the original plan of taking all their furs to York where they could be sold. However, they would also visit the Mississauga camp, near the lakeshore just west of Annis Creek, and speak with the chief. They had no idea what they would find there, and it might be a tense situation. In any case, they would pursue justice for John Sharp and, at the same time, try to keep their trading business alive.

CHAPTER 2

OVER THE SCUGOG CARRYING PLACE

The brothers were up before dawn the next morning. They had a quick breakfast, closed up the cabin, and packed their canoes for the trip across Lake Scugog. They were pulling away from shore as the sun made its appearance to the east. The sky looked good for a day of travel and the two young men put their backs to the paddles, propelling the canoes easily through the light waves. It was over thirty kilometres to the shore of Lake Ontario, most of it by land, and they wanted to cover the distance in one day. Even with perfect weather and no mishaps, it would be a long trip.

They headed in a southwesterly direction, toward the south shore of Lake Scugog three kilometres away. Here they would meet the northern terminus of the trail called the Scugog Carrying Place,[1] which the Mississauga people had used for many generations to travel between Lake Scugog and Lake Ontario. It began near the shore of Lake Ontario, on the west side of what we now call Harmony Creek. Not far north, in the first concession, the trail split into two, sending one branch to the west up Annis Creek and another north and east. The eastern branch would provide the brothers with a path to the lake on this day.

Moody Farewell used this quiet time to think about what was to come. Top of mind was the image of his pretty young wife down at the Annis farm, and he revelled in the thought of wrapping her in his arms after an absence of several weeks. He knew the fur trade required lots of travel, but now that he was married, the long absences were tough to swallow. The situation required serious thought.

One idea was already in the works. Moody had his eye on a piece of land immediately north of Benjamin Wilson's farm, Lot 4 in the first concession. He had discussed the matter with his father-in-law, Charles Annis, as well as with Wilson, and all seemed thrilled with the idea. This would require a visit to a lawyer and the land office in York. The more that Moody thought about it, the more he saw it as a good thing, especially now that he was married. Certainly, his wife was all for it. Frankly, it was inevitable that he would end up a farmer, like so many young men at this time.

But right now, Moody needed to focus on the load of pelts that represented income for him and William. The death of John Sharp meant that the brothers were compelled to travel to York in short order, so they could report the murder to the authorities. At the same time, their pelts would have to end up in York in order to bring a reasonable price. The problem was, there were far more furs in their canoes than the brothers could carry on land by themselves. They would have to make some kind of arrangement to have them transported down the Scugog Carrying Place to the shore of Lake Ontario, and from there to York.

As they approached the shore, they could see the wigwams of several Mississauga families in the woods. They were in the vicinity of the modern village of Caesarea, which has a popular marina.[2] This was the northern terminus of the Scugog Carrying Place. Any key point in a commonly used trail would draw a few enterprising families who engaged in what was simply called the carrying trade. Arrangements could be made with the elders to have goods carried overland to Lake Ontario. The Mississauga men who lived here were anxious to engage in this business because it meant money in their pouches.

Two young men helped William and Moody drag their canoes up the beach and, using what very limited English they knew, guided the traders to a clearing in front of the wigwams where the elders sat. In 1804, most Mississauga people did not speak English, although many were developing sign language and learning a few common English terms. The effectiveness of this method of communication grew as more settlers came into the area and the traders engaged more directly with the people in their camps. It was often not very pretty, but everyone wanted to benefit from the exchange, so patience and humour went a long way, on both sides.

The Farewell brothers had done business here before, and so they knew what to expect. A smoking circle was convened. Then, as the whole family joined in the assembly, food and drink were passed around. Many Englishmen were impatient with this preamble. The passing of a pipe and the feasting seemed like a waste of time to them, when they were just interested in making a deal.

That's not how the Mississauga people dealt with each other, however, and not how they would deal with newcomers. It was their tradition to engage in social interaction with people before agreeing to any deal that required trust between the parties. It was a way of establishing a relationship as a basis for a business arrangement.[3] European immigrants to Canada learned that if they did not take time for this, the Mississauga people would take it as a sign of disrespect and be less likely to agree to whatever was being offered. Sometimes, the price would go up.

After the prescribed ceremonies, the Farewells engaged in serious discussion, reaching an agreement that would see their pelts transported the twenty miles down the Scugog Carrying Place in the next few days. They were to be delivered to the farm of Charles Annis at the mouth of Annis Creek. In exchange for this, the brothers agreed to bring back a dozen blankets and two new metal traps, as well as some fish hooks, when they returned from York. Another smoking circle ensued, and everyone was happy.

The furs were piled inside one of the wigwams. William and Moody said their goodbyes and, canoes on their shoulders, began the long trek over the Scugog Carrying Place. The trail headed straight south over flat ground. In modern terms, they walked south from Caesarea, along Regional Road 57. The path was well-marked and not so much cleared as trampled down by many feet over decades of use. The forest was unbroken except for small meadows here and there. There was a slight rise in the land, but it was hardly noticeable from underneath a canoe. They just kept walking.

Although it edged slightly west, the beaten track was as straight as it could be until it neared the modern village of Blackstock, where it moved farther west. Here they encountered long inclines that made walking more difficult. The travellers stopped for water and a snack, but mostly kept moving. They crossed into the northwest corner of Darlington Township, now part of Clarington, where the trail entered the eighth concession of Whitby Township.

The walking was easier once the land started downhill toward the lake, and the forest provided cooling shade as they trekked south along the western side of Harmony Creek. Soon they came to the branch in the trail near the bottom of the first concession. Here, they headed west along the broken front past small patches of cleared fields and private trails to the Annis farm.

Beginning in the early 1790s with Benjamin Wilson,[4] several families had settled in the first two concessions of Whitby Township, near the mouth of Annis Creek. Wilson moved into an abandoned trading post, on Lot 5 of the broken front, just east of Annis Creek.[5] Eleazer Lockwood,[6] a teenager when his widowed mother married Benjamin Wilson, took Lot 7, just to the west of Wilson's. Charles Annis[7] arrived in 1796 and settled just west of his neighbours, at the mouth of the large creek that was named for him.

It was nearly sunset when the Farewell brothers walked up to the Annis farmhouse and dropped their canoes. They were both tired and sore and very happy the trip was over. A warm reception awaited them, not least of which was the embrace of an excited young bride. Food and drink were spread out on the Annis kitchen table as everyone filled up on nourishment and news. Moody told all about the discovery of John Sharp's body and then sat back, astonished as Charles Annis recounted the events that had occurred here at the lakeshore.

The Mississauga people had established their spring camp in their traditional location, which happened to occupy part of the Annis farm and nearby Eleazer Lockwood's farm. On the previous day, there was much excitement in the camp after a group of young men came back from the north with tales of violence. Word went around that a white trader had been struck down during a confrontation at the trading post on Lake Scugog.

Just as Charles Annis was explaining these events to William and Moody, Eleazer Lockwood came in. Eleazer recounted how he had been working on his farm when he saw and heard a young Mississauga man, named Ogetonicut,[8] demonstrating graphically to his comrades exactly how he had bashed in the trader's head with a club. While Lockwood had been alarmed to witness this admission, he observed that the young man appeared very pleased with himself.

That was not all. News of the murder caused major anxiety among the elders of the Mississauga families camped here. They knew very well that the death of an Englishman at the hands of an Indigenous man could destroy the relationship that they had been working so hard to build with both the authorities in York and the newcomers along the lakeshore. Trouble like this might result in red-coated soldiers with muskets loaded, marching into their camp one day. There would be arrests and they might be told to leave. Worse could be imagined.

The situation in the camp was relieved to some degree by the intervention of Chief Wabbekisheco,[9] who was leader of the Mississauga people along the north shore of Lake Ontario east of York. He was known to be a wise and moderate man who had the respect of his own people as well as the English. It was evident that the chief had worked very hard to maintain peace between the two peoples over the past two decades and would show up at any place where trouble was brewing.

One well-known story of the chief's wisdom and authority, often repeated by the settlers,[10] was how he assisted Benjamin Wilson when he first settled in Whitby Township. Shortly after Wilson arrived at his new home, a group of young Mississauga men came to his cabin and confiscated many of the tools and supplies he had been allocated by the government to help him get started farming. They told Wilson in no uncertain terms that he was not welcome on land that belonged to the Mississauga people, and he should get in his boat and leave, never to return. In fact, the boat was the only thing left to the terrified family, so they boarded it and made haste for Ganaraska, the next settlement to the east, where Port Hope is located today.

By a stroke of luck, Chief Wabbekisheco happened to be there, working with trader and interpreter William Peak.[11] When Wilson described his family's ordeal, with Peak translating, the chief's response was strong and swift. He insisted that they all return to the Wilson cabin so he could correct this injustice. When they arrived, Chief Wabbekisheco went among his people and held some very intense discussions. The Wilsons were still very fearful because they were defying the clear warning to stay away.

The chief told his people that he knew very well the newcomers had made no arrangement with the Mississauga people to use the land along the lakeshore. The normal procedure would have been for the parties to sit down and negotiate an agreement for sharing the land, respecting the rights of all those involved. Benjamin Wilson had not done this and was therefore, by traditional Mississauga custom, trespassing on the land. This was seen as disrespectful, which is why the young men took it upon themselves to show the newcomers that they were not welcome.

On the other hand, the chief explained, respected leaders of the Mississauga people had placed their sign on an agreement that allowed the English settlers to use the land along the lakeshore.[12] What he did not know at this time, so could not tell his people, would become clear in the years to come. The treaty was written in English and not translated into the language of the people who had negotiated and signed it. In effect, they took the word of the English participants regarding what was in the treaty.

As a final, passionate plea, Chief Wabbekisheco tried to convince his people of what he knew in his heart. The Mississauga people were in a weak position. Their population had dwindled from more than one thousand in 1780 to a few hundred scattered over a wide area. Disease and the ravages of strong drink had disrupted their communities, and now English settlers were pushing into their traditional camping and hunting areas. The picture was not a positive one.[13]

After speaking frankly to his people, Chief Wabbekisheco came to the Wilson cabin with the leader of the group who had threatened them. With William Peak translating, the chief insisted that the young man return all the goods that had been removed. When he heard that not everything was still available, the chief ordered an equivalent value in furs be provided to the Wilsons to ensure they were fairly compensated.

Then, to emphasize the importance of peace between his people and the English, Chief Wabbekisheco called for a wampum belt,[14] which he gave to Benjamin Wilson, stating that as long as that beaded belt appeared above his door, no member of the Mississauga people would do them any harm. In effect, this episode set the stage for years of peace between the Mississauga people and the settlers in this area.

Now, in the spring of 1804, the death of John Sharp threatened to undo all that good will, and Chief Wabbekisheco was involved again. He interviewed Ogetonicut and others who were involved in the incident at the trading post. There was no attempt to hide the truth. The young man was proud that he had finally gained proper restitution for the death of his brother, Whistling Duck. Ojibwa tradition required that the families sit down and negotiate restitution in the case of wrongdoing. They did not want blood for blood but expected meaningful signs of remorse along with practical compensation.[15] The Mississauga people of Lake Scugog shared this custom.

In the case of Ogetonicut, the chief felt he had to take decisive action immediately in order to protect his people. He decided that the perpetrator must be given over to the authorities at York without delay. The very next morning, most of the people at the camp, including the frightened young man, took to their canoes and a flotilla made its way west along the shore of Lake Ontario heading for York.[16]

Before sunrise on the following day, Moody Farewell and Eleazer Lockwood set out in a light canoe, following the same path as the chief. As their paddles cut quickly through the waves, the two young men discussed how they would present what they knew about the crime. They expected there would be a lengthy interrogation and their words would be recorded. Later, they might have to testify as witnesses at a trial. It was a scary prospect.

Moody Farewell was grateful for a night with his bride and hated to leave again so soon, but duty called. As he paddled, he thought about having a cabin of his own, where his wife could set up house and care for the children they planned to have. He was warming up to this idea more and more all the time. Right now, however, he had to dig into the waves and concentrate on the task at hand. They needed to get to York.

CHAPTER 3

ALONG THE SHORE TO YORK

The north shore of Lake Ontario was still in a natural state in 1804. There were only a few scattered settlers, mostly along the new Danforth Road and farther inland, taking advantage of good farm land in the interior. The road had been pushed through from York to Kingston in 1799 but, after only a few years, had become overgrown in many places and was hardly recognized as more than a trail. Travellers generally preferred canoeing along the shoreline to the discomfort and danger of the land route.

As Moody Farewell and Eleazer Lockwood paddled west, they would have seen Mississauga camps near the mouths of major rivers and creeks, similar to the one at Annis Creek. The Mississauga people followed a traditional lifestyle, guided by the moon in pursuit of natural food sources. Grant Karcich explains the seasonal moves in his book *The Legacy of Vanished Trails*: "The different seasons focused around the cycles of the moon. The Mississauga people gave each moon a name that was associated with a plant species. The first moon was the sugar-making moon (sizubakud kegizis) and started after February 26."[1] As the snow melted and the land began to warm up, small groups went out to the sugar bushes to draw sap and make sugar, which was an important supplement to their diet.

In April came the sucker moon, sometimes also called the blossom moon, when groups would move down to the shore of Lake Ontario to catch fish, one of their most important sources of food. Families camped at the same locations for generations, beside waterways such as Annis Creek, but also farther east at the mouths of the Moira, Trent, and Ganaraska rivers, and west at the Rouge, Humber, and Credit rivers. In many of these locations, they constructed extensive fishing weirs in the shallows, designed to divert and trap the fish. These installations required constant maintenance and were the responsibility of certain families over many decades.

Moody and Eleazer may have seen a camp at the mouth of what we call Lynde Creek, near the future town of Perry's Corners, which would later be Whitby, although Windsor Harbour was still in a natural state.[2] They were more likely to find a large camp at Duffin's Creek, a significant waterway that the Mississauga people had called Salmon Creek due to the profusion of fish there for the taking. The name Duffin was given to this creek by Augustus Jones when he surveyed the area in 1793. Recent detailed research has determined that the name derives from William Duffin, an Irishman who worked as a trader at Niagara for a number of years (both before and during the War of Independence), then established a trading post here for a short time before returning to Ireland.[3]

Most of the canoe traffic would be Mississauga people heading to York to trade or moving between camps on the lakeshore to visit and trade with their brothers. Settlers also paddled to and from York to sell produce or buy manufactured goods. In some cases, they travelled to conduct business with a lawyer or the Crown Land Office, as Moody Farewell was planning to do.

Occasionally, a schooner or brig could be seen sailing farther out on the lake, delivering office-seekers to the muddy streets of York or carrying tons of food, clothing, and tools to the Mohawk settlements near the west end of Lake Ontario. Joseph Brant, who signed his name Thayendanega,[4] was a famous war chief who fought with the British during the War of Independence. After the war, he led his people to a new home in Upper Canada, all the while pressing the British hard to provide the best possible conditions. He negotiated persistently for the maximum quantity of goods to be delivered, and the authorities scrambled to meet delivery schedules set out in contracts.

The Mohawks had been stalwart allies of the British Crown during the War of Independence, so it was only fair that the British should provide them with land and a safe home in Upper Canada after the war. In order to accomplish this, the British initially allocated a parcel of land at the Bay of Quinte, where Chief John Deserontyon was the leader. Later, a second tract of land, this one on the Grand River, was provided for Joseph Brant and his people. All of these lands had been purchased from the Mississauga people, who were the recognized owners of the land north of the lakes.[5]

Most of the goods destined for Brant's people were carried by British gunboats, officially called His Majesty's Armed Vessels. There were only three or four of these ships operational on the lake at any one time; never enough, it seemed, to meet the growing demand for shipping. These gunboats were what we might call government taxis, not well-built and often difficult to sail, but providing a critical service to the government and community.

In the spring of 1804, two ships that Moody and Eleazer may have seen on the lake were the identical gunboats HMS *Swift* and HMS *Speedy*, which had been launched together in September of 1798 at the shipyards of Point Frederick, near Kingston.[6] Built specifically to provide more capacity on Lake Ontario for moving goods and people, they were about fifty-six feet long with twin masts and two small cannons, one at the bow and one at the stern, to warrant the description of gunboat. In practice, however, the weaponry was mostly for show; the real work during sailing season was the mundane drudgery of carrying tons of cargo with a few passengers, day in and day out.

In another class, there was the *Toronto Yacht*, which was launched to much acclaim at York in September 1799.[7] This ship was slightly larger than earlier ships and had cabins for a few special passengers, such as the lieutenant-governor, who preferred it for the many trips he made up and down Lake Ontario.[8] The *Duke of Kent*, launched in 1801, represented the next generation of design and technology, which outclassed the older boats in both comfort and efficiency.[9]

When they were about forty kilometres from York, Moody and Eleazer would have passed a significant deep bay that was separated from the lake by a spit of sand and gravel. This had been called Frenchman's Bay for some time, another example of earlier times when French traders did business with the Mississauga people who lived north of points along the lakeshore. Decades later, Pickering Village would take shape along the Kingston Road, a bit inland from the bay.

The largest Mississauga camp the canoeists saw may have been at the mouth of the Rouge River, a significant waterway that drained a large area to the north and west across Scarborough Township. It was an important gathering point for the Mississauga people, due not only to the plentiful fish in the river, but also because this had traditionally been the southern terminus of an ancient trail, the eastern branch of the Toronto Carrying Place.[10]

The Rouge River ran swiftly between high banks of a narrow valley as it approached Lake Ontario. This limited the value of the river for north–south transportation in its lower reaches and presented a major obstacle to east–west transportation along the major roads that crossed the valley. Local history is full of stories of accidents and delays, first on the Danforth Highway and later the Kingston Road, at the very dangerous Rouge River crossing. For most of the nineteenth century, this would be considered the most dangerous place between Toronto and Kingston.[11]

Not long after the canoe passed the Rouge River, another significant watercourse, called Highland Creek, came into sight. This was also a popular gathering place for the Mississauga people, because of the extensive wetlands at the lakeshore. At this time, it was also the destination for the earliest settlers in Scarborough Township. Just a couple of miles up the creek, a group of Scottish immigrants were establishing farms and making homes for themselves.

The banks along the shore grew taller as the men paddled along the Scarborough Highlands, today called the Scarborough Bluffs. This spectacular landform has been characterized as the CN Tower[12] of the early period when lake travellers approached from the east. Even if you were in a hurry, it was hard not to be moved by the sight. The two young men in the canoe would no doubt rest their weary arms for a few minutes in front of the tallest part, which towered three hundred feet over the water. They had sailed or paddled this way many times before, but the sight of the majestic cliffs would always be a source of wonder.

Their reaction was similar to that of Lady Simcoe, inquisitive spouse of John Graves Simcoe, first lieutenant-governor of Upper Canada. She approached the scene from the west while on a pleasant canoe ride in 1793. She wrote in her memoirs, "After rowing a mile we came within sight of what is named, in the map, the highlands of Toronto. The shore is extremely bold, and has the appearance of chalk cliffs, but I believe they are only white sand. They appeared so well that we talked of building a summer residence there and calling it Scarborough."[13] What could be better than naming a unique landform in the colonies after a familiar place in England? In fact, the surveyor took the hint and applied this name to the surrounding country, resulting in Scarborough Township.

Today we can view the Scarborough Bluffs from every direction and still marvel at their unique beauty. We must remember, though, that especially in the area west of the highest cliffs, significant parts of the original Scarborough Highlands have not survived industrial and residential developments. Erosion has also reduced the extent and appearance of the cliffs, a process that is ongoing.[14]

As the young men resumed paddling, the cliffs on their right gave way to four sandy beaches, which Torontonians now call The Beaches or The Beach (take your pick). The York Southeast Township map in the *Belden County Atlas* of 1878 shows Balmy Beach[15] as the only name at that time. In 1804, the beaches were a sign to the canoeists that they were approaching York. The route they would take from here into the town can be traced on William Chewett's 1802 map,[16] which includes a very clear illustration of the harbour, the spits, and the marshy area to the east.

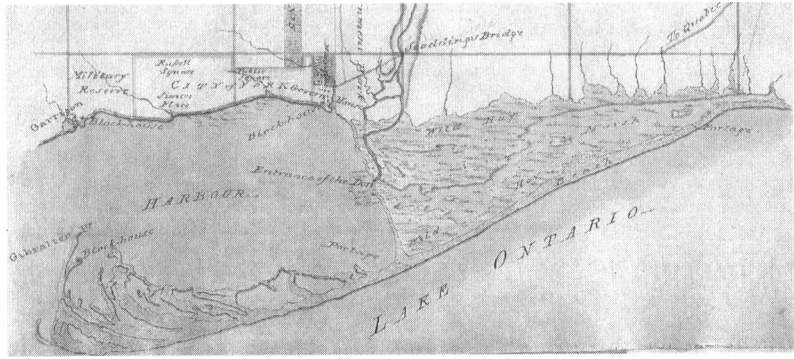

William Chewett's map of York in 1802 provides a clear picture of York Harbour, the sand spits and islands to the south, and the swampy area on the east we now call Ashbridge's Bay. The portage in the middle would have been used by Moody Farewell and Eleazer Lockwood, as they travelled to York.

Chewett's map shows the beaches as a long, narrow spit separating the lake from a large swampy area to the north that we now call Ashbridge's Bay. The spit continues west to form the Toronto Islands. Not far along the shore is a portage to cross over into Ashbridge's Bay, which was named for the family who had settled along the north shore. The bay was filled with many channels, along with large tracts labelled "Wild Hay."

Moody Farewell was very familiar with this area, having been back and forth several times between Whitby Township and York in the previous few years. His habit was to paddle on west to the second portage labelled on Chewett's map, south of the mouth of the Don River. Here, Moody and Eleazer hoisted the canoe onto their shoulders and walked the few dozen yards across the sandspit to the harbour side, where they embarked again, this time into the southeast corner of York Harbour. Moody preferred this route because it avoided a lot of unpredictable marshland and, later in the season, clouds of mosquitoes. Of course, if they carried any amount of cargo, rather than manhandling it across the portage, they could easily paddle all the way around the sandy islands, entering York Harbour from the west. On this day, the middle route was an obvious choice.

Owen Staples was a Toronto artist who, in 1909, produced this painting of the shoreline of York as it may have appeared in 1803. His inspiration was the work of Edward Walsh, a surgeon with the Forty-ninth Regiment who was in York at the time of the *Speedy* and painted the York shoreline.

The canoe slid easily across the calm, clear waters of York Harbour. Off to their left, the two men could see a few canoes where the Mississauga people were casting their nets and spearing a ready supply of fish. Moody was curious about the situation at the camp on Gibraltar Point, on the far west end of the harbour. The Mississauga people traditionally made their camp there because it provided easy access to the fishing grounds to the east in the bay and allowed them a clear vantage point for any activity on the water. For this community, the narrow fingers of sand and surrounding swampy land represented a healing place of cool breezes and isolation from the English who kept to themselves on the north shore. By 1804, however, they came to these islands less often than before, largely because of the growing presence of the English. They would come even less frequently as time went by.

The two young men began to see their destination across the blue waters to the north. There was the blockhouse guarding the shoreline near the east end of the bay, and just behind that they could see the roof of Parliament House, the town's largest building at the time. There were small boats out from the north shore, most of them fishing in the bay, and they could see a schooner moored off the landing place. They were minutes from York.

CHAPTER 4

MUDDY LITTLE YORK

In 1804, the town of York had been in existence for only a decade, but its location had been important for controlling the fur trade for about a century. In the late 1690s, the Ojibwa and their allies pushed the Iroquois south of the lakes and began the slow process of consolidating their presence north of the lakes, from Fort Frontenac to York.[1] The French had a trading post and fort at Toronto, which was destroyed before the British took over in 1763. Then the location became an important British harbour and trading centre.

One of the best descriptions of Toronto Harbour was produced by the deputy surveyor general for Quebec, John Collins.[2] On a visit there in 1788, Collins wrote,

> The Harbour of Toronto is near two miles in length from the entrance on the west to the isthmus between it and a large morass on the eastward. The breadth of the entrance is about half a mile, but the navigable channel for vessels is only about 500 yards, having from three to three and a half fathoms water. The north or main shore, the whole length of the harbour, is a clay bank from twelve to twenty feet high, and rising gradually behind, apparently good land, and fit for settlement. The

water is rather shoal near the shore, having but one fathom
depth at one hundred yards distance, two fathoms at two hundred yards; and when I sounded here, the waters of the Lake
were very high. There is good and safe anchorage everywhere
within the harbour, being either a soft or sandy bottom.[3]

Despite all the positives about this location, in the early 1790s, there
was considerable debate about whether the capital of Upper Canada
should reside there. When Simcoe announced in 1794 that the capital
would move to York from Newark, many officials disagreed strongly because they already had homes and businesses established in
Newark. Even Simcoe himself was not wholeheartedly behind the
move. Certainly, the capital of the province needed to be farther away
from the American border, as a matter of basic security, but Simcoe
had become enamoured by the idea of a new town called London that
he envisaged on the Thames River in the southwestern part of the
province. His bosses did not support his recommendation, however,
and insisted the capital be located on the north side of Lake Ontario.

By 1803, York covered 420 acres and counted 456 inhabitants.[4] It
was laid out in a grid pattern, centred around King Street. The names
applied to its streets were, as Henry Scadding suggests in *Toronto of
Old*, "intended as loyal compliments to members of the reigning family."[5] King Street was named for King George III, and the town itself was
called York after the King's heir, the Duke of York. Not everyone was
happy with the new names, and a bill was brought before Parliament
early in 1804 to restore the old names which were "more familiar and
agreeable to the inhabitants."[6] The bill went nowhere.

The north–south street that approached closest to the Parliament
buildings was Princes Street. According to Scadding, Princes Street was
so named in honour of the King's other sons, "the Duke of Clarence,
the Duke of Kent, the Duke of Cumberland, the Duke of Sussex, and
the Duke of Cambridge."[7] The next street to the west was named for
Caroline, the Princess of Wales, who was, as the venerable Toronto

historian puts it, "afterwards so unhappily famous as George the Fourth's Queen Caroline."[8] The modern reader will recognize the name Sherbourne Street, which was applied to Caroline Street in the 1840s due to the influence of the Ridout family, who had major land holdings to the north. Frederick was a brother of the Duke of York, and his name was given to the next north–south street. Not to be left out, the Prince of Wales, heir apparent and namesake of the King, gave his name to George Street.

Maps from this time show New Street as the next street to the west. This seems like an odd name, but it had practical origins. By 1797, the government anticipated an influx of people to support the growth in commercial activity and public services.[9] There are numerous diagrams and lists in archives concerning the area west of New Street, including names of people who wanted lots in the area of Yonge and Bay streets. In 1804, the functional centre of York was around Frederick Street, although that would gradually move west to Yonge Street.

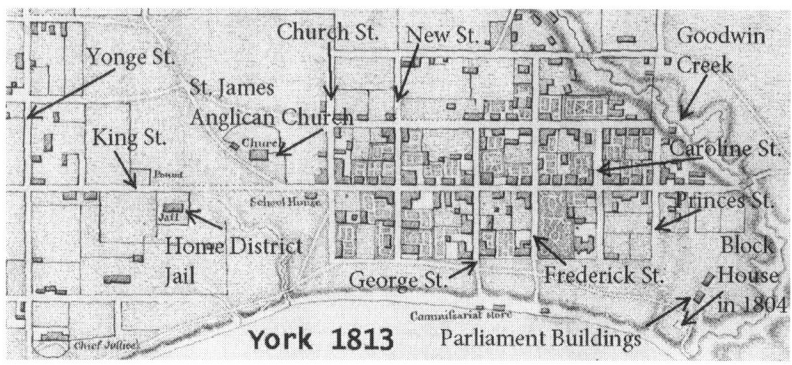

In order to imagine York in 1804, we can use part of a map done in 1813 by George Williams. It shows the streets and buildings of the time. The author has added arrows and labels to highlight locations pertinent to the *Speedy* story.

While the streets of York had been laid out in an organized manner, within the blocks bounded by the streets anything but orderliness prevailed. York was a work in progress in every way. The sound of hammers pounding and saws cutting mingled with the barking of dogs and squawking of seagulls to create a sense of energy and motion. Add to this the occasional shouts of men and shrieks of laughter from children, and the visitor from the country became immediately aware that this was a small but dynamic place. It seemed to grow as you watched.

Underlying all of this was the mud. From its earliest days, the town of York was referred to by visitors as "Muddy Little York,"[10] which delivered two gibes at once. The constant, clinging mud was obvious to anyone walking the streets, and the size of the place in relation to New York in the United States or even York in England, was grounds for a joke.[11]

The *Upper Canada Gazette* was the only newspaper in York, and by 1800 it had been enlarged to include more local ordinances and information about public behaviour. In regard to fire protection, an item on April 12, 1800, announced that "every housekeeper in the Town of York aforesaid shall, on or before the first day of October next ensuing, provide and keep TWO BUCKETS for carrying water, when any house shall happen to be on fire."[12] And that was not all. "It is also ordered that every house keeper in the said Town shall keep two ladders, the one to reach from the ground to the eaves of the house, and the other to be properly secured and fixed with hooks or bolts on the roof near the chimney."[13] Oh, yes, there would be a fine of five shillings "for every neglect of having said buckets and ladders, or either of them."[14]

Keeping the streets clear was also an issue at the turn of the century. Another decree stated "that whoever shall leave any wood or stone or suffer any nuisance to remain in the said streets, opposite their respective premises after the 12th day of May next, will be prosecuted as the law directs."[15] No messing around here. Keep the streets clear of junk, or else.

As Moody Farewell approached York with Eleazer Lockwood in May 1804, he knew the best place to land was a stone's throw west of the blockhouse at the far-east end of the shoreline. The canoe made straight for this familiar spot. *Landmarks of Toronto* has an excellent description of York at that time: "Extending from the grounds which surrounded the Parliament Buildings in the east all the way to the fort at the entrance of the harbour in the west there was a succession of fine forest trees, especially oak, underneath and by the side of which the upper surface of the precipitous, but nowhere very elevated, cliff, was carpeted with thick green sward."[16] Sward was the term used for thick green grass; it was mentioned often as part of the shoreline until development edged south and found more lucrative use for valuable waterfront property. The same source goes on to describe the landing place: "In the interval between the points where now Princess and Sherbourne streets descend to the water's edge was a favourite landing place for small craft of the bay — a wide and clean gravelly beach with a convenient ascent to the cliff above."[17]

The Parliament Buildings at York (locals used the term Parliament House) were the most impressive structures in the town in 1804. Built in 1796, they housed the offices of government and administration in the fledgling province. The American attack in 1813 would target these buildings as symbols of British power in the region, and Parliament House was burned to the ground, along with the library and archives.

On this mild spring afternoon, the two canoeists directed their attention to Parliament House. Completed in 1796, these buildings were described as "humble but commodious structures, of wood. . . . two elegant halls, with convenient offices for the accommodation of the Legislature and the courts of justice . . . [each] 40 x 25 feet, and standing a hundred feet apart, a space which was afterwards filled up by additional buildings."[18] This first Parliament House was torched during the War of 1812 when the Americans attacked York. Unfortunately, the loss was not confined to the structures; the contents of the library were also destroyed, depriving us of what would undoubtedly be a fascinating collection of historical documents.[19]

The young travellers knew they needed to tell their story to someone in these buildings. As they approached the shore at the landing place, they stopped paddling and let the canoe slide onto the beach. In a few swift motions, they drew their canoe out of the water, hoisted it onto their shoulders, and stepped smartly down the beach toward the blockhouse. Just before they got there, they turned up a dry creek bed and soon came to the well-worn path through the sward that ran across the shoreline. Turning right, onto the path, a few more steps took them to the wide yard in front of Parliament House.

They felt intimidated, simply being in this august location. Powerful people such as Upper Canada's Lieutenant-Governor Peter Hunter[20] worked here along with the members of the executive council. Mighty figures like that were unlikely to pay any attention to a couple of sweaty country boys, but Moody and Eleazer were on their toes, just in case.

They found an open space by some trees to one side of the buildings, where they set down their canoe, turned it over, and stowed their belongings underneath. Without knowing exactly how to go about what needed to be done, they walked over to a sentry and stood respectfully until he asked them what they wanted. Moody was the talker, as usual. Gathering his courage, he said they must speak to a constable or someone who could register a complaint about a murder. The sentry immediately perked up and told the pair to wait while he fetched someone who could help.

A few minutes later, the sentry returned with a man dressed in a military uniform who smiled warmly and shook hands with the men before ushering them into a room inside the building. He introduced himself as Lieutenant Colonel James Green,[21] military secretary to Lt-Gov. Hunter. His boss held two positions, one civil, as lieutenant-governor, the other military, as lieutenant general, commanding His Majesty's Forces in Upper and Lower Canada. Green served in York in the military context, but his responsibilities were varied, based mostly on what his boss needed.

Born in Sweden in 1751 to a very poor family, James Green was an exceptional case of self-improvement in a time of family influence and nepotism. He had no sponsor when he enlisted in the British Army in 1772, but by 1776 he was promoted to sergeant major when his regiment came to Quebec and he saw action during the American attacks. The next year he was among many soldiers captured with the defeat of General Burgoyne and spent ten months as a prisoner of war.

After his release, Green was given several jobs by the governor in Quebec that provided valuable exposure to the elite in government and military circles. Following a trip to England, where he married, he came back to Quebec and was appointed military secretary to Lord Dorchester, a position he would continue to hold through Dorchester's successors, including Lt.-Gov. Hunter. In 1799, Green brought his young family to York, adding an air of military dignity to the rough-and-tumble nature of the new town, especially inside the offices at Parliament House. He would also offer a more civil tone in dealing with the townsfolk, compared to the often gruff and sharp impression left by his boss.

As military secretary, Green performed many duties in support of Lt.-Gov. Hunter. One very important task was management of correspondence between the lieutenant-governor and the authorities in Kingston, Quebec City, and other points in Upper and Lower Canada. The British Military and Naval Records, which are held in Library and Archives Canada, provide a rich collection of letters and reports, many signed by James Green, who would then provide information to his boss. From 1799 he signed himself as Major Green[22] and then, after his promotion in March 1804, he was Lieutenant Colonel Green.[23]

Green listened carefully as Moody began to explain why he and Eleazer had come to York. Immediately grasping the significance of the situation and the potential dangers it raised, he asked Moody to stop and wait for him to find the right person to deal with this delicate matter. Soon, Green was back with a well-dressed man who had the appearance of being in charge. He greeted the young men with a certain condescension common in British office-holders of the time, then he led them into another room and bade them to take chairs at a large table. He sat down opposite them, while Green sat with paper, pen, and ink at a small writing table nearby. The proceedings would be recorded.

The well-dressed man across the table was Henry Allcock,[24] chief justice of Upper Canada. He was an experienced judge and a favourite of Hunter's, but he was also a man most folks found difficult to like. Allcock was an excellent example of an aggressive office-seeker, so typical in British colonies of the time. He was over-confident in his knowledge and abilities due to the inherent notion that everyone British was superior to all others. At the same time, he was extremely insecure about his position in regard to both his authority and his wealth.

Moody talked, Allcock nodded, and Green's quill pen scratched. At a certain point in the story, Moody looked over at his friend, and Eleazer Lockwood nervously told the part about Ogetonicut and the Mississauga people coming to York. Allcock leaned forward in his chair when this was revealed and asked Lockwood several questions to make sure he had the story right. The chief justice then appeared agitated and suddenly stood up, exiting the room without so much as a nod.

Moody and Eleazer sat in silence as Lt. Col. Green continued to write. After a few minutes, he signed the paper and set his pen down. Smiling at the two nervous young men, he told them they had done well and would be required to assist further, so they should not leave town. He suggested they wait outside for further instructions.

Green took the record he had created to the office of Lt.-Gov. Hunter, where Chief Justice Allcock was already waiting. He read the document aloud. His words set off alarm bells. This was serious. If it became common knowledge that an ex-British soldier had been murdered by a Mississauga man, the potential for unrest was high among the residents of York as well as the wider settler community. There was still a strong mythical image in the minds of most European immigrants to the New World that "Indians" were savages, always on the verge of performing bloody acts. The fact that the Mississauga people had been peaceful over the previous two decades did not enter into the equation. Right or wrong, it was simply the majority view among the settlers.

At the same time, the governor in Quebec and the authorities in London were strongly urging Lt.-Gov. Hunter to maintain good relations with all the Indigenous people of Upper Canada. It was apparent that the Americans would attack at some point and that the small number of British regulars would need the assistance of local militia as well as Indigenous warriors in the fight. The crucial nature of this alliance would be borne out in less than a decade during the War of 1812.

It was rumoured that Chief Wabbekisheco and his Mississauga people were encamped on Gibraltar Point, just across the bay from York. Some thought it odd, even concerning, because this group normally stayed well to the east. However, nothing was done to communicate with them. As often happened, a failure to communicate led to speculation and wild rumours on the streets of York. At least now the officials at Parliament House knew the reason for the camp. It was time for the justice system to take action and make it very clear to the public that things were under control.

Hunter and Allcock discussed the problem at length and agreed that the highest priority at this point was to arrest the young man named Ogetonicut. It seemed from the story that they had just heard, Chief Wabbekisheco must have come to York with the express purpose of turning Ogetonicut over to the authorities. This needed to be accomplished quickly, with as little muss and fuss as possible.

The chief justice sent a soldier into York to fetch two men who would be instrumental in the arrest. The first was John Fisk, recently appointed high constable of Home District.[25] The soldier found Fisk on King Street, speaking to his friend, James Ruggles, a merchant and magistrate of York.[26] Everybody in York knew if you greeted Ruggles you could kiss your next hour goodbye. Conversation would quickly turn to Ruggles's famous uncle, Brigadier General Timothy Ruggles,[27] who had been one of the most prominent Loyalists in Massachusetts and ended up in Nova Scotia after the war. Not surprisingly, Fisk welcomed the interruption from the Ruggles epic and gratefully hurried back to Parliament House to see what orders Allcock had for him. As high constable, John Fisk was the top law officer in the Home District and would be responsible for the arrest and subsequent incarceration of Ogetonicut.

The soldier carried on west and found the second gentleman at his home. Colonel James Givins[28] was the assistant superintendent of the Indian Department. At this time, he was the senior member of that organization in York, since his boss, Superintendent William Claus, was in Detroit. Givins would be the representative of the Indian Department in these proceedings and act as interpreter between the authorities and the Mississauga people.

At Parliament House, Chief Justice Allcock informed Fisk and Givins of the situation and outlined what was expected of them. They were to proceed to Gibraltar Point and request that Chief Wabbekisheco hand over the young man, Ogetonicut. They were to confirm the identity of the accused, take him into custody, and transport him to the jail in York. Allcock made it very clear that this prisoner must not escape and, throughout it all, the Mississauga people on Gibraltar Point were to be kept quiet. The requirements of the law must be strictly upheld. There was to be no incident that might be exaggerated by certain parties on the north side of the bay. The arrest needed to be quick and clean.

Allcock called on all the pomp and circumstance he could muster to impress upon Fisk and Givins the importance of these tasks, as well as to underline his own authority as the chief justice of Upper Canada. John Fisk had been in his position for less than a month and was still feeling his way around the circumstances at York and the internal politics at Parliament House. One thing he knew for sure was that Allcock was Hunter's favourite, to the exclusion of better men, some thought. In any case, Fisk knew he must do as the powerful man said if he wanted to keep his job.

Fisk had turned fifty the previous year and was now in the job he had worked toward all his life. He was born in Connecticut and during the War of Independence had been assigned to guard British prisoners of war. When the war ended, he moved his family to Grand Isle, Vermont, near the Quebec border. By 1801, he was settled in King Township, north of York, where his experience in policing was put to good use.[29]

James Givins had a completely different background. Born in Ireland, he immigrated to Detroit around the beginning of the War of Independence and worked in the fur trade, spending time with the Ojibwa of the area and learning their language. In 1791, Givins was appointed lieutenant in the newly formed Queen's Rangers. A few years later, Lt.-Gov. Simcoe, who was very impressed by this young man, recommended him for a position in the Indian Department. Givins proved adept at communicating with the various Indigenous groups around Upper Canada and gained the trust of most of the chiefs. As a result, in November 1803, Givins was appointed assistant to William Claus.[30] He is better known in Canadian history, however, for his service during the War of 1812, when he led a small group of Mississauga men in defence of York against the American attack.[31] His name is also prominent in the history of Toronto because of the house he built on Queen Street West, probably around this time, later known as the Givins Homestead.[32]

Fisk and Givins met Moody Farewell and Eleazer Lockwood outside Parliament House on that May afternoon in 1804 and reassured the young men that they had done their duty honourably and should be proud. However, the high constable said he would need their assistance with one more task. Since they were the only witnesses who could identify the man suspected of killing John Sharp, it would be necessary for them to go to the Mississauga camp on Gibraltar Point, to positively identify the accused before the arrest. The two young men looked nervously at each other. They did not like the idea of going to the camp but could see it was their duty to assist in this manner. They would do it.

Fisk handed a piece of paper to a soldier and instructed him to deliver it immediately to the garrison commander. It was a request by Chief Justice Allcock for the loan of a bateau as well as a squad of six armed men to act as escorts on the trip across the bay to Gibraltar Point and back with the accused. Bateaux were common along the St. Lawrence River and the shores of the lakes at the time. They were flat-bottomed and came in various sizes, according to use, but most were from thirty-five to forty feet long with a relatively narrow beam of about five feet, six inches.[33]

When the bateau arrived at the landing place, the four men climbed aboard and the soldiers smartly reversed the craft to the west, edging south toward the northern tip of Gibraltar Point, where a blockhouse and two storehouses had been built. Once they'd beached on the east side of the point, Fisk, Givins, and the two witnesses quickly disembarked, and four of the soldiers formed up behind them. The latter, according to Fisk's instructions, were to march six feet behind the delegation and do nothing else unless directly ordered by him. They must anticipate a tense situation.

John Fisk led the way, trying to look as officious as possible. James Givins walked to one side, just behind. Moody and Eleazer came next. Through the woods they could see the camp's wigwams; when they approached the central meeting grounds, they stopped and waited. Dozens of people stood around silently, staring at the visitors from York. The atmosphere was tense, but the people seemed more curious than hostile.

Soon, Chief Wabbekisheco stepped out of one of the wigwams, followed by three young men. As they walked slowly toward the delegation, several others joined them. When they met, Fisk and Chief Wabbekisheco shook hands. Givins shook the chief's hand too and spoke to him in his own language for a moment, then Fisk introduced Moody Farewell and Eleazer Lockwood.

With Givins translating for the chief, Fisk got right to the point. He told Chief Wabbekisheco that they had come to arrest Ogetonicut on suspicion of murdering the trader John Sharp at Lake Scugog. The chief nodded solemnly and reached back to grasp Ogetonicut's shoulder. The young man reluctantly stepped forward. Fisk turned to Eleazer Lockwood and asked him if this was the man he had seen talking about Sharp's murder. Lockwood said that it was. Givins made sure to translate this for the chief, who nodded that he understood. With that, Fisk announced that he was arresting Ogetonicut for the murder of John Sharp and that he must come with them peaceably. The young man glanced at his chief beseechingly, without speaking. The chief knew enough English to understand Fisk and responded in English that he accepted the need to arrest his kinsman.

With this, Fisk fastened a pair of handcuffs on the prisoner's wrists and installed a set of manacles on his ankles. He turned to thank Chief Wabbekisheco for his co-operation and shook hands with him again. James Givins did the same, speaking in the chief's own language. Chief Wabbekisheco stood stoically, trying to hold back his tears. Turning over Ogetonicut was the last thing he wanted to do, but he knew it was his only option under the circumstances. He looked around at his people, some crying and others standing sullenly, eyes averted. His next job would be to keep the angry young men under control as the family awaited the fate of their son. It was a very sad day for the Mississauga people of Lake Scugog.

This extraction of a member of their community was seen as another example of the brutal and immoral nature of the English. If this sort of problem arose between two Mississauga families, they would gather together, feast and smoke, and then negotiate a mutually acceptable exchange. Many of the people who stood outside their wigwams and

watched the young man being manacled and led away by English soldiers, were angry at this indignity. It showed a serious lack of respect
for the Mississauga people. In practical terms, they were powerless to
respond in any way, but they would not forget.

The delegation, followed by the soldiers, made its way back to the
bateau and shoved off for York. Squatting in the middle of the boat,
with an armed soldier at each side, Ogetonicut looked very small. He
stared at the floor, not looking up, even when spoken to. He was terrified and felt abandoned.

Moody Farewell wished to be anywhere else on earth. As he stood
with his friend near the stern, watching the soldiers row toward the
north shore, he tried so hard to keep his eyes away from the prisoner,
but something stronger, deep in his gut, forced him to look. And the
sight of the accused man put Moody right back at that bloody scene
among the trees at the trading post. It was hard to fathom the reality
that the young man cowering in the boat had perpetrated such a horrible crime. This moment would never fade away for Moody Farewell,
as long as he lived.

The bateau soon crunched on the gravel at the landing place, and
the entire party disembarked and formed up for the march to the Home
District Jail on King Street. Once again, Fisk and Givins would lead the
way, followed by Moody and Eleazer. The six soldiers formed a box
around the prisoner and followed a short distance behind. The parade
was a unique sight for the residents of York. They were accustomed to
seeing soldiers performing various tasks, even escorting prisoners to
jail, but this was a much more elaborate show of force by the authorities than anyone had seen before.

The procession stepped slowly up the dry creek bed, turned onto
the footpath and followed it westward, along the south side of the
town. Green sward surrounded the group as they passed below Princes
Street, then Caroline Street. Pedestrians stepped back into the grass
and waited for the marchers to pass by, watching curiously until they
moved out of sight.

Between Frederick Street and George Street, the path edged north, closer to the occupied lots of the town. People working in their fields and gardens stopped to watch. At the bottom of New Street, the track ran along the southern boundary of the town to Church Street, where the group turned north. It was not many steps to King Street, and the group turned left to head west again. Along the road on their left was a schoolhouse where William Cooper[34] was the schoolmaster. A little farther along on the north side of the street, behind some trees, they could see the lot that had been set aside in 1797 for a church. In July 1803 there had been a meeting of subscribers, hoping for a new Anglican chapel.[35]

The procession continued along King Street, through a swampy area that was the source of a small creek to the south. Finally, on their left, the members of the group could see the Home District Jail, an excellent description of which is found in the *Upper Canada Gazette* of July 25, 1807: "It was the first jail in York, built in 1800, on the south side of King street. The building was a squat, unpainted one, with hipped roof, concealed from persons passing in the street by a tall cedar stockade. At the outer entrance hung a billet of wood suspended by a chain, communicating with a bell within."[36]

The *Gazette* would later boast about the lack of tenants in the facility. "We sincerely compliment the country that at the last General Quarter Sessions so little was to be done, and that the House of Correction has remained so long unoccupied by either misfortune or irregularity. The prospect is truly gratifying to every benevolent mind, and a subject of peculiar pride to the Home District."[37]

On this day in May 1804, however, the jail would have an occupant. The procession marched up to the front door, and Fisk pulled a chain that rang a bell inside the building. The jailer, William Knott, peeked through a hole in the door and was greeted by Fisk, and the heavy door swung open, its rusty hinges squeaking in complaint.

William Knott had come to Canada in 1792 with the Queen's Rangers and was married at Newark to another soldier's widow. The

following year, the young couple moved to York with John Graves
Simcoe, commander of the Queen's Rangers, and assisted in the creation of the town.[38] Knott was known as a busy tailor but, always
looking for more reliable income, he became the first jailer of York
when the new jail was built in 1800.[39]

The procession entered the yard inside the stockade and stopped
in front of the building. Moody Farewell and Eleazer Lockwood stood
aside, having no desire to enter the jail. Four of the soldiers formed a
guard outside the front door and the other two marched behind the
prisoner, muskets at the ready. Knott led the way, through the front
office and down a hallway to the cells. Ogetonicut was pushed inside
the first cell, shoulders hunched, handcuffs and manacles still in place,
and the heavy wooden door with a barred window swung shut behind
him. This would be his home for the next four months.

Givins stood outside the cell, speaking to the prisoner in his own
language for a time, attempting to tell him what was happening and
what he might expect. Knott brought some water and bread, setting it
on the floor inside the cell door. However, the prisoner was not interested in food at this point. He shuffled to the cot along one wall and sat
down, head hanging and eyes closed. He ignored the two men outside
the door of his cell. Finally, they got the message and left him alone.

The job was done. The murder suspect had been arrested and was
secure. John Fisk left the jail, heading back down King Street, intent
on reporting to Henry Allcock that his instructions had been carried
out. Givins walked toward his home west of town. The two soldiers
who had escorted the prisoner inside the jail stood guard on either side
of his cell door. The four others took up positions in front of the jail
building and on the street in front of the stockade. They would be relieved every six hours by other soldiers from the garrison. There would
be a twenty-four-hour guard on this prisoner. Allcock was taking no
chances.

One can only imagine the living conditions in the Home District
Jail in 1804. A few years later, the jailer and sheriff lobbied for better

facilities, reporting that "the prisoners in the cells of the jail of the Home District suffer much from cold and damp, there being no method of communicating heat from the chimneys nor any bedsteads to raise the straw from the floors which lie nearly, if not altogether, on the ground. A small stove in the lobby of each range of cells, together with some rugs or blankets will add much to the comfort of the unhappy persons confined."[40] In those days, simply being in jail was hazardous to one's health.

Moody Farewell and Eleazer Lockwood stood on King Street outside the jail and talked for a few minutes, sharing their thoughts of what had transpired and their desire to return home. However, each had visits to make before they could leave York. Moody would visit his mother, who lived to the west in Etobicoke Township. Eleazer also had relatives in town with whom he would stay overnight. In the morning, Moody would meet with a lawyer and then speak to the agent at the Crown Land Department regarding the acquisition of the land in Whitby Township. Afterward, the two young men would meet up at Parliament House, where their canoe was stowed, and begin the journey back down the lake. Home looked very good to both of them right now.

CHAPTER 5

A CRITICAL QUESTION

In the days following the arrest of Ogetonicut, the offices and meeting rooms at Parliament House were abuzz with discussion. Much of the talk was between Chief Justice Henry Allcock and Lieutenant-Governor Peter Hunter, although Solicitor General Robert Isaac Dey Gray[1] became involved in anticipation of a criminal trial. At thirty-two, Gray was still quite young, but he was known as a very conscientious lawyer. He would be the Crown's representative in court.

In those days, it was expected that a man in high position would also run for a seat in the House of Assembly, which young Robert Gray had done, representing his home riding of Stormont and Russell in the Eastern District. His work as a member of the House of Assembly was constructive but low-key, as he applied tact and common sense to all questions, an approach that rather set him apart from the developing partisan rancour of the time.

Lt.-Gov. Simcoe had recommended Gray to be the first Solicitor General in the fall of 1794. He was looking for ambitious young men to make up the government and judiciary in the new province and had seen great promise in the twenty-two-year-old barrister of Cornwall, although his background may have been even more important. Robert's father, James Gray, a Highlander, had been a captain in the Black Watch who escaped to Quebec after the War of Independence ended. For his

service, James received large land grants east of Cornwall.[2] Whatever
the reasons, Simcoe's favour had given Robert Gray a chance to obtain
legal education in England. He returned to the colonies ready to serve
his King and country and was confirmed as Solicitor General of Upper
Canada in 1798.

While Gray was seen to be a good lawyer and participating member of the House of Assembly, he was also known as a bon vivant
around York. He was a single man with money to spend and was often
seen dining at the best houses, indulging in the finest food and drink
that could be brought to York from Kingston. Alexander Macdonell's
diary mentions that the Solicitor General had a rather elegant vehicle
driven by a servant, which he often used to pick up friends on the
streets of York. "Walked to the Garrison, met Allcock and shortly after
was overtaken by the Solicitor in his Cariole who was also going to the
Garrison, got in with him."[3]

A trial of the importance of Ogetonicut's required detailed paperwork, and a man in Gray's position would delegate most of that work
to an underling of some sort. He chose law student John Anderson[4]
to be his assistant. Just turned twenty, Anderson was Gray's cousin,
which is probably how he gained a much-coveted law student position in York, as well as the trial work. Active family connections were
common across the provinces of Upper and Lower Canada at this time.

While the technical work in preparation of the murder trial began,
behind the scenes the talk swung around to the broader issues of politics. Lt.-Gov. Hunter was well aware of the public sentiment around
York and out in the countryside. He knew that the mere presence of
a Mississauga man shackled in the Home District Jail awaiting trial
for the murder of an Englishman was provocative. Even worse, the
Mississauga people that were still camped on Gibraltar Point seemed to
present an ominous threat to public peace. Hunter was also aware that
the citizens of York expected swift justice, according to the rules and
regulations of the British judicial system, which was being persistently
implanted in this new colony.

Peter Hunter came from landed gentry in Perthshire, Scotland, which allowed him to purchase an ensign's commission in 1767 at the age of twenty-one. He was stationed at Minorca, went back to England and then to the West Indies before being posted in 1786 to Halifax, where he soon became commander of the western posts of Quebec, stationed at Fort Niagara, which today is Youngstown, New York.

When he was first stationed at Upper Canada, Hunter was forty years old and known as a serious, efficient officer. As events unfolded in the wilderness posting of the Western District of Quebec, he established a reputation for making his own decisions based on conditions on the ground, then working things out with his superiors after the fact. One controversial decision was his authorizing the distribution of provisions during the terrible famine year of 1787 without waiting for orders from Quebec. It was charged that he acted hastily, and two wealthy merchants managed to profit financially from his orders. The fact that many of the new settlers in Upper and Lower Canada were prevented from starving due to Hunter's decisive action, was less important for those who were jealous of his influence.

Upper Canada would seem far from the pulse of world activities for an ambitious army officer in his forties, so Hunter returned to England on leave in 1789. While there, he was appointed temporary superintendent of British Honduras, now called Belize, where he took a strict authoritarian approach to governance and gained very useful experience in colonial administration.

Hunter returned to England in 1791 and was promoted to colonel. He served on the continent, in the Caribbean, and during the Irish Rebellion of 1798. The following year, he was appointed lieutenant-governor of Upper Canada, and when the Duke of Kent returned to England in 1800, Hunter also assumed command of His Majesty's Forces in the Canadian colonies with the rank of lieutenant general. As a result, he would often be called General Hunter. He now faced the challenge of doing two equally important and demanding jobs at the same time. Since he was first and foremost a military man, a conventional authoritarian approach was natural for him, and he applied this style to improving the military strength of the colonies as well as to the governance of Upper Canada.

The person most impacted by Hunter's appointment was Peter Russell,[5] who was the administrator of Upper Canada but lost his job as soon as Hunter arrived. Russell had been appointed administrator when Lt.-Gov. Simcoe returned to England in 1796. For more than three years, Russell was responsible for the governance of Upper Canada but was still subject to the authority of Simcoe. In fact, Russell expected to be named lieutenant-governor at any time, and so he was bitterly disappointed when Peter Hunter appeared in York to take the job. Simcoe tried to smooth things over when he wrote a letter recommending that Russell be provided with support because of his important service,[6] but others had different ideas.

Peter Russell was shunted aside because the powerful men in London insisted that a military man be in charge. Simply put, he was no longer in favour. He was named receiver general and became a member of Hunter's new executive council, but he never had any real power, and he resented it. Russell expressed his feelings in a letter to John King on September 22, 1799: "The consequence is that I have now the Mortification of being commanded by those to whom I was so lately Superior; without having done anything to merit this Degradation but on the Contrary having been honored by my Sovereign with his entire approbation of my Conduct."[7]

The arrival of the new lieutenant-governor at York was reported in the *Canada Constellation*, a short-lived newspaper at Niagara, on August 23, 1799. "His Excellency, Governor Hunter, arrived at York on Friday morning last [August 16] in the *Speedy*."[8] Hunter's first decision was to arrange for the ongoing governance of Upper Canada while he spent the winters in Quebec. The position of commander of His Majesty's Forces in the Canadian colonies was centred on Quebec, and Hunter used this as the premise for spending half the year in Upper Canada and half in Lower Canada. The real reason, however, may have been that Hunter disliked the puny little settlement at York and preferred the much more civilized people and culture he found in Montreal and Quebec City.

To address the issue, Hunter appointed a committee to administer the government at York while he was away in Lower Canada. He did not consult Peter Russell on how this would work, and it is doubtful that Hunter was amused by Russell's rather obtuse comment "And tho' this mode may not display all the Splendor and Respectability of a more efficient Government, it might possibly preserve at least the appearance of One, & by immediately providing for the more pressing wants of the Province prevent such a temporary Suspension from being felt or noticed by the People."[9]

The executive council[10] would be responsible for carrying out the orders of the lieutenant-governor, whether he was in the Upper or Lower province. It had little real power, as Hunter insisted in making all the decisions. Clearly, Peter Russell felt much abused in the process. However, he would take some consolation in the acquisition of significant land grants arising from his service to the Crown and would serve patiently, no matter the situation.

The executive council continued functioning while Hunter was in York, but, after a few years, he found that the complexity of the civil government of Upper Canada and the growing military tensions demanded his presence in York for the full year. By 1804, he was staying in York most of the time and making short trips to Quebec when he could arrange the time. York was a busy place.

Hunter became known around York as a strict disciplinarian and a sharp, cold man focused only on his work. He was fifty-eight years of age in 1804 and seemed both unwilling and unable to make friends in the community. This seems a far cry from the forty-year-old officer who had made his own decision to send life-saving supplies to the settlers in 1787. Military life and elevation to governance can have severe effects on a man.

A recollection about Hunter at York comes from John Baker, one of Robert Gray's servants. It was uttered decades later and is obviously not objective, but it paints a picture. "Governor Hunter was a severe and wicked old man. He wore leather breeches. In one pocket he carried tobacco, in another snuff. When giving orders he would take out a handful of snuff, and it would fall over his white ruffled shirt. He always wore shoes with silver buckles; never saw him with a boot on."[11]

It was no secret around town that Hunter preferred Chief Justice Allcock. He liked Allcock not only because he supported his ideas without reservation, but also because he was an effective administrator at a time when the nuts and bolts of governing were in very early stages of development. In particular, Hunter appreciated how Allcock had taken charge of the land grant administration system, reducing the time it took for settlers to receive their paperwork and take full possession of their lots.

The John Sharp murder case was a problem that resulted in some candid discussions between the two men. Hunter voiced serious trepidations about having a murder trial in York that would inevitably lead to the hanging of the accused at the Home District Jail. Top of mind for both men was the question of how the Mississauga people camped on Gibraltar Point might react.

It might be difficult for the modern reader to understand the fear that pervaded the minds of people in Upper Canada at this time. John McGill,[12] the commissariat officer at York, was thinking out loud in a letter to David William Smith in England, on October 4, 1804, when he wrote "What appearance as to the so long threatened invasion . . . will it take place or not?"[13] Nobody knew, but it was prominent in the public mind.

There had been many false alarms about invasions from the south over the previous years, and there were even arrests for espionage. One plot[14] suggested that the French were going to provide an army to march up the Mississippi Valley, gathering Indigenous allies as they moved north. The Mohawks and Ojibwa of Upper Canada were expected to rise up and massacre all the English in alliance with the Americans and the French. These threats proved to be pure fantasy but, for a people who still believed that the Native population was capable of the kind of extreme and grotesque violence vividly expressed in the salacious penny press, it was all very frightening and real. Both the lieutenant-governor and the chief justice felt it was their first job to protect the citizens of York and Upper Canada from any possible incitement at this emotional time.

Luckily, they came up with a solution. It's not clear from the records, but it could be that Allcock reminded his boss of a law which said that a murder trial must be held in the courthouse of the district in which the crime took place. While the law was clear, its application in the murder of John Sharp was not so obvious. In fact, they did not know where the crime had been committed, at least not exactly.

The town of York was in the Home District. The eastern border of Home District was just east of today's Oshawa, with Newcastle District extending east from there to the Trent River. The border between these two districts had not yet been surveyed north of the first couple of concessions, which meant that the exact border farther north was unknown. Travellers would have general knowledge, of course, but the law required more exact information.

Hunter and Allcock knew that Sharp had been murdered in the marshy area in the northeastern reaches of what would later be called Lake Scugog, but they could not tell which of the two districts had jurisdiction. This was a critical question. If the murder happened in Home District, the trial must take place at York, the county town for Home District. If the murder took place in Newcastle District, the trial would be held in the small town of Newcastle, down on Presqu'ile Point, 155 kilometres east of York. Finding the answer to this question became their most pressing problem.

A document in the Archives of Ontario provides a brief but fascinating glimpse into Allcock's thinking at this time. It appears to be a note to self, just a scrap of paper with some scratches on it. All things considered, we might be amazed that it has survived. The date "31 May 1804" is clearly written at the top.[15] The next line is "Went to the

Gov'r about the wait for London,"[16] which demonstrates that his highest priority at the moment was his plan to move back to England. Then "The Indian taken"[17] indicates that Ogetonicut had been arrested not long before May 31. Following this Allcock wrote "Survey of the place where murder committed"[18] to show that he was planning for a survey soon after the arrest. On that point, he concludes his note with "That it would do if survey made in the last of July."[19]

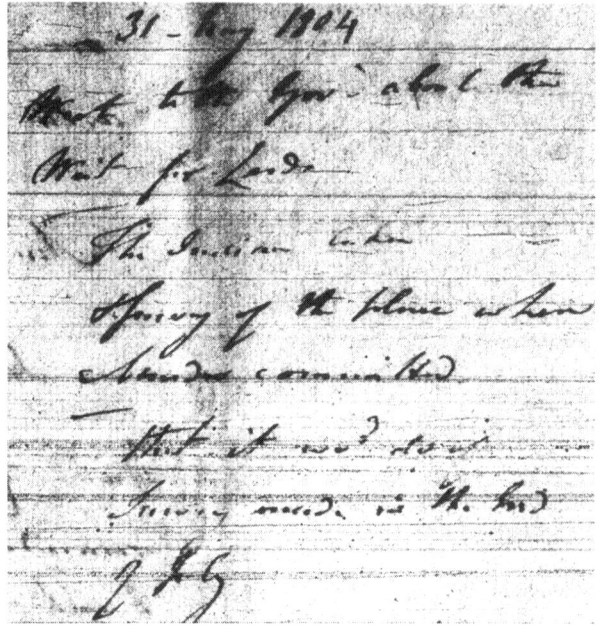

Chief Justice Henry Allcock scratched this note-to-self on May 31, 1804. It shows us that the idea of a survey was established very soon after Ogetonicut was arrested.

According to this, by the last day of May, Henry Allcock was planning to have a survey done to determine the location of the murder in relation to the border between Home and Newcastle districts. The hope for a late July time frame was not realized, but plans for the survey were set in motion.

CHAPTER 6

THE SURVEY

The delay in starting a survey of the border between Home and Newcastle districts in the summer of 1804 may have been due partly to the lack of a surveyor. There were only a few experienced men available to do this work and it was an extremely busy time for them, as the government rushed to open townships and prepare for more settlers. In fact, homesteaders were lining up for lots before townships were even laid out, and the surveyors were scrambling to keep up.

John Stegmann[1] was one of the best deputy surveyors in the province at this time. He had been one of twelve thousand Hessian soldiers who arrived on Staten Island, New York, in 1776 to fight as mercenaries with the British against the Patriots. After the war, he stayed in North America and got married in Quebec. As a result of his war service, he was granted land in Osnabruck Township, Stormont County, near Cornwall.[2]

Through his commission as an officer, Stegmann had received an appointment as a surveyor, but work had been scarce. By 1792, he was anxious to find a steady job to support his family. To this end, he wrote a letter to the Surveyor General's Office (SGO) in York.[3] The letter shows decent handwriting, dodgy spelling, and a respectful tone covered by self-deprecation. He explains, "The struggles natural in a New

Country augment to me by being a stranger and engaged in a calling to which I was hither entirely ignorant of, but am in hopes that you soon will employ a number of Surveyors in the Province. Therefore, I take the liberty to offer you my humbly service, and beg that you will have the goodness to employ me."[4] His confidence was rewarded. He was employed by the SGO of Upper Canada, transferred to York in 1797, and granted land in Vaughan Township, York County. Now that he and his family were near the hub of activity for his profession, he would have constant work.

By 1804, Stegmann was a veteran in the SGO and had become accustomed to the frustrations of the job. For example, he wrote to his office on June 15, 1804, "In my going along was questioned by a number of persons respecting the Township of Elmsley who all expected to make locations immediately. I then thought proper to tell them that I had done no work yet, and that the best way for them would be to explore the township after the survey was done, which would be by the end of July."[5] Apparently, one of the settlers was in a big hurry and was not satisfied with the response from the surveyor. He felt it necessary to complain directly to the surveyor general. It was a sign of the times.

A lack of surveyors added to the problem. Earlier in the year, when Stegmann was reporting about the survey of Elmsley Township in Lanark County, some three hundred kilometres northeast of York, he said that his efforts had been limited by thick snow. However, he made it clear that the snow paled in comparison with the fact "that I could get no hands to go on the survey for the wages allowed by Government."[6] Civil servants will always complain about their wages, but this was a matter of competing for young men who had other options.

The erratic delivery of letters between Stegmann and the SGO added to his discontent. There was no real mail service in Upper Canada yet, so when a surveyor was out in the bush, he had to rely on chance meetings with someone who might be in York sometime soon. This method often resulted in lost mail or, at the very least, long delays.

A letter he wrote to the SGO on June 15 shows his sensitivity about being blamed for these delays. "Your letter of the 22nd of May I received and am sorry to see that his Honor the Chief Justice supposes me to be neglectful in my office. I have answered every letter received from your Office by the first opportunity I could get but for the want of a Post, being obliged to send often letters by Travellers; some of which have never reached your office, and by which means I must bear the blame — The last return I sent to Samuel Sherwood, requesting the favour to forward the letter without loss of Time."[7] Stegmann was not shy in pushing back on the authorities in York, who knew nothing about the real facts on the ground.

In late July, as he was wrapping up the survey of Elmsley Township, Stegmann was asked by the SGO to provide an estimate for a survey of the line between Home and Newcastle districts. By August 11, he was back in York and responded like the experienced hand that he was, saying "a real Estimate cannot be maid, not knowing the distance of the Survey, neither what wages Labourers may be had."[8] Of course, he sweetened the pot a little with a platitude, "But then all necessary precaution will be taken to perform the Survey agreeable to the Instructions, and as economically as possible."[9] You had to deal carefully with the people in authority.

On August 13, Stegmann concluded the Elmsley survey with a visit to the Surveyor General's Office in York, where he presented his diary and field notes as expected. The next day, he met with officials, or, as he said in his diary "Waited on the Honorable the Executive Council."[10] There would be no time to visit his home north of York. The chief justice was in a big hurry.

The chief justice delivered the official order to the SGO, approved by Lieutenant-Governor Peter Hunter, on August 15. It read, in part:

You are hereby required and directed to cause a Survey to be performed, so as to determine the exact position, or situation of the House of Moody Farewell, where a murder is

supposed to have been committed on the Body of John Sharpe
— that is [to] say whether the Said House falls into the District
of Newcastle, or into that of the Home District, so that the
Surveyor may be enabled to declare the same upon oath. This
Survey, if in the nature of possibility to be returned by the
Surveyor on the seventh day of September next, to the Court
Held at Newcastle where he is to remain in waiting after he
has finished his Survey, until he is called upon by the Said
Court, and this shall be your Order & Authority for so doing.[11]

The Surveyor General of Upper Canada at this time was Charles
Burton Wyatt,[12] just arrived from England. He had obtained the position through the influence of his father, the renowned architect, James
Wyatt. This privileged young man, aged twenty-six, would bring his
upper-class attitudes to Upper Canada. Until Wyatt was up to speed,
however, William Chewett[13] and Thomas Ridout[14] were appointed joint-
ly to do the job. They signed all documents with the title "Acting for
the Surveyor General." These two gentlemen were both experienced
deputy surveyors and saw themselves as rivals for the top position one
day. It wasn't an ideal situation at the head of a very busy and critical
government department, but they would muddle through, as always.

In due course, the letter from Chief Justice Allcock passed into the
hands of John Stegmann, who recalled hearing about the death of John
Sharp and immediately realized the critical nature of this survey. As an
active surveyor, he had been able to avoid direct contact with Allcock
because he was not in York very much. However, the presence of a
rookie surveyor general, who knew nothing of these matters, meant
that for all intents and purposes he would report directly to the chief
justice for this survey.

Reading the letter, Stegmann noticed the wording "the house of
Moody Farewell."[15] He understood the term to mean the trading post
operated by the Farewell brothers. For him, the key point of the order was that the surveyor "may be enabled to declare the same upon

oath."[16] This survey would not be undertaken for the usual purpose of laying out lots for settlers or running a road through the wilderness. No, it would be conducted to gain solid, technical evidence that would stand up in court.

The last sentence was even more concerning. It stated that the survey must be completed by September 7, which was not a problem for Stegmann, as long as he could get started in the next few days. Then it said that the survey must be returned "to the Court held at Newcastle where he is to remain in waiting after he has finished his Survey."[17] What? This was clearly another example of the higher-ups in the government and judiciary having little knowledge or concern about the practical issues around doing this type of survey. Contrary to orders, Stegmann would return to York after the survey in order to pay off his crew and produce the required report for the SGO. He could not sit at Newcastle and wait for the trial to begin.

The modern reader may wonder about the final sentence of the letter. It seems clear that Allcock knew very well what the outcome of the survey would be, weeks before it was completed. He assumed that the trial would be held at Newcastle, which means he already knew the Farewell trading post was in Newcastle District. We should see this in the context of Allcock and Hunter being worried about the consequences of a trial in York. It could be that they were simply taking no chances. They had their best man on the survey and were optimistic he would come back with the results they needed.

The first problem Stegmann faced was a shortage of money. In a letter to the SGO on August 15, he complains, "My want of cash to the amount of Thirty Pounds Halifax Currency, not being able to procure in this Town by a Bill on the Surveyor General's Office."[18] This issue was resolved, and the next day Stegmann engaged several experienced and reliable men he knew for a survey crew, which typically consisted of eight axemen and two chain bearers. He then purchased all the provisions they would need, including the necessary drawing tools, as indicated in a receipt for an order he picked up at the Surveyor

General's Office. It listed "Two sheets of drawing paper, Two black lead pencils, 2 black memo Books, 1 Quire paper."[19] The crew was ready to set out from York first thing in the morning.

Luckily, Stegmann's survey notes from this trip are available in the Archives of Ontario in two different forms. There are copies of the actual memo book in which he wrote his diary, and there is also the official transcription of the diary by a clerk at the Surveyor General's Office. The former shows Stegmann's excellent handwriting as well as some of his favourite spelling idiosyncrasies, such as "maid" instead of "made."[20] In any case, his words are clear, crisp, and unadorned. This fellow knew his business and wasted no time.

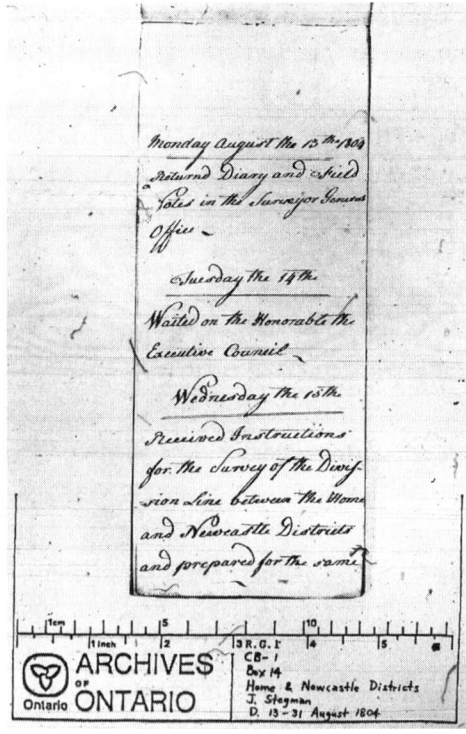

John Stegmann was an experienced deputy surveyor with meticulous habits. During the survey he took notes in a small flip-page notebook. Copies of this, as well as a transcription of his notes, are available in the Archives of Ontario.

After a quick canoe ride down the shore of the lake on August 19, the crew arrived at the boundary line between Whitby and Darlington Townships, the subject of the survey. From the shoreline they travelled straight north, confirming the line as they went, all the way to the 9th Concession, at the top end of Whitby Township. On August 21, they worked north into Reach Township and "began to open the Division Line."[21] This means they followed a compass heading and cut a trail in the bush, planting signposts at intervals along the line.

When the crew reached the western shore of Scugog Island, they stopped. On August 24, Stegmann reports in surveyor jargon, they "Scaled the Lake Beobescugog and the Large Bay by intersection."[22] This was the objective of the trip. Stegmann was able to project a line east from this point, across the island, and then over to the estimated location of the Farewell trading post. He could report, in technical terms, that John Sharp was murdered east of the boundary between Home and Newcastle districts. This was exactly what was expected of him.

On August 25, the survey was finished and the crew returned south to the lakeshore. They were paid off and discharged in York on August 28 and, the next day, according to his diary, Stegmann "Protracted the Survey and returned a Plan of the same in the Surveyor General's Office."[23] The survey report was concise and to the point. The most important words were "that the exact and positive situation of the house of Moody Farewell is seven miles eastward of the division line between the Township of Whitby & Darlington."[24] There it is, in a nutshell. The deputy surveyor had done his job. No doubt Mr. Allcock was pleased.

What is curious for the modern researcher is that the "plan" John Stegmann drew as part of the report for this survey did not accompany his diary and report to the Surveyor General's Office. At least, it is not in the same collection of records in the Archives of Ontario. Luckily, it came to light in the 1980s due to the work of Paul Arculus, an active historian from Port Perry, who found Stegmann's survey plan[25] in a collection of maps at Queen's Park in Toronto. Apparently, it had been misfiled years ago.

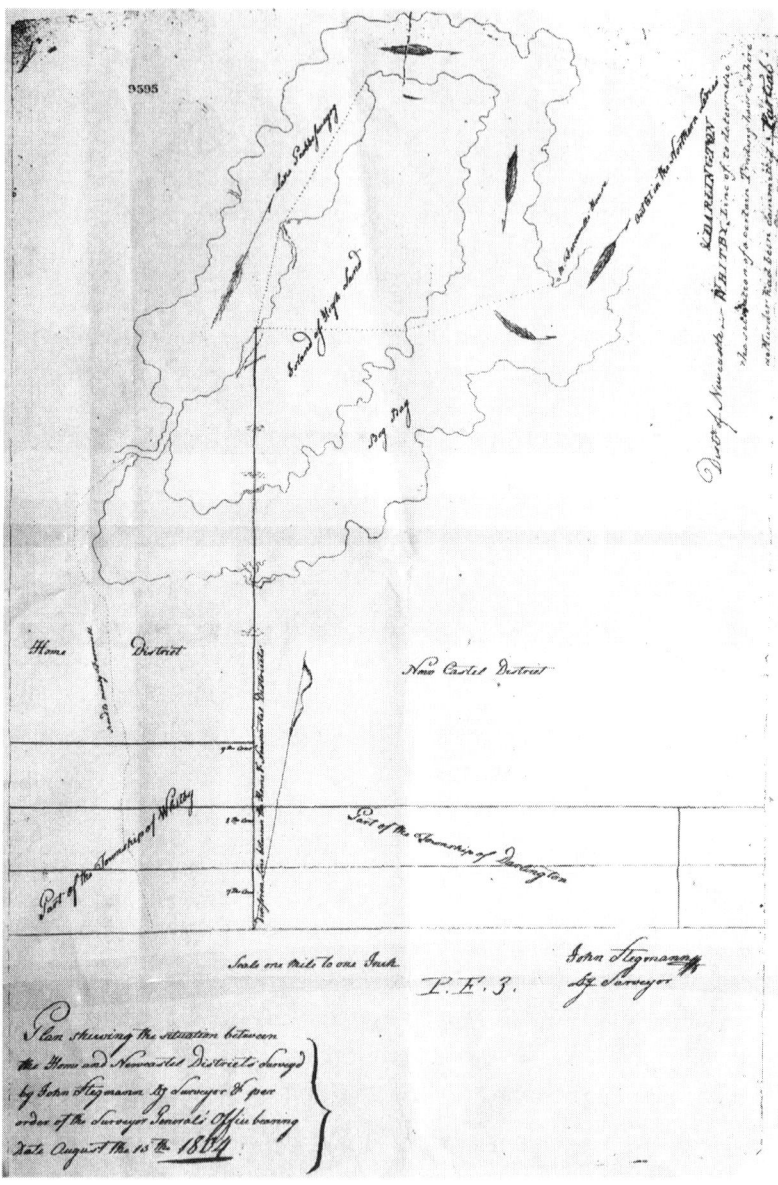

John Stegmann created a map (they called it a plan) after the survey. It shows a dark line up from the lakeshore to the western shore of Scugog Island. A dotted line goes east to M. Farewells House, showing that the murder of John Sharp took place in Newcastle District. This was exactly the point of the survey, no more, no less.

The survey map is rough, simple, and to the point. It shows the boundary between Home and Newcastle districts as a dark line up from the south, cutting across what he labelled "Island of High Land." The dark line goes only as far as the western shore of the island. From there, a dotted line goes across the island to the eastern body of water he calls "Beg Bay," then angles northeast a bit. It comes to a stop at the south end of a large peninsula jutting down from the north, which is not named. However, on the very south end of it, there is a small square with the words "M. Farewells House."

John Stegmann did not travel to the location of the Farewell trading post in August of 1804. He had finished the job and was under great pressure to get back to York and report his findings to the chief justice. He would have known the general location of the post from speaking with Moody Farewell and others who knew its location. The sketch he created was not meant to be a survey of the land in this area (that would not happen until 1816[26]), but only to provide that critical line between the districts. All he needed to know was that the post was east of the line, in Newcastle District. Mission accomplished!

CHAPTER 7

PLANNING FOR A TRIAL

With Newcastle now confirmed as the location for the murder trial, arrangements had to be made to transport a significant number of people 155 kilometres from York east to Presqu'ile Point. The first step was determining exactly who would take the trip.

Justice Thomas Cochran was only twenty-seven in September of 1804 when he was ordered to take over Ogetonicut's trial by his superior Henry Allcock, who then sailed for England. A native of Halifax, Cochran had been appointed chief justice of Prince Edward Island in 1801,[1] but he gave up that job to move up the career ladder. He was very young to be a judge on the Court of King's Bench in Upper Canada,[2] but Chief Justice Allcock had been much impressed with Cochran's obvious abilities and potential and was happy to welcome him to York. Of course, It was well-noted that the new judge came from a prominent family.[3]

Cochran would step easily into the trial preparations and proceedings. The previous year, he had conducted the fall assizes at the Newcastle District Courthouse, the first to be held there,[4] so he was familiar with the location and the building's custodians, Charles and Elizabeth Selleck. During the early weeks of September, letters were sent to the Sellecks with instructions about the next session to begin

October 10. Next, a list of all individuals to be included in the trial would be drawn up and correspondence initiated with them to ensure their attendance.

Judge Cochran would be ably assisted in these preparations by Solicitor General Robert Gray and Gray's assistant, John Anderson. Gray had plenty of experience travelling on Lake Ontario and the St. Lawrence River, since he occasionally visited his hometown of Cornwall, some 430 kilometres from York. The trip to Newcastle was much shorter, but it would still take him away from his comforts and social life. Such were the trials of public service.

In spite of his youth, Gray had accumulated significant property and other assets that would require disposition in the unlikely event of his death. He felt great responsibility regarding his family, so he set about preparing for his trip to Newcastle by making a will. The Gray family had owned slaves as household servants and farm workers for many years, which was not unusual for wealthy landowners at that time. When his father, James Gray, died in 1795, Robert inherited large land holdings near Cornwall and ownership of the slaves.[5] His ultimate plan was to free them.

Abolitionists had been busy in England for decades, and the Somerset decision in 1772[6] stated clearly that slavery was not supported by British common law. In Upper Canada, Lt.-Gov. Simcoe had attempted to abolish slavery in 1793 but was forced to compromise in favour of a gradual approach. Most men in the government held slaves, and they were not willing to give up one of their most valuable assets all at once. They agreed, instead, to prohibit importation of slaves into Upper Canada and decreed that all current slaves should be freed when they reached the age of twenty-five. They thought slavery would fade away of its own accord under these conditions. Unfortunately, the law was largely ignored.[7]

The Slave Trade Act of 1807[8] would prohibit the slave trade in the British Empire, and emancipation would become law in 1834 when Parliament agreed to pay compensation to the owners. But thirty years earlier, as Gray's will shows, liberal-minded people were moving away from their traditional attitudes, toward the practical steps that each family could take to free their own slaves.

Robert Gray felt very close to Dorine Baker, who had raised him, and he was protective of her two sons, John and Simon. In his will he wrote, "I feel it a duty incumbent on me, in consequence of the long and faithful services of Dorine, my black woman servant, rendered to my family, to release, manumit and discharge her from the state of slavery in which she now is, and to give her and all her children their freedom."[9]

While the sentiment was not unique in Upper Canada at this time, direct actions resulting in financial loss were less common. For example, Robert Gray's approach was in stark contrast to the cold, dollars-and-cents approach of Peter Russell, who had been administrator of Upper Canada before Hunter arrived and was now receiver general. In 1806 he advertised in the *Upper Canada Gazette* regarding the sale of two slaves:

> To be sold: A Black Woman named Peggy, aged forty years, and a Black Boy, her son, named Jupiter, aged about fifteen years, both of them the property of the subscriber. The woman is a tolerable cook and washerwoman, and perfectly under-stands making soap and candles. The boy is tall and strong for his age, and has been employed in the country business, but brought up principally as a house servant. They are each of them servants for life. The price of the woman is one hundred and fifty dollars. For the boy two hundred dollars, payable in three years, with interest from the day of sale, and to be se-cured by bond, &c. But one-fourth less will be taken for ready money. York, Feb. 19th, 1806. Peter Russell.[10]

As Robert Gray was completing his will, John Stegmann received a letter from the Surveyor General's Office dated September 28 that said,

"Sir, the Chief Justice on the day of his departure said that you was to attend the Court House for the District of New Castle on the 10th of October but perceiving the hurry the Chief was in when you were last here, he may have only thought he gave you this charge, we now repeat it, as from him. We are, Sir, Your most Obedient, for the Surv. Gen'l. Chewett & Ridout."[11]

Stegmann had been planning to sail to Newcastle for the fall assizes, and this letter made it official. He would be present and ready to testify for the Crown in the trial of Ogetonicut. As a forty-four-year-old man with a wife and a house full of young children, however, Stegmann dreaded the trip. He had a lovely farm at Pine Grove in Vaughan Township,[12] north of York, and was beginning to begrudge the time away from his family. He knew he earned a good living because his skills and knowledge were in great demand, but he hoped to stay around home a bit more in the future. The family would love that.

Angus Macdonell[13] would go to Newcastle as well. He was one of the best lawyers in York and had been appointed defence counsel for the accused. A single man, his closest family in York was his brother, Alexander Macdonell,[14] also still single, though planning to be married in the next year. Although both brothers were members of the House of Assembly, they seldom worked together on legislative issues. It was obvious to everyone that being defence counsel when the trial result was a foregone conclusion was not the most satisfying work, but Angus Macdonell had shown a streak of independence that was sorely lacking in most office-seekers in York. He would do the best he could with what he was given.

John Fisk, the fifty-two-year-old high constable of Home District, would be responsible for escorting the accused, Ogetonicut, to Newcastle. Fisk's home was in King Township,[15] north of York, where his wife, Levine Dean, tended to the farm and the kids while he was away in York. This was a relatively new situation for the family, since Fisk had been appointed high constable of Home District only in

April.[16] Certainly, the trip was not something he looked forward to, but he was anxious to perform his duties as high constable.

James Ruggles would also make the trip to Newcastle, in his capacity as a Justice of the Peace for York County. His job was to assist John Fisk in ensuring the security and condition of the accused. Ruggles immigrated to York in 1796 from Massachusetts, married in 1801,[17] and had been involved as a commissioner in several developments in Upper Canada in recent years. He was a member of the commission that provided major repairs for the bridge at Burlington Bay[18] and he participated in the plans to improve fire safety practices in York.[19] Just a few weeks before, Ruggles had performed one of his more routine tasks when he travelled to Markham Township to determine whether the person recorded for a certain lot had, in fact, settled there and done improvements.[20] His report to Chief Justice Allcock confirmed that another homestead was in the making and they could check that lot off their list. Earlier in the summer, Ruggles's thoughts were also on culture and education, according to a friend who recorded in his diary for July 22, 1804, that "Jas. Ruggles & me had a deal of talk about a Library which we wished to establish."[21]

George Cowan was probably the most colourful of all the people who would go to Newcastle for this trial. Born in Scotland, Cowan came to North America as a boy and found himself captured by the French at Fort Pitt, where he lived near the Indigenous people of the area. A bright boy, he quickly mastered several Indigenous languages, which served him well when he made his way to Michilimackinac to engage in the fur trade. He established a home and trading post on the south end of Georgian Bay, called Matchedash,[22] which included the large house everyone knew as "The Two Chimneys"[23] due to two impressive towers that could be seen from well out in the bay.

Through years of fair trading and honest treatment of all alike, Cowan gained the trust and co-operation of the Indigenous people in the area. Lt.-Gov. Simcoe visited Matchedash in 1793[24] and was much impressed by this man who seemed to live and work as well with the

English traders as the Indigenous ones. He recommended Cowan for a position as an interpreter with the government in order to take advantage of this man's long experience.

The role of interpreter was essential to carrying out government policy at this time. Most English traders and officials did not speak any of the Indigenous languages, and the chiefs of the Mississauga, Ojibwa, Chippewa, and Mohawk seldom knew more than a few words of English. A good interpreter could smooth over the chasm between the two sides as they sat in a meeting, ready to discuss important topics like land surrenders and military alliances.[25]

Cowan's services had been critical during tense negotiations at Penetanguishene in 1797 after survey crews were accosted by a group of angry men who insisted the English had no right surveying for a road because the land did not belong to them. A provisional agreement for the purchase of a large tract of land hung in the balance. The government desperately offered Cowan large land grants and other benefits if he would apply his skills to the problem.[26] The Indigenous people in the area trusted Cowan, but these situations would test that trust.

Peter Russell, the administrator of Upper Canada at the time, made it clear to Cowan that it was not just his skills as an interpreter that they needed. He wrote "You are to do your utmost to discover the Dispositions, Movements, and Intentions of the Lake Indians toward Lakes Simcoe & Huron, and fail not to transmit to me the earliest Intelligence of every matter that may come to your knowledge, which you shall judge likely to affect the Kings Interest or the Welfare of this Province."[27]

Compared to this, the job of interpreting for an accused murderer must have seemed rather tame to Cowan, just another paying job. We might wonder why such an experienced interpreter was sent to Newcastle for this murder case. Perhaps this was another reflection of Lt.-Gov. Hunter's desire to make sure this trial went off without a hitch. He wanted no possibility of complaints after the trial that the accused was not treated fairly due to inadequate understanding of the proceedings. No matter the cost, he would have the best interpreter in the province on the job.

When the list of participants was complete, it was clear that the trip to Newcastle would include a significant slice of Upper Canada's most experienced and productive professionals.

CHAPTER 8

THE SHIP
AND THE CAPTAIN

One afternoon in the middle of September, Peter Hunter and James Green sat under a shade tree near Parliament House, enjoying the cool breezes off the bay. It was a welcome break from the meetings and discussions that had filled their day to that point. Hunter was anxious to move ahead with the construction of new and larger Parliament buildings to accommodate the growing number of officials and functions at York. He was also hoping for a more dignified and aesthetically pleasing edifice that would impress residents of York as well as visitors. The capital of Upper Canada was a place of significance, and it should look the part.

An ambitious plan for the new structure had been presented by Edward Walsh,[1] a surgeon with the Forty-ninth Regiment, which came to York in May of 1803 to replace the Forty-first Regiment at the garrison. The plan matched Hunter's expectations. It had a large hexagonal hall with galleries and a dome, as well as large chambers for the legislative council and House of Assembly. There was space for a library and much-needed practical features such as water closets, kitchens, and storage rooms. Walsh insisted the new buildings could be built of wood and brick for no more than £1,000 sterling.

This all sounded wonderful, but the discussion quickly turned toward the practical matter of finance. Walsh's proposal might have been a little too ambitious for the times. Both men knew that the Napoleonic Wars were ramping up and huge amounts of money were being directed toward growing armies on the continent as well as the British Navy. It was starting to look like their ambitious plans would have to wait, at least for now.

Hunter and Green gazed down the shoreline and took notice of a ship being tied up at the small wharf at the garrison. Looking more closely with his spyglass, Hunter confirmed it was HMS *Speedy*, one of His Majesty's Armed Vessels on Lake Ontario. The ship was letting off stores and a few passengers, and there would soon be a messenger running across the green sward with a pack of letters. Arrivals and departures of the various ships on the lake were anticipated to some degree, but the vagaries of weather and ship conditions often caused delays of several days. It was impossible to know exactly when any given ship would arrive at its destination, but they were always welcome, if only for the mail.

The flurry of preparations going on around York regarding the trial of Ogetonicut had, by this time, focused on the very practical issue of transportation. The fall assizes were scheduled to begin at Newcastle on October 10, so the contingent of officials, assistants, witnesses, plus the constables and, of course, the accused, must leave York no later than the seventh. During the last week of September, several of the ships that were active on the lake at this time came and went according to their normal habits. Now, only a week before the planned departure for Newcastle, it was time to select a ship for this special duty.

Setting down his spyglass, Hunter shook his head in a gesture that said, "Oh, dear!" The two men looked at each other and grimaced. HMS *Speedy* was one of several British gunboats that plied the Great Lakes at this time. They were built and managed by the Provincial Marine, the organization that represented the British Navy in the British North American colonies. Many of the ship captains and sailors in these ships came out of the British Navy by one path or another, but the organization was commanded by the British Army, which had its headquarters in Quebec City. Hunter knew HMS *Speedy* as the vessel that had delivered him to York in August 1799, amid ceremony and celebration.[2] It was a typical workhorse for the Provincial Marine. Government officials and military officers travelled between Kingston, York, and Fort George on these ships and, at the same time, decks were piled high with all kinds of cargo.

Launched at Kingston in the fall of 1798,[3] at the same time as the identical HMS *Swift*, the *Speedy* was a modest gunboat, about fifty-five feet long, with twin masts. Hunter recalled that the launch of both ships had been delayed several months in order to build an extra two feet of height on the sides of the deck.[4] The demand for shipping space was growing every year, and this modification was done to increase the tonnage carried by each ship. Unfortunately, it would also make them difficult to sail in rough weather.

As he squinted again through the spyglass, Hunter had the unsettling feeling that both he and HMS *Speedy* were a bit worse for wear. His gout was a persistent annoyance, and the long-standing stomach ailments he had picked up in the tropics made him crankier than normal. The ship was at the end of a stormy sailing season and had a sad, ragged appearance. What Hunter remembered about his trips on this conveyance was the discomfort of travelling with meagre passenger comforts. The *Toronto Yacht*, which he much preferred for his trips across the lake, had a private cabin that he appreciated.

Knowing the history of HMS *Speedy*, neither Hunter nor Green would have willingly chosen it for the Newcastle trip. In the fall of 1804, it was six years old and nearing the end of its useful life. Its construction had followed the common practice of the Provincial Marine at the time, using timber that was uncured, or green. This resulted in high maintenance and a short lifespan. In 1795, the Duke of La Rochefoucauld had noted "All these vessels are built of timber fresh cut down and not seasoned, and for this reason last never longer than six or eight years. To preserve them, even to this time, requires a thorough repair."[5] Nothing much had changed in a decade. In fact, the British Military and Naval Records, held in the collection of Library and Archives Canada, show there were plans afoot to repair the *Speedy* that fall[6] in the hope that it might gain one more shipping season before it would have to be replaced. This kind of major refit was repeated every winter for these ships, in order to make sure they would be ready for the next sailing season.

Normally, the cargo carried by *Speedy* and the other vessels of the Provincial Marine was very mundane. On April 17, 1804, Lt. Earle wrote from Kingston that "I intend to load the Speedy this week with Pease to go on to Amherstburg."[7] A request from Kingston on August 13, 1801, asked "to forward fifty bushels of Indian Corn for the use of His Majesty's Service. I have ordered Lt. Paxton to take them on board the Speedy."[8] A year later, the cargo may have been somewhat more anticipated when "the Speedy, after receiving some repairs, is now receiving a cargo of port on board for the upper country."[9]

Another kind of function for HMS *Speedy* is found in a letter sent to Hunter by Lieutenant Colonel Isaac Brock,[10] commander at Fort George, on October 1, 1803. "At the request of Mrs. Powell, who arrived here just in time to take her last farewell of her son, the lawyer who died the day before yesterday, I consented to delay the sailing of the *Speedy* till this evening, that she might be accommodated with a package back to York. Indeed, the little wind that blew the whole of yesterday was so very contrary, I much doubt whether the *Speedy* could have made any way, had she attempted to sail."[11]

In another letter to Hunter, while he was still at Fort George, Brock said at the bottom, "I am by this conveyance requesting the General's acceptance four brace and a half of very fine quails."[12] There was always room for networking, after all. We expect the quail were appreciated and the lieutenant-governor made note of the gesture. In fact, this was typical of Brock, who is better known as the tragic hero of Queenston Heights, where he was killed fighting the Americans in 1812.

Hunter and Green were both army men. They were imbued with the traditions and beliefs of that very strong institution, which meant that they distrusted sailors and, in particular, uppity ship captains who questioned or directly disobeyed orders. The Provincial Marine was seen as an unruly organization, full of prima donnas, misfits, and criminals. Many a fist fight occurred in pubs where sailors and soldiers were enjoying a pint, the quarrel erupting over nothing more than partisan pride. Soldiers and sailors were not a good mix.

The captain of HMS *Speedy* was a good example of this conflict. Thomas Paxton[13] had been promoted to first lieutenant in 1790, second lieutenant in 1791, and became a full lieutenant, on August 1, 1797, as ordered by Robert Prescott, commander of the British forces in the colonies. Paxton was expected "carefully and diligently to discharge the duty of Lieutenant,"[14] a responsibility he took very seriously. He was a career Navy man.

Lt. Paxton had been captain of HMS *Speedy* from its first day on the water. His long experience and extensive knowledge of sailing on Lake Ontario made him an obvious choice. Less welcome in the authoritarian world of the British Army was his willingness to bend the rules and his propensity for voicing his own opinion.

On the positive side, it was useful to have the man's expertise in the constant boards of survey that were held at Kingston in order to evaluate the condition of a ship and outline the material and labour required to put the ship back in service. Paxton served on dozens of these boards from the time he was commissioned as a full lieutenant.[15] There was also a consensus that young sailors would receive excellent tutoring from this old salt, and newcomers were assigned to his ships deliberately to spread his knowledge around.

However, there had been several instances where the arrival of important stores was delayed or, in some cases, cargo was damaged by storms or accidents. The authorities always blamed the captain. In addition, Paxton was not shy about complaining when he could not obtain the quantity of firewood and candles he expected and needed for his growing family in Kingston.[16] Even more damning, as far as the army was concerned, was an incident in which Paxton went ashore at Kingston to spend the night at home with his family rather than stay on board the ship to make sure no sailors deserted. It was common knowledge that sailors in the Provincial Marine were undesirable fellows, just waiting for the opportunity to desert. News of desertions passed around Kingston, York and Newark routinely, and authorities complained constantly about how tough it was to keep enough men to man the ships. When two of Paxton's men deserted that night, the captain was blamed, and he had another blot on his record.[17]

Two events in particular caused the authorities to question Paxton's loyalty and general fitness for service. In 1798, Peter Russell, administrator of Upper Canada, wrote General Prescott, commander at Quebec, asking for a favour. He said he had approval from the Duke of Portland that "gives me leave to build a small armed Vessel for the Service of the Civil Government of this Province, I had contracted with a Ship Wright in this place to build one, and I had promised Lieut. Paxton of the Lake Marine to give him the Command of her, if he could obtain your Excellency's Permission to take it without injuring the Progress of his Rank in the line in which he is now serving."[18]

This was a terrific opportunity for Paxton. The new ship would be much larger and better equipped, which meant it would be safer and make his work on the lake much easier. Also, the pay would be considerably more than the meagre stipend he received from the Provincial Marine. On the other hand, he knew that his rank as lieutenant in the British Navy was critical to his long-term financial stability. He was forty-four years old, with a wife and five children. He could not do anything to jeopardize the well-being of his family. In this context, Lt. Paxton kept very quiet, so as not to give away his preference.

From the standpoint of the Provincial Marine and the authorities in York, experienced ship captains were very scarce on the Great Lakes and they wanted to keep Paxton in the fold. They were quite willing to threaten the captain with loss of rank if he took leave to sail on a ship for the civil government, although they were not ready to raise his salary to keep him in place. The Provincial Marine was under strict financial regulation and was not inclined to increase the pay of sailors. The result was poor service on the lakes and a constant shortage of sailors and shipping. It also explains many of the desertions. In the end, General Prescott did not approve Russell's proposal and Lt. Paxton stayed at the helm of HMS *Speedy*.[19]

A more sensational episode in 1800 caused much disruption and confusion. The commodore of the Provincial Marine at this time was Jean-Baptiste Bouchette,[20] a long-time mariner and one of the most experienced sailors in the colonies. His claim to fame was his daring rescue of Guy Carleton[21] in 1775, while the Americans were attacking Quebec, and he owed his later success to favours from Carleton, who later became Lord Dorchester. In 1800, Bouchette was sixty-four years old and nearing the end of his career. He had been appointed commodore in 1794 and had assumed this meant he had full control. The army commander at Point Frederick had very different orders, and the two clashed constantly.

As the commodore became increasingly obnoxious and unreasonable, a group of senior members of the Provincial Marine insisted on a court of inquiry to highlight his dangerous and damaging behaviour. A telling part of its report reads: "I am led to believe that the want of respect and improper conduct in the Lieutenants Fortie, Paxton and Earl [sic], towards their superior officer, Captain Bouchette, is owing in a great measure, to his not adhering to the established rules, and orders given him for the government of the Marine Department under his command."[22]

Fortie, Paxton, and Earle would succeed in their attempts to force the commodore to resign, although it would take another two years of disruption and anxiety before he finally left, more because of ill health than any desire to retire. While this was a good result for the men of the Provincial Marine, it marked the three lieutenants, all excellent professionals in their field, as troublemakers lacking the proper respect for tradition and authority. This cloud hung over Thomas Paxton long after the Bouchette affair was over.

When *HMS Speedy* docked at York in late September 1804, all Captain Paxton wanted to do was unload his ship, have a few things repaired, then set off for Kingston on the last trip of the season. There were major repairs already scheduled at Point Frederick, amounting to a full swapping of sails and rigging with HMS *Swift*. On September 27, Captain D.W. Edwards, the officer in command of the dockyards at Kingston, wrote James Green, saying "I have spoken to Captain Steel respecting the exchange of sails between the *Speedy* and *Swift*, which is to take place as soon as Paxton's vessel arrives and I shall then report the number of each articles exchanged."[23]

There was damage to the sails and rigging of both ships that had been caused by a series of storms, and temporary, makeshift repairs had been made to carry them through the last few months of the shipping season. Over the winter, the captain would oversee the full repair of his ship and spend some welcome time with his family at their home in Kingston. Now fifty years old, Paxton was starting to feel the wear and tear of three decades on the water.

In spite of their trepidations, Green told Hunter that he would summon Paxton to speak with the lieutenant-governor about the trip to Newcastle. The next day, in response to the order, Captain Thomas Paxton walked into Parliament House and put himself at Hunter's disposal. He had no idea why he had been called in, but he had enough experience to expect that it would not be agreeable. Indeed, he did not like what he heard.

Green watched as the Captain's face changed expression and his cheeks reddened. Not only would he not sail for Kingston on the next fair wind, Hunter told him, but he would have to prepare his ship for more than twenty passengers along with their baggage. The old sea dog tried to control his anger but was not altogether successful. Green attempted to mediate, but the message was clear. These three men were all direct and simple talkers. Nobody had to guess what the other was thinking.

When it was his turn to speak, Captain Paxton ran through a long list of issues, as he saw them. He emphasized the dangers of loading passengers on this ship at this time. HMS *Speedy* was not designed to take twenty passengers down the length of Lake Ontario, especially not in October, when storms could come up quickly and be extremely dangerous. If they had to put the accused and a constable down below, that would force passengers onto the open deck of the ship for more than twenty-four hours of October weather. How would he feed them, or carry enough water for them all? How would they keep warm? It was just impossible.

The captain described his ship's condition. The damage of the past sailing season, mitigated only to a degree by temporary repairs, had left him with a vessel that was ungainly, clumsy, and very difficult to navigate. HMS *Speedy* had never been a swan out on the lake, even from the first day off the blocks, partly because of the extra two feet of deck height that made it top-heavy when fully loaded. The heightened deck made the ship less manageable in difficult seas. Add to that the rotten condition of timbers in the hull, which needed major repairs every winter, and you had a ship that was not in good shape.

Paxton then reviewed the list of passengers for this trip. It included the Solicitor General, a judge, a barrister, the high constable, a magistrate, the surveyor, and more. This was simply too much. The straight-talking sea captain told Lt.-Gov. Hunter that he could not possibly be responsible for the lives of all these people under such dangerous conditions. He would not sail!

As one might expect, however, the lieutenant-governor had the final say. If Lt. Paxton refused an order from his superior, Hunter said, he would immediately be arrested. Then, he would face court martial, losing all his rank and seniority. He might spend considerable time in jail. That was the choice. Thomas Paxton staggered backward as if hit by a shovel. He was shocked at the brutal and uncompromising nature of Hunter's threat. His mind went immediately to his family and the destitution that would result from the loss of his income. He was not willing to let that happen, no matter what he was forced to do.

His orders had been written up before the meeting. Lt. Col. Green handed them over as Paxton stepped quietly out of Parliament House. He strode smartly down the path to his ship. Now that it was established that he would sail HMS *Speedy* to Newcastle, he turned his mind to all the tasks that needed to be done to ensure a safe and timely journey for all. As always, Captain Paxton would do the best he could under the conditions he was given.

Contemporary records do not mention this exchange between Paxton and Hunter. The only reference we have to this sharp application of authority comes from a petition in 1827 by one of the captain's sons, Thomas Paxton Jr.,[24] who lived in Amherstburg. He was asking for permission to purchase Fighting Island,[25] in the Detroit River, for business purposes. He already had a licence to use the land, but now he wanted to buy the land or, better yet, have it granted to him. A grant would be appropriate, he felt, because he had not yet received any land grants from the government, in spite of his service during the War of 1812 and his father's extensive service with the Provincial Marine.

It is interesting that Paxton Jr. leads his petition with the accusation that Lt.-Gov. Hunter "peremptorily ordered"[26] his father to sail HMS *Speedy* in spite of the fact that Captain Paxton "remonstrated alledging the utter unworthiness of the vessel to go to sea."[27] Thomas Paxton Jr. was just ten years old in 1804, but he would have heard about it from family and friends as he grew up. It would be a tangible lesson about the real relationship between most folks in the community and the few who held final authority. There was no doubt, in the case of this episode between Paxton and Hunter, that the authority of the state had won.

CHAPTER 9

THE ACCUSED
AND THE LAW

After Ogetonicut was arrested, John Fisk, the high constable of Home District, worked closely with William Knott, the jailer, to ensure that this important prisoner was treated well and that security was maintained with no exceptions. The garrison commander co-operated by arranging for a squad of soldiers from the Forty-ninth Regiment to guard the jail and watch its only inmate very closely. This patrol changed three times a day in such a punctual routine that nearby residents could determine the time by seeing the soldiers tramping back and forth between the jail and the garrison.

Through the summer of 1804, John Fisk also paid special attention to the Mississauga camp at Gibraltar Point. The initial perception of this site as a threat to public peace proved unfounded, as the Mississauga people kept to the islands and sandspits across the bay. Chief Wabbekisheco was true to his word in keeping the younger men under control, and there were routine meetings between the chief, the high constable, and Ruggles, the magistrate, to deal with any concerns of the authorities at York or complaints from the citizens. It had been a quiet summer.

Soon after Ogetonicut was incarcerated, his family began visiting the jail, bringing clothing and food, and spending time with the young man. They often performed rituals and ceremonies meant to encourage the spirits of the jail to protect their son. William Knott was very tolerant of these visits, having instructions from the Solicitor General to accommodate the needs of the Mississauga people to the greatest degree possible. It was important to keep them from causing any trouble, so moderation was the best approach.

Of greater concern was the occasional presence of tents in the green sward along the shoreline when small family groups came to York and stayed for a few days. This was not unusual in the context of normal trade and commercial activity around the town. In fact, most often these campers were not the Mississauga people from Gibraltar Point but others from the Credit River or Georgian Bay. Sometimes they were settlers who came to York for business or to visit relatives. Of course, for most townsfolk, one tent looked pretty much the same as any other, so tensions remained just below the surface.

The lawyer appointed to defend Ogetonicut, Angus Macdonell, was busy through the summer trying to mount a credible defence for the accused. He had come to the jail several times with the interpreter, to get the story from the point of view of the accused. It had been difficult, because Ogetonicut was not very receptive and said little. They spoke to his family members and they were helpful, but the best information the lawyer could find was James Green's transcript of the interview with Moody Farewell and Eleazer Lockwood. Their words were enough for Macdonell to understand the events and their context.

What Macdonell heard from Ogetonicut, when he would speak, and from his relatives when they visited, was a persistent and heartfelt expression of anger. His family and, in fact, their whole Mississauga community, felt insulted and degraded by the absence of compensation for the death of Whistling Duck a year before. The authorities at York had hoped this episode was behind them, but they did not understand the deep-seated traditions of the Mississauga people and their basic need for restitution in the face of tragic loss. The two sides were worlds apart on this issue.

An account of Whistling Duck's demise is found in T.E. Kaiser's *Historic Sketches of Oshawa*. It is included in a passage about Ogetonicut murdering John Sharp: "This Indian was a brother to Whistling Duck, who had been killed by a white man the winter previous, at Cozens, in what is now the township of Clarke. Whistling Duck had tried to thrust a muskrat spear through an American, but missed his aim, and had his skull cracked. The Governor promised there should be blood for blood, and this is why Sharp was killed."[1]

Samuel D. Cozens owned property close to the lakeshore in Clarke Township,[2] near the home of Robert Baldwin.[3] Samuel's father, Daniel Cozens, had been a dedicated Loyalist from New Jersey who had performed significant service to the Crown and was granted several thousand acres of land in Upper Canada. Much of this land was in or near the town of York, and his sons would inherit property of considerable value.[4]

That Samuel Cozens killed Whistling Duck would be confirmed much later by recollections of neighbour Mary Warren Baldwin.[5] She was only eleven years old in 1803 when another event occurred a few months after the Whistling Duck incident. At the time, the Baldwin household included old Mr. Baldwin, his young daughters Alice and Mary, and a French maid. Mary's daughter, Maria, would tell the story in 1859, using her mother's words.[6] (The full text can be found in Appendix D.)

It happened on a Sunday, after Mr. Baldwin had gone over to Samuel Cozens's place. A group of Mississauga men came to their home and demanded alcohol, which the daughters refused. It was well-known that the Baldwins had a cache of whisky somewhere under the house, so the men persisted. The maid tried to go to the Cozens's house to get help but was waylaid and sent back home.

Many of the intruders, who numbered about forty and were well-armed, were already intoxicated. The maid and the Baldwin girls feared for their lives but still refused to produce the whisky. After a time, Mr. Baldwin returned home with his neighbour, Samuel Cozens. At the sight of Cozens, one of the Mississauga men stepped forward. As Maria explained, "No sooner did the Indians see him than one man drew his knife and showed it to my mother, saying, 'Cozens kill my brother, I kill Cozens.'"[7] Whisky was reluctantly handed over and the ordeal ended peacefully.

This story provides a tantalizing glimpse into the mind of Ogetonicut and his family regarding the lack of action on the part of the authorities to bring Whistling Duck's killer to justice. In fact, the person who said, "Cozens kill my brother, I kill Cozens" may have been Ogetonicut himself. The word "brother" could be used very broadly in the Mississauga culture, so it could refer to someone else in the immediate family group. However, all the references to this relationship use the word brother, and they are all from non-Indigenous writers, historians and even some from the Baldwin family. In this context, it is very likely to mean exactly what it says, his brother.

From the standpoint of the legal authorities in York, the incident between Samuel Cozens and Whistling Duck had been a clear case of self-defence, and there would be no legal action taken. Unfortunately, according to Kaiser, "The Governor promised there should be blood for blood, and this is why Sharp was killed."[8] This was typical of the kind of language used by the authorities in York. They had no intention of doing anything in this case, but promises to the chiefs would keep things quiet for the time being.

From Ogetonicut's point of view, this totally missed the point. Over centuries, the Mississauga and their parent group, the Ojibwa, had devised an effective way to identify and recognize an evil deed, especially if someone was harmed. There were elaborate ceremonies and rituals through which the guilty party and his family had an opportunity to provide gifts and promises of support. If the parties could not agree, the chiefs and elders would negotiate a solution that would not only satisfy both parties but would bind the two groups together even more closely in the future. It was an opportunity for community building and helped maintain fair and equitable relationships between members. It had worked well for many generations and was integral to the Mississauga culture.

J.R. Miller tells us in *Skyscrapers Hide the Heavens: A History of Native-Newcomer Relations in Canada* that "In societies without coercive authority or police functions, a major deterrent to violence against people was the requirement that those whose kin or tribesmen had been killed avenge the fallen. A family that had lost a member to another in the nation was theoretically obliged to kill a member of that other family, though in practice such obligations were transmuted into acceptance of a compensatory payment for the loss."[9]

Sure, the young men would often have revenge in mind, but the community was less interested in determining guilt than engaging in negotiation toward compensation. They had lost a member of their family and it was expected that someone from Samuel Cozens's family or the government would offer them something. They were willing to accept gifts that would smooth the whole thing over.

This story also provides a stark illustration of the fear that settlers still felt regarding the presence of the Mississauga people in the area. Raids on known liquor caches were not uncommon at this time, usually by groups of young men whom the chiefs found it impossible to control. They wanted firewater. After they got it, they normally sat down, drank it all, slept it off, then went away.

How had it come to this? The path is not difficult to discern. After the British defeated the French at the Plains of Abraham in 1759, the Indigenous people around the Great Lakes dealt with English traders, who were supported by the British government. The traders in Boston learned that rum could be an effective tool for controlling the Indigenous men who came to them with furs. In collaboration, the governing authorities would turn a blind eye, or even participate when it served their purposes. It proved to be a very effective approach, and would become one of those wink-wink, nod-nod policies.

The situation has been explained like this:

'The free sale of rum will destroy them more effectually than fire and sword.' There is more evidence to indicate that this became the government's method of dealing with potential uprisings. In 1761 traders had been forbidden to carry, sell, or give strong liquor to the Indians, but on 27 April 1763 Bouquet was calculating the expense and equipment required for 375 packhorses to carry 18,000 gallons of liquor to Fort Pitt. Again, given the social disintegration caused by alcoholism among the Indians, it is possible that there was an unwritten policy in this regard following the peace and the resumption of trade.[10]

The meagre regulations for selling liquor were ignored by traders who were intent on making profits, and competition between aggressive individuals made matters worse. "Under such conditions, the loyalty to the British, the contentment of the various Ojibwa bands, and the degree of tranquility in the Great Lakes depended to a considerable extent on the acceptability of the local English trader. Each band of Indians and each trader determined the law 'or lawlessness' among themselves. Because of this situation, the unity of the Ojibwa Nation was not enhanced. These various bands, therefore, were less prepared to withstand the impact that would hit them in the last decades of the eighteenth century."[11]

Four decades of this practice decimated Indigenous families and communities across the region. In the Lake Scugog area, we don't have evidence of the Farewell brothers selling liquor to the Mississauga people, but we can expect they operated under standard habits of the time. Working under the auspices of Lawrence and Jacob Herkimer, who had several trading posts in the area, the Farewells were new to the trade and probably keen on doing what they were told.

The Herkimer brothers were known to be aggressive businessmen, intent on making profits, like most traders of the time. Their father, "John Jost Herkimer, a fur trader who had settled at Cataraqui as a Loyalist in 1784 or 1785,"[12] was also known back in the United States, with "a reputation for selling excessive quantities of rum."[13] Whatever the immediate circumstances for the Farewell brothers' trading post at Lake Scugog, the aggressive selling of rum and whisky to the Mississauga people was an accepted part of the fur trade.

Another killing on the minds of all Indigenous people of Upper Canada at this time was that of Mississauga Chief Wabakinine[14] at York on August 20, 1796. An altercation with a soldier at the shoreline ended in the death of both Chief Wabakinine and his wife.[15] It was well-known that the soldier was guilty of criminal behaviour. As part of the investigation, the authorities asked for the exhumation of the bodies of the chief and his wife. There were rumours that the chief was not actually dead, and they wanted to examine the bodies in order to be certain a crime had been committed. Any disturbance of a burial site was completely contrary to cultural norms for the Mississauga people, and the request was rejected. Eventually, the perpetrator went free, to the outrage of the Indigenous community. Peter Russell, the administrator of Upper Canada at that time, was hard pressed to placate the Indigenous people with gifts and supplies, in order to keep order in the province.[16]

Here was another clear example of the difficult relations between these two very different societies. Cultural practices as simple as aversion to exhumation, along with very different ideas about fairness in achieving justice, combined to create tragic situations that left scars in the public consciousness for decades to come. The Mississauga people knew they were unlikely to get justice for wrongs done to one of their members, but the Ogetonicut episode demonstrates how the English would rush to make sure a young Mississauga man paid with his life in order to placate the settler community. Justice was a one-sided coin in Upper Canada.

CHAPTER 10

PREPARATIONS AT NEWCASTLE

Preparations for the fall assizes moved into high gear in Newcastle in September. Charles and Elizabeth Selleck[1] were custodians of the new courthouse and jail, where the trial would take place. They set to work cleaning third-floor guest rooms and stocking the kitchen and tavern for the large group of important visitors coming from York. They had hosted the first court session the previous year, but this one would be much different. Besides run-of-the-mill larceny and fraud cases, it would include a murder trial that was the talk of the province. The anticipation was palpable.

Charles Selleck was an experienced ship captain who came from a large seafaring family in Stamford, Connecticut.[2] In the last years of the War of Independence, when he was barely twenty years old, Charles enlisted with His Majesty's Marine Department and worked on British gunboats, where he gained the rank of lieutenant.[3] After the war, he immigrated to Upper Canada, and in 1797 married Elizabeth Gibson,[4] daughter of George Gibson, a ship carpenter.

Both men had been engaged in the shipping of people and goods from Newark to York in support of the transfer of the capital in 1794.[5] Selleck was for a time captain of the *Duchess of York*, according to an

item in the Newark newspaper, the *Canada Constellation*, which reported in 1799 that "If Jonathan A. Pell will return and pay Captain Selleck
for the freight of the salt which he took from on board the Duchess
of York without leave, it will be thankfully received and no questions
asked."[6] Unfortunately, the same ship was lost off Devil's Nose, near
Rochester, New York, in December 1799,[7] an example of how dangerous
it could be on Lake Ontario outside the normal sailing season.

At Presqu'ile, Selleck and Gibson operated their own ship called
the *Lady Murray*. They had settled permanently with their families in
the new town of Newcastle in 1802, and the following summer worked
together to build the new courthouse and jail: "a large frame building,
thirty feet in width and fifty feet in length and three stories high, on
a heavy stone basement."[8] For a short time, it had been the largest
building between the Trent River and York. When it was complete,
the Selleck family moved in. During the summer of 1804, Selleck and
Gibson also built a new wharf at the shoreline near the courthouse, in
exchange for the grant of one acre of land for the purpose.[9] The town
of Newcastle would develop due to the enterprise and skills of these
two men.

News from York that the fall assizes would begin October 10 had
identified the ship that would be carrying the participants to Newcastle
as the familiar HMS *Speedy* with their old friend, Lieutenant Thomas
Paxton. The joke was that Paxton had drawn the short straw to make
a trip with this kind of cargo, at this time of year. Charles Selleck was
out of the military at this point and could more freely voice his opinion
of the terrible treatment Provincial Marine ship captains received, and
how meagre their pay. In any case, he was sympathetic to the reality
that this was an order from above and his friend had no choice. He and
Gibson would do everything they could to make Captain Paxton feel
welcome and comfortable at Newcastle.

The wharf was a major improvement at Newcastle, but it did little
to solve a real problem that was becoming more and more evident to
ship captains who sailed into Presqu'ile Bay. Soundings in the water off

the east end of Presqu'ile Point showed that there were major shoals extending almost all the way across the mouth of the bay, to the shore of Stony Point. A deeper channel had been discovered, but it was well toward the eastern side of the mouth of the bay.[10]

A survey by W.P. Anderson in 1893 produced an excellent chart[11] illustrating the bay's tricky entrance. It shows the Middle Ground, a large area of shoals immediately east of Presqu'ile Point, and north of that, the old channel running east and west into the bay. The chart also shows the new, direct channel, just east of the point, which was dredged in the 1870s after it was determined that the old channel was simply not adequate.[12]

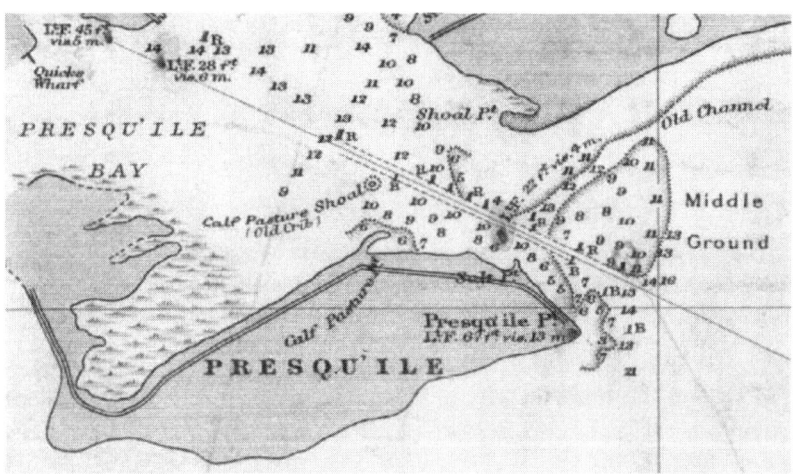

This chart is from a survey by W. P. Anderson in 1893. It shows the large and shallow Middle Ground shoal off the east end of Presqu'ile Point. The Old Channel is shown starting far to the east, extending west to the deeper bay waters near Salt Point. In the 1870s a deeper and more direct channel was dredged into the bay, not far from the lighthouse.

In 1804, ship captains were learning how to deal with the old channel. A ship approaching the bay from the west had to sail all the way east, past the mouth of the bay, to find the deeper channel. A sharp turn to the west was required to enter the channel, then the ship followed the course to Salt Point, which jutted out from the shore a few yards east of the courthouse and jail. Once they rounded the north end of Salt Point, they could safely turn south and sail into the calm waters in a small cove where the new wharf would welcome them to Newcastle.

Sailors running between Kingston and York knew very well that Presqu'ile Bay could be a safe place to ride out a storm. However, the entrance into the bay was a serious problem that would continue to challenge ship captains until the direct channel was dredged. Experienced ship captains could handle this difficult entry under most conditions, but bad weather on the lake added an element of difficulty that caused even seasoned sailors to plan ahead very carefully.

Of course, ship captains in 1804 did not have the benefit of a lighthouse, either on the end of Presqu'ile Point or at various points around the area. In those days, a beacon fire was the best method of assisting sailors in bad weather, and the responsibility fell to Charles and Elizabeth Selleck to build such fires when and where needed. In some cases, it might be on the very east end of the point, where the big lighthouse is today,[13] but the most effective spot was typically the eastern shore of Salt Point, toward the north end. A large fire there would provide ship captains with an obvious visual destination as they turned into the bay and followed the old channel. At least, that was the theory.

One of the jobs, therefore, in preparing for the arrival of Captain Paxton and the *Speedy*, was to make sure there were enough logs and branches on Salt Point to build a large beacon fire on short notice and keep it going for several hours, likely in the rain. There was a pile of refuse from the building of the courthouse that the Sellecks and Gibsons had been using for firewood, and they carried a good portion of that to Salt Point.

Charles Selleck and George Gibson had one last job requested by the authorities in York. They had to build the gallows. Leftover construction material was used to erect a simple platform with a post set upright and a crosspiece high enough to give Ogetonicut plenty of room to swing. A stout piece of rope from Selleck's ship, *Lady Murray*, added the finishing touch. It was distasteful work for the two men but, when it was done, they consoled themselves with some rum at the tavern Mrs. Selleck ran in one corner of the courthouse.

CHAPTER 11

ALL ABOARD!

Captain Thomas Paxton had worked hard to have HMS *Speedy* repaired in the short time he had before departure. Even then, he was not happy with its condition. There were still leaks in the hold, and the sails were unruly. He could only pray they would not encounter too much severe weather on the way to Newcastle. The sailing season of 1804 had been particularly bad for storms. Recently, persistent rain had caused major flooding on the creeks and rivers along the north shore of Lake Ontario.[1] If this continued, Paxton could not be optimistic.

Besides unpredictable weather, his sleep was disturbed by thoughts of all the important people from York who would be under his care, most of whom he knew. As an experienced ship captain, and a full lieutenant in the Provincial Marine, he was supposed to be confident in his ability to protect his passengers. In this case, however, he could only try to reduce the danger.

Looking out his office window, Lieutenant-Governor Peter Hunter saw the ship anchoring about two hundred yards off the landing place, and a blue flag[2] being hoisted to indicate it had orders to proceed to Kingston. Hunter felt some satisfaction at this because he had established the procedure of raising different coloured flags exactly so he, or anyone else at Parliament House or the garrison, could see the intended destination of the ships anchored in the bay. In this case, the ship was destined for Newcastle but would proceed to Kingston after the trial, so the blue flag was appropriate. While Hunter would have a clear view of the embarkation procedures from Parliament House, what he was most interested in seeing was the stern of the ship as it passed out of the bay, and the sooner the better.

Nearby, John Fisk was meeting with William Knott and James Ruggles to discuss the task of moving Ogetonicut from the jail to the ship. They were relieved that the landing place would be their destination rather than the garrison, because it was much closer, so the procession escorting the accused would be mercifully short.

There was a rumour that this approach had been taken so Hunter could watch the proceedings first-hand, and not many argued with that. Whatever the actual reasons, there was nothing unusual in this arrangement. Residents of York were familiar with small boats transporting people and supplies to schooners anchored offshore. The shoreline was gravelly and firm in this area, so cargo could be temporarily piled up at the landing, and it was a convenient spot to beach bateaux, rowboats, and canoes.

Captain Paxton visited the jail to check the condition of the prisoner. He was uneasy about having him chained in the hold of his ship but saw no alternative. He also agreed that Ogetonicut should be taken from the jail to the landing place early Sunday morning when fewer people would be out on the streets. That would also allow them to install him in the hold without interference from other passengers and the loading of cargo. This ship was not designed to accommodate prisoners, but they would work out the details as they went along.

All the planning turned into action early on the morning of Sunday, October 7. At the jail, Knott was up before five o'clock and gave Ogetonicut breakfast. Fisk and Ruggles came in soon after, and then George Cowan, the interpreter, who explained to the accused what was about to happen. It was a frightening experience for the prisoner, who would have no direct support from family members during the trip, and Cowan's main objective was to keep him calm and compliant.

Ogetonicut was sullen, as usual. From the time the shackles were clamped on his arms and legs at Gibraltar Point in May, he had been resigned to his fate. He knew his life was over. Even so, he would honour his father and his ancestors by behaving with dignity, pride, and bravery, no matter what the English did to him. When his family came to his cell to conduct ceremonies, he spoke to the spirits and was confident he would be viewed with favour for his role in gaining restitution for the family.

A glimpse of dawn appeared in the east as a squad of a dozen soldiers from the Forty-ninth Regiment at the garrison formed a square on King Street outside the jail. A torch at each end of the formation illuminated the very young faces of the soldiers and lit the way for Ogetonicut as he was led out to the street. The irons on his ankles caused him to shuffle across the uneven, muddy ground, and stumble over the ruts. The soldiers escorting him now handed him over to the squad on King Street, and they positioned him in the middle of the square. Their sergeant gave a terse command and the group stepped forward in unison.

All the soldiers were dressed in the traditional red wool tunic that was specific to the Forty-ninth Regiment and easily recognized by the green facing used on the tunic's collar, cuffs, and epaulettes. They also wore the familiar stovepipe headgear, called a shako. On this morning, some would have mud splattered on their grey wool trousers although the distinctive wool half-gaiters with small pewter buttons would keep the muck out of their boots.[3]

Two soldiers, one on either side of Ogetonicut, struggled to hold their muskets in the proper manner, while grabbing the prisoner by the arms to hold him up and urge him forward. Fisk, Ruggles, and Cowan followed the procession as it marched along the wet street. Hardly anyone was out this early, as the authorities had predicted, but a few curious folks looked out their windows or stood watching at their front doors.

The procession took the same route used to bring Ogetonicut to the jail in May, just in reverse.[4] When it arrived at the shoreline, a bateau was there with several soldiers already manning the oars. The accused was lifted on board and his manacles tied to the mast in the middle of the boat. The two soldiers who assisted him down the path stood beside him, muskets at the ready. A few minutes later, the prisoner was lifted on board HMS *Speedy* and quickly taken down to the hold, where his chains were locked in place. The two soldiers who had escorted Ogetonicut on board would accompany him to Newcastle, taking shifts in the hold so both could enjoy time on deck. At least this was better than guarding the stockade at the garrison.

Once the prisoner was secured in the hold, Fisk and Ruggles returned home to complete their own preparations for the trip. They would board later in the morning. Cowan stayed on the *Speedy*, ready to act as interpreter for the prisoner if needed.

Through the early morning, Captain Paxton oversaw the loading of cargo. Numerous trunks and bags, mostly personal property of the passengers, had been delivered to the landing place. The hold was not very large, and Captain Paxton tried to place a limit on how much each passenger could take, but social rank prevailed. Several trunks arrived from the Solicitor General's household, so the crew took them below. More would arrive later in the morning.

Captain Paxton made sure that he personally supervised one particular piece of cargo, which was being delivered by a bateau that bumped alongside the *Speedy*. John Bennett, Printer to the King at York,[5] stepped onto the deck, followed quickly by several strong lads hefting a captain's chest. Their grunts indicated it was full of something substantial, and the solid padlock on the front proved its value. Paxton barked out orders for this item to be taken to a particularly secure corner of the hold, tied down, and covered by a tarp.

The chest contained six copies of the *Statutes of Upper Canada*. The printing office had notified the residents of York in the *Upper Canada Gazette* on September 8, 1804: "In the course of a few days will be ready for sale, the Revised Statutes of Upper Canada, comprising all the laws enacted in the first, second and third parliaments of this Province — such British Statutes also as relate to Upper and Lower Canada are annexed to this work, to which is affixed a copious alphabetical index. The nature and expense of the above undertaking and other circumstances immediately connected therewith, entirely preclude all possibility of the printer giving credit for a single copy; it is therefore hoped no such application will be made."[6]

Printing of the statutes had been ordered by the lieutenant-governor, with the further instruction that copies be made available to the magistrates and judges of all districts in the province. Since the statutes were ready to go and HMS *Speedy* was headed to Newcastle, the copies slated for Newcastle District would hitch a ride. The fact that they would not be sold on credit indicates the value that the authorities placed on these documents, thus the padlock and careful treatment.

Less care was taken with a wood-and-wire chicken coop containing a respectable collection of agitated, clucking travellers, which was hefted aboard by the crew. This was a common item on Provincial Marine ships at the time, the hens used mainly as food for the crew.[7] Considering the unusual number of passengers in this case, the captain had ordered the coop painted red to indicate that it belonged to the crew and its contents were not for sale. However, if the weather allowed, he would ask the crew to wring some necks and the pot-bellied stove in the hold would be employed to fix up a chicken dinner for anyone who cared to indulge.

Captain Paxton had arranged for passengers to board during the late morning, with the idea of an early afternoon sailing. The ship's bell began to ring every hour in order to alert them that it was time to embark.[8] There were lots of details to oversee, and Paxton hurried his crew along. Fisk and Ruggles boarded and went into the hold to see the prisoner and speak to the interpreter, to make sure everything was ready for the trip. Judge Thomas Cochran came aboard with a servant, and lawyer Angus Macdonell boarded with boxes of paper, ready to defend the accused at trial.

The noise level increased dramatically as a boat carrying Solicitor General Robert Gray and his retinue came alongside. Many of those on board moved to the rail to see what all the commotion was about. Gray was dressed in his Sunday best, as was his servant, Simon Baker. Simon's younger brother, John, would recollect many years later that "Simon was master's body servant, and dressed finer than his master, with a beaver hat and gold chain."[9]

Robert Gray may have looked his best as he boarded the *Speedy*, but he was not his normal jovial, fun-loving self. He dreaded the idea of sailing to Newcastle on any ship, let alone the dubious *Speedy*. In fact, he had planned to travel by land with William Weekes,[10] another lawyer, because both of them preferred a horse to a boat. However, Judge Cochran had prevailed on Gray to join him on board, so here he was.

John Anderson also boarded with Gray, carrying a leather case containing all the documents related to the murder case that would be heard at Newcastle. He was very familiar with Simon and would spend considerable time teasing him, trying to solicit an extreme response, which would generate laughter from anyone listening in, along with a bemused grin from Gray.

As the sun rose higher in the clear sky, Captain Paxton eyed his passenger list and watched the landing place for the stragglers. Soon, there was a flurry of activity as a foaming horse raced down the cut and onto the beach. The rider jumped off and quickly hired a young man in a canoe to take him across to the *Speedy*. John Stegmann had travelled all the way from his home in Vaughan Township[11] and, now, muddy and out of breath, the surveyor stepped aboard the ship, carrying a valise of papers that contained his testimony for the Crown.

While Stegmann was getting settled on the deck, there was more activity on the beach. Joseph Willcocks[12] arrived in a wagon accompanied by two small children. A boat was hired, and he and the children came alongside the ship. Willcocks had only recently been appointed sheriff of Home District,[13] after much lobbying with authorities, and Captain Paxton greeted him warily as he stepped aboard. This man was known to be an inveterate office-seeker, recently appointed to the position of sheriff due to friends in high places.

Willcocks explained to the captain that these two children were to sail on the *Speedy* to Kingston. Their parents were indigent[14] and could not afford the fare for sailing to Montreal where they had family, so they were travelling by land. The authorities had stepped in and decided to send the children on the next ship to sail in that direction, at the cost of the state. Captain Paxton was surprised and annoyed and stated this clearly to Willcocks, who shrugged off his protests with his normal arrogance and disdain. There was no choice. The children were brought on board.

Captain Paxton fumed but was powerless. After all, it was not his ship. It belonged to the government of Upper Canada. With his long experience dealing with functionaries and office-seekers, he knew he would have to accommodate Willcocks. But how? Who would care for these little children during an overnight trip on Lake Ontario? Robert Gray overheard the discussion between the sheriff and the captain and stepped forward to offer his assistance. He and his servant would care for the children.

The captain took another look at his passenger list. There was one last name, which had been added just yesterday. He was not going to wait much longer but paced the deck for a few minutes, just in case. Much to his delight, activity at the landing place indicated that Jacob Herkimer was on his way. A canoe delivered the merchant and trader to the ship, and once on board, he found a place for himself and his bag. Herkimer would testify as part-owner of the trading post and would then visit family in Kingston after the trial.

With the last name checked off the passenger list, the captain turned to the boatswain, who confirmed that all the repairs were done, the cargo stowed, and the crew ready to sail. Then, the ship's mate reported that the passengers were in place and as comfortable as possible. With that, the captain ordered the anchor raised. At the same time, he instructed that the ship's bell be rung to announce to the passengers on board, as well as to the folks in York, that the ship was departing. The name "HMS Speedy" was proudly displayed on the side of the bell as it delivered the message. With that, the trip to Newcastle began.

CHAPTER 12

ON THE WAY
TO NEWCASTLE

Early surveyors reported many good things about the town of York, including the excellent harbour. However, they usually had a word of caution about the western entrance to the bay and the problem of prevailing winds. "It will appear that the harbour of Toronto is capacious, safe and well sheltered; but the entrance being from the westward is a great disadvantage to it, as the prevailing winds are from that quarter; and as this is a fair wind from hence down the Lake, of course it is that which vessels in general would take their departure from; but they may frequently find it difficult to get out of the harbour."[1]

Another surveyor,[2] who conducted a detailed survey of the harbour, included soundings all around the bay and the sandspits to the south and east. The survey documented the shallow nature of the north shore, which was confirmed by very low readings close to the shore and well out into the bay. The channel the *Speedy* would take to exit the harbour at the west end was seldom more than three fathoms deep. Even though the entrance into the harbour was half a mile wide, only a narrow channel, about five hundred yards wide, was safe for sailing ships to use.

Captain Paxton had sailed in and out of this harbour dozens of times in various ships, under all weather conditions, so he knew quite well where the channel was located and how tricky it could be toward the west end of the harbour, especially if the winds did not co-operate. It was always a challenge but, with his experience, a decent crew, and a ship that would respond to his orders, he was confident of a safe passage through.

The *Speedy* eased into the deeper channel and swung around to head west, toward the exit from York Harbour. Hunter and Green watched from Parliament House as their plans to diffuse a dangerous political situation finally came to fruition. Literally, their problems were sailing out of York Harbour.

C. H. J. Snider used his expertise in design and construction of Lake Ontario sailing ships to create a sketch of HMS *Speedy* to accompany the story he wrote for his column in the *Toronto Telegram* called *Schooner Days*, in 1949. Owen Staples, a well-known Toronto artist, then added water colors to produce this stunning image. It is the most widely recognized image of HMS *Speedy*.

Normally, it would take about twenty-four hours to sail from York to Newcastle, and it had been done in less time under ideal conditions. Departing early Sunday afternoon, a ship would be expected to approach Newcastle in the middle of the second day, in daylight. However, HMS *Speedy* was loaded with cargo and passengers and not in ideal shape. Captain Paxton considered the issues, including the unpredictable October forecast, and anticipated that the trip might take longer than he hoped. It all depended on the weather.

Well, maybe not only the weather. There is one account of what may have happened next that only came to light decades later. On December 22, 1860, Reverend George Okill Stuart[3] wrote a two-page letter to his long-time friend John Beverley Robinson,[4] in which he says, "I am reminded of her running aground on leaving the harbour of York. The occurrence delayed her departure, nearly two hours."[5] The delay would have pushed back *Speedy*'s departure time, which matches a report from the *Upper Canada Gazette* that the *Speedy* had "left this port on Sunday evening."[6] A similar time frame is suggested in John Baker's recollections: "The schooner started between four and five in the afternoon."[7]

If we believe these accounts, we might picture Captain Paxton on the deck, all the passengers sitting or standing around the places normally used by captain, crew, and cargo. He is using the sextant and compass located on the binnacle to navigate the ship and is barking orders to the mate and boatswain as the *Speedy* sails uneasily westward, down the channel. The wind kicks up and tosses the ship toward the north shore. The crew has trouble responding due to the bad condition of the sails, which are scheduled to be replaced after this trip. Soon, with a sickening thud and jerk, the *Speedy* runs aground on one of the many sandbars in the harbour.

One can imagine the language that emanated from the captain at this point. The crew would scramble to adjust the sails in order to edge the ship back into the channel. When this was of no avail, Captain Paxton would signal to the soldiers at the garrison that he needed help. It would have been very evident that the *Speedy* was in trouble, and a couple of rowboats would already be heading toward the ship. They would assist the crew in manoeuvring the ship back into deeper water. Since HMS *Speedy* had been grounded on one of the many shifting sandbars in the area, no serious damage would have been done to the hull.

Over the years, this incident, true or false, has been analyzed and various meanings applied. Cynics have speculated that Captain Paxton deliberately ran his ship aground in order to protest the unequivocal orders he had received. Or, to take it a step further, that he was so afraid of the unseaworthy nature of his ship, he ran aground to prevent the trip altogether. A thorough study of the man makes this idea seem absurd. Lieutenant Thomas Paxton was an extremely conscientious sailor and citizen. Sure, he was an independent thinker, but he also had a wife and young family back in Kingston and he knew how to take orders. He would not for a moment countenance so childish and dangerous a prank. He was just too good a man for that. If the grounding happened,[8] it was an accident, plain and simple.

In any case, Captain Paxton set sail again, this time late in the afternoon as darkness was falling. The ship passed through the entrance at the west end of the harbour and proceeded out into Lake Ontario. Finally, they were under way. The matching blue flag at the garrison fluttered in the mild northwest breeze, waving farewell and Godspeed to the crew and passengers. Over at Parliament House, Lt.-Gov. Hunter finally sat down at his desk and went back to work, happy to see the ship, and especially the accused, leaving his town. It's great when a plan works to perfection.

Captain Paxton barked orders to the crew as the sails took hold of the breeze and the ship surged forward. Soon, they were around the headlands at the west end of the Toronto Islands and edging by the southern, lakeside beaches. The captain looked to the western sky. It was a pleasant evening for early October in Upper Canada, but he knew that the temperature would gradually drop overnight and hoped the passengers were prepared for the cold.

The nature of the *Speedy* soon became evident. The masts and spars squeaked and squawked, sometimes in unison. The deck and the hull seemed to groan and complain with every wave. Down below, the crew kept a constant vigil on the bilge pumps. It was clear that the hull leaked in several places, but the captain and crew felt that recent repairs along with constant attention to the pumps would keep the problem under control. It was constant, back-breaking work, but the crew was well-trained and had lots of practice. Besides, it gave them a very good excuse to be away from the nattering passengers. The sailors were accustomed to dealing with full loads of cargo, not people.

Sailors of the Provincial Marine had no prescribed attire, as was the case in the Royal Navy,[9] but officers were proud to wear the distinctive blue-and-white uniform with rows of shiny brass buttons[10] that everyone in Upper Canada could recognize. Captain Paxton stood near his binnacle and watched over to port as the Scarborough Highlands slowly passed by. He wore his lieutenant's uniform with pride. His crew, although a boisterous lot, respected him and obeyed his commands, not because of all those shiny buttons, but because of the way he treated them. They all knew he had a lifetime of sailing knowledge, and they were most gratified by his sense of fairness in dealing with them.

The captain had ordered the crew to sail about a mile offshore, which was standard practice along Lake Ontario's north shore.[11] He and the mate then discussed timing. The delay in York Harbour meant their arrival at Newcastle would likely be postponed until Monday evening, probably well after dark. If weather conditions at the time were not too bad, they might enter Presqu'ile Bay with assistance from the folks at Newcastle, who would build a beacon fire on Salt Point to guide them in. If conditions were difficult, they could sail over to Wellers Bay, east of the entrance to Presqu'ile Bay, and wait until the winds subsided. This was a common practice. In the end, the weather would dictate the approach.

As dusk came over the ship, a few hens were sacrificed to the public good and the passengers pulled out bread, meat, and vegetables from pockets and bags, enjoying a pleasant supper while gazing at the sunset off the stern. As the crew enjoyed their evening allotment of rum, the gentlemen pulled out their flasks, passing them around to their friends. Pockets of talk developed around the ship. The crew talked with the crew, the lawyers with the lawyers, and the captain kept watch.

Lamps were lit at the bow and stern, which cast shadows across the deck and gave the billowing sails an eerie glow, imparting to passengers a sense of being inside a moving cathedral. The lantern on the binnacle was lit as well, allowing the captain and mate to read the compass through the night.

With the darkness came the cold. Blankets and robes were pulled out and the deck became a mountain of fur and wool, with humans huddled somewhere underneath. Captain Paxton merely pulled his cloak closer around his shoulders and rested on his chair beside the binnacle. There was a small cabin space on the *Speedy*, but it was so cramped that it was hardly functional; the captain preferred to be near the navigational instruments. He may have heard about the request from Kingston to provide measurements for cabin stoves that might be installed in ships next year,[12] but he would have to see that to believe it.

Robert Gray worked with Simon to arrange a large bearskin cloak over themselves and the two children, to keep them warm through the night. While Simon complained about having to look after the little ones, he also worked hard to keep them comfortable and content, telling stories and jokes to distract them from the noises of the ship and the constant motion. Gray chuckled to himself that even Simon might make a good father one day.

George Cowan took a lantern to the far end of the hold where Ogetonicut was chained. He covered the prisoner with a cloak, then sat and spoke to him in his own language, hoping to calm his agitation so that he might sleep. The young man listened to Cowan for a moment, then gave a slight nod as thanks and pulled the cloak over his head. He preferred to be left alone.

The interpreter had seen many young men like Ogetonicut at his Two Chimneys trading post on Matchedash Bay over the decades he had been there.[13] The pockmarks on the prisoner's face spoke of survival through smallpox epidemics[14] that ravaged the Indigenous people in the 1790s, before the inoculation programs reached into the back country.[15] Sullen, angry eyes reflected years of imposition on the lives of his people by a force they could not understand and had no power to oppose.

Cowan left the prisoner to his own thoughts and returned to the deck. He found an open spot to lie down, stretched his legs, and took a deep breath of fresh, cold air. John Stegmann was sitting beside him, staring at the deck, deep in thought. He was grateful for the company and the two men began to talk.

Stegmann never liked sailing on Lake Ontario, especially when the wind and waves picked up, and his fear was well-grounded. In September of 1779, he had been one of several thousand Hessian soldiers on board a fleet of British Navy ships that set sail from New York, headed for Nova Scotia. A massive hurricane struck the fleet, dispersing the ships, and causing each to make its own way, as best it could. Many were sunk, killing all on board, and several were captured by the Patriots, meaning those soldiers spent the rest of the war in captivity.[16]

Stegmann had been on a ship that managed to make its way to Nova Scotia. He was battered and bruised from the violence of the storm and stunned by the knowledge that so many of his compatriots had not survived. From that moment on, he dreaded sailing on any of the larger waterways. It seemed like he had already been given a reprieve and should not press his luck. George Cowan pulled out a flask, handed it to his neighbour, and the two men took turns sampling the rum within.

While the *Speedy* was a mile out on Lake Ontario, making its way slowly toward Newcastle, several individuals were heading the same way on land or by canoe. Lawyer William Weekes had left York a few days before on horseback and was riding slowly along the Danforth

Highway,[17] using the primitive trail established only four years earlier. He spent a good deal of time navigating through stretches that had fallen into disrepair. In some places, it was hard to see there was a road at all.

Several canoes had left York Harbour long before HMS *Speedy* and were making their way along the shoreline of the lake. Some of the canoes may have held family and friends of Ogetonicut. Many of his people on Gibraltar Point had moved back down to Annis Creek and on to their autumn camps in the interior. Those still at the camp had been amused and confused by the sight of the *Speedy* running aground on the sandbar, but they watched with sadness as the ship finally sailed out into the lake. Ceremonies were undertaken to encourage the spirits of the lake and the ship to help their son, and possibly bring him back to them. After that, they would depart to join the others at Annis Creek.

There is no record of any Mississauga people from Gibraltar Point going to Newcastle for the trial of Ogetonicut. This lack of documentation could be due to the fact that English people wrote the story and did not feel it was important to consider the involvement of the Indigenous people. In the dozens of accounts of the *Speedy* story that have been written over the years, we don't learn so much as the age of Ogetonicut, or his father's name. It was a common practice in the past to discount the participation and experiences of Indigenous people in the telling of Canadian history. Thankfully, that approach is no longer acceptable.

Under the circumstances, it is likely that someone from the group would go to Newcastle, at the very least to deal with Ogetonicut's body after his inevitable hanging. Frankly, whether the accused was Indigenous or English, family members would be involved, probably on the periphery, waiting to see the outcome. It's not difficult to picture a couple of canoes filled with solemn members of Ogetonicut's family, paddling to Newcastle.

Another canoe headed to Newcastle on October 7 was paddled by Moody Farewell and Eleazer Lockwood. They had served as witnesses for the arrest of Ogetonicut in the spring, and now they would testify at his trial. They were both nervous at the prospect of standing in front of a judge and the court but were intent on doing their duty. It was all they could do for John Sharp at this point.

The northwest breeze remained fairly steady through the night, kicking up at times but then subsiding for periods, which becalmed the ship on the lake. The passengers had settled down to sleep and the crew took turns keeping watch, with Captain Paxton taking the first shift.

Dawn arrived quickly and passengers roused to marvel at the sunrise over the eastern end of the lake. Soon the blankets were stowed, and they settled in for a day of sailing, accepting that time did not pass more quickly if you complained about it. As the crew set about their normal tasks, Captain Paxton hovered near his binnacle.

The swells on the lake were now a little more pronounced and the moderate breeze from the northwest, though still mild, was more persistent. The captain watched the western sky with trepidation as he sensed that less benign weather was coming. He hoped it would hold off until the ship was tied up at the wharf at Newcastle. Still, HMS *Speedy* was making good time with moderate seas and Captain Paxton was pleased enough to order a few more capons prepared for lunch.

Moody Farewell and Eleazer Lockwood were making good progress in their canoe as well. They had camped on shore overnight and made an early start. In the early afternoon, however, cloud covered the sky and the sun disappeared. The temperature dropped slightly, and the air took on a summer mugginess that was unusual in October. Farewell and Lockwood kept close to the shoreline to avoid rougher waters out on the lake, but over the course of the day, the lake came to life and their progress slowed. They took occasional breaks during the afternoon as the wind picked up and the waves grew stronger and more persistent. Late in the afternoon, approaching evening, the two men decided it was too rough on the water and it was time to find a place to camp for the night.

Aware that they were approaching the settlement of Smith's Creek, which later became the town of Port Hope,[18] they paddled a mile or so farther east, beaching the canoe at the mouth of a smaller creek, then named Dean's Creek[19] after the family who had recently settled along the creek in the second concession.[20] Today, it is called Gages Creek.[21]

While they made camp, Moody watched the lake to see if the *Speedy* might come into sight. At one point, he did see the ship being tossed about in the wind.[22] It was a fleeting glance, but it raised the anxiety he felt for the poor souls on HMS *Speedy*. They were still a few hours from Newcastle, about fifty kilometres as the crow flies. As the men ate their supper, the wind howled and the waves crashed against the shore. They hunkered down to wait out the weather, uncertain what the morning would bring.

CHAPTER 13

BEACON FIRE

Late Monday afternoon, almost twenty-four hours after HMS *Speedy* left York, Charles Selleck stood on the wharf at Newcastle and gazed west over Presqu'ile Bay. The stiff wind in his face and the choppiness of the bay suggested that conditions on the lake were growing nasty. George Gibson joined him, and together they walked to the eastern point of the peninsula to look for the ship. What they saw was disturbing. The sky was darkening and the wind had whipped up large whitecaps. This did not look good. They searched the lake with a spyglass but saw no sign of the ship. As the sun went down, the two men walked back to their homes.

About the same time, on board the *Speedy*, Captain Thomas Paxton was growing impatient with the slow progress the ship was making in the face of increasing wind and rain. The crew was busy making adjustments and repairs to sails and rigging. Looking up into the heaving canvases, the captain wished they had replaced the sails earlier in the season. Oh well, he would make do with what he had.

The crew cooked up a few hens for an early supper; Paxton wanted the meal finished before it got too rough. They made sure the cargo was secure and maintained their attention on the pumps in the hold. The passengers huddled down, sensing the cold in the air. Soon after sunset, rain began to come down steadily, drenching the blankets on the deck and causing passengers to crowd together. Water ran down the faces of the crew and soaked their clothing, but they ignored the discomfort, intent on the job at hand.

All the *Speedy*'s crew were accustomed to working in the elements, both topside and in the hold. Dealing with leaks was as a matter of routine. A year earlier, Major James Green had received a letter from the commander at Kingston, dated November 7, 1803, saying "Captain Steel acquaints me that the very leaky state of the Speedy is in at present will prevent her from making another trip this season without being previously repaired, after which he thinks it will be too late to send her, as the weather is so very variable at this season of the year."[1] One year later, HMS *Speedy* was in no better condition, possibly worse.

Captain Paxton stood at the binnacle and consulted his compass. They were late, but the ship was in a good position, approaching the entrance to Presqu'ile Bay from the west. He would try to navigate the ship closer to the shore, intent on sighting the bluff off the west end of Presqu'ile Point, which would give him a good idea how far to go before turning into the bay. With the storm up like this, it might be tricky, but he had negotiated it many times before, so was confident it could be done.

Charles Selleck and George Gibson sat with their families for supper but were too uneasy to relax afterward. They walked out to the point again, alarmed at the escalation in the wind and waves on the lake. Peering though the dark and seeing nothing, they decided to build a beacon fire. They did not know whether Captain Paxton was in a position to make use of the beacon, but they had to make sure it was there if needed.

Gibson called on his son Joseph,[2] and he and Selleck, accompanied by the sixteen-year-old, hurried out to Salt Point. They struggled to light the kindling under the big pile of wood they had placed there. In spite of the rain, the dry branches and boards ignited, and, within a few minutes, a fire was blazing away, illuminating the shoreline and sending sparks out onto the bay. Joseph stayed at the fire with instructions to feed it wood and keep it going as long as possible.

The two men returned to the south shore, where the rain was now driving almost horizontally and the winds gusting wildly. They huddled in a bark lean-to near the stone beach, pulling their coats tightly around their shoulders. The temperature was dropping as the storm intensified, all bad signs for the safety of the ship they knew was out there on the lake. They waited.

On the *Speedy*, Captain Paxton could sense the irresistible power of the westerly wind and doubted he could make the turn into Presqu'ile Bay. Even if he could, he would not have the kind of navigational control of the ship that was called for to find the channel and follow the beacon into the bay. He began to think that riding out the storm on Wellers Bay might be the only viable option.

Whether the captain actually saw the beacon fire on Salt Point that night, we will never know. What we do know is that he was not able to navigate into Presqu'ile Bay. Selleck and Gibson waited on the beach for a couple of hours, but seeing no sign of the *Speedy*, they went back to Salt Point to see how young Joseph was doing. The fire was still burning but on the wane, the fuel almost gone.

Later that evening, while the three stood on the edge of the point, wondering what else they could do, they sensed a change in the air. In only a few minutes, they felt the wind turn from the west to the northeast, while the temperature dropped dramatically. These experienced sailors knew what this meant. They were in for a nor'easter.

A nor'easter is an occasional weather phenomenon, well-known around the Great Lakes.[3] It is a powerful winter storm that roars out of central Quebec, loaded with snow and frigid temperatures, heading in a southwesterly direction, down across the lakes, wiping out whatever moderate weather might be in its path. In sailing days, it was dangerous weather for ships on the lake not just because of its suddenness but also because of its force. Heavy winds were full of wet snow and sleet, followed by a deep freeze that coated tree branches and topsails alike with a heavy layer of ice. Nobody wanted to be on the lake when a nor'easter hit.

This was a game changer. The three men quickly left Salt Point and returned to their homes. They agonized over the fate of the *Speedy* and all those on board, but they had their own families and homes to worry about right now. They could only hope that Captain Paxton had managed to sail off into Wellers Bay before the nor'easter hit. Anything else was awful to contemplate.

Camped on the shoreline west of Newcastle, Moody Farewell and Eleazer Lockwood were also aware that a nor'easter was coming. They immediately set about improving their temporary abode, which was likely to be a little less temporary than expected. They moved their lean-to around, so that the back faced east, and then set their canoe behind the back of the lean-to, to act as a windbreak. They cut more branches to build up the top and sides, and to reduce the size of the front opening, and tightly lashed down everything. Then they settled in to wait out the storm. They had good shelter, lots of warm clothes, and enough food to get them through a couple of days. In a pinch, they could walk back to Smith's Creek where there were homesteads and settlers. In the meantime, they bided their time.

The storm raged for two days. The Sellecks and Gibsons at Newcastle stayed inside as much as possible but ventured out a few times to see if they might sight the *Speedy* off the shore. The conditions were horrible, and they saw nothing.

On Wednesday morning, the storm finally ended. Farewell and Lockwood decided to break camp and begin walking to Newcastle, carrying their canoe. They passed by the few log houses at Grafton[4] and then the small settlement at Keeler's Creek, today's Lakeport.[5] Later in the day, the waves calmed to the point the men could safely paddle. As they passed along the shoreline of Cramahe Township, approaching Presqu'ile Point, they could see to their right the land that would be called High Bluff Island. At the long, wide beach, their canoe slid easily and quietly onto the soft sand.

Hoisting the canoe onto their shoulders, the men trudged through the sand on the portage that took them across the narrow isthmus connecting Presqu'ile Point to the mainland. Today, a strip of that same sand holds a fine paved road that leads cottage owners to part of the Municipality of Brighton and takes visitors to the entrance to Presqu'ile Provincial Park.[6]

On the east side of the portage, Farewell and Lockwood launched their canoe into the calm waters of Presqu'ile Bay and paddled east toward Newcastle. As they manoeuvred through the marshes and out into clear water, the air was alive with ducks and geese and the water swarmed with fish. They hurried along at a good pace.

As they approached the town, they could see the *Lady Murray*,[7] Selleck's ship, tied up beside the wharf near the courthouse and jail building. Several canoes and rowboats were beached nearby, and a group of people were on the wharf watching and waiting for the new arrivals. Charles Selleck and his wife, Elizabeth, stood beside George Gibson and his son Joseph. Several people who owned lots at Newcastle were there as well, waving at the young men as they pulled their canoe onto the gravel beach. All were anxious for news about the fate of the *Speedy*, but it quickly became evident that nobody knew anything.

Selleck was interested, but not surprised, to hear that Farewell and Lockwood had seen the *Speedy* around dusk on Monday evening, since it confirmed that the ship had actually sailed that far and was coming toward Presqu'ile Point on a westerly storm. The information, however, only deepened their anxiety about the fate of the *Speedy* and the twenty souls on board.

Mrs. Selleck made Moody Farewell and Eleazer Lockwood comfortable in rooms on the third floor of the courthouse building. There were lots available since the passengers on the *Speedy* had not yet arrived. Afterward, the group sat around the table and casually reminisced about Captain Paxton and the others they knew but, beneath the surface, there was dread.

Over the next few days, William Weekes, the only lawyer there, handled the details related to the fall assizes. The session was formally opened and adjourned each day, as a matter of procedure. Most of the people in the community set about the task of searching along the shore on foot and in canoes and rowboats, looking for any trace of the *Speedy*. Selleck and Gibson took *Lady Murray* out and searched farther up the shore in both directions, out to the western bluff and east into Wellers Bay. Nobody found anything.

Finally, in the obvious absence of a judge, the fall assizes were cancelled. Moody Farewell and Eleazer Lockwood made the decision to head back home. They bade goodbye to the sad group on the wharf at Newcastle and paddled into Presqu'ile Bay, steering for Whitby Township.

CHAPTER 14

A STOP TO ALL BUSINESS AT YORK

On Monday, October 15, 1804, eight days after the *Speedy* set sail from York, William Ross, commander at Kingston, sent a letter to Lieutenant-Governor Peter Hunter, saying "The Speedy's non-arrival prevents my sending the pay list for Ryerson to sign."[1] This is mundane administrative fare, but it represents the first documented reference to the fact that HMS *Speedy* did not arrive in Kingston as expected.

It was not unusual in those days for ships to experience major delays, so a few days' wait would not necessarily cause alarm. Routine schedules were interrupted, mail was late, and passengers had to wait, but the ship usually showed up. In this case, however, Kingston was *Speedy*'s second port of call; it had not yet arrived at its first, Newcastle. Officials would have been very concerned, as would friends and family of crew and passengers.

Ten days later, word of the possible fate of HMS *Speedy* arrived at York in a letter from Lieutenant Colonel John Vincent,[2] commander at Fort George, at the mouth of the Niagara River. "I feel much regret. I have it not in my power to remove the General's alarm for the fate of the Speedy. On Friday last, an account came here that a boat had broken up, a top mast, a binnacle, mast and hen coop painted red, with some spars."[3]

Vincent had received this news on October 19 and took immediate steps to confirm the information. In his subsequent letter, he notes "a Mr. McDonald has just arrived from that place who reports that he saw there articles at Mr. Fuller's and that the name of Paxton was on the lantern of the binnacle."[4] The items had been found on the south shore of Lake Ontario, at a place called Oak Orchard Creek, about fifty-two kilometres east of Fort George in the state of New York.

Today, at the mouth of Oak Orchard Creek lies the town of Carlton[5] in Orleans County. A map of Lake Ontario shows that Carlton is about a hundred kilometres from Presqu'ile Point, mostly south but a bit west. It is not difficult to see that a ship, or debris from a shipwreck, starting in the water near Prince Edward County, Ontario, could be blown across the lake in a severe two-day nor'easter. It is feasible that the items from HMS *Speedy* could have washed up on the shore at Carlton, New York, a week or ten days after the ship sank off Presqu'ile.

There have been questions about the veracity of these reports. The physical logistics of that kind of trip in 1804 might seem a bit outside our normal expectations, and the nature of communication at that time could add to the skepticism. However, when we look carefully at a map, then consider the commander's words in the letter to his boss, we must take the reports to be accurate. The specific mention of the name Paxton on the binnacle should convince the skeptics.

In York, the news spread fast. A local resident wrote in his diary on Thursday, October 25, 1804: "The Town of York was in confusion by the loss of the Schooner Speedy on her way to Newcastle with a Number of Passengers from York; her loss had been supposed some time but now was authenticated."[6]

The next day, Peter Russell, the former administrator of Upper Canada and now the receiver general, wrote a letter to an old friend in England, reporting what he knew. "We have lately suffered a most serious misfortune to the Province in the loss of one of the King's vessels which sailed from hence on the evening of the 7th instant, And as she did not arrive at her port and nothing has been heard of her since, it is concluded that she must have foundered in a violent storm which happened on the 9th following, and that every person on board perished."[7]

On the same day, J.W. Steel, commodore of the Provincial Marine, stationed at Kingston, sent a letter to York that reflected his personal connection with the ship's sailors and his concern for their families. "I am to express the utmost regret in the loss of the Speedy . . . from circumstances there cannot be a doubt. His Excellency, if so, I have no doubt, will cause some provisions to be made for the widow Paxton who is left with eight small children without a farthing to support them, as also Gerrard the Boatswain, who has left a wife and two children, & Francis Labard, a seaman, has left a wife and two children. I can attest to these men to be Old faithful servants."[8]

We can expect that Commodore Steel, who was a very experienced sailor himself, would know the sailors and their families who had homes in Kingston. In particular, he would have been personally familiar with Captain Paxton, since both of them had been serving for so long. In any case, his concern was genuine and heartfelt. There was no life insurance in those days, and the loss of a breadwinner put a widow and children at serious risk. His mention of the families of boatswain Gerrard and seaman Francis Labard gives us the only contemporary reference to these men as part of the crew of the Speedy at the time it was lost.

The community of York was in shock. Judge Thomas Cochran was just twenty-eight at the time of his death, only beginning what promised to be a productive career. In York, Cochran had made a positive impression on many people and, in particular, he was good friends with old school chum George Okill Stuart, the young minister from Kingston. George's father commented in a letter "George is again able to perform his public Duty; although he has sustained an irreparable Loss in the Death of J. Cochran, such a Friend as cannot be replaced.

George feels severely on the melancholy Occasion, not only for him but for Gray, Herkimer, & etc."[9]

The word "Public," with a very deliberate capital P, was often used in speaking about the feelings and emotions of people in York as well as the wider community of Upper Canada. In the exchange of letters between family members, we see "The Public will feel the loss as well as Individuals."[10] In fact, this event was felt deeply by the whole province, both in the immediate days after the news arrived and for many years to come.

Fifty-six years later, George Okill Stuart would express the degree and depth of feeling due to the horrible loss and tragedy in a letter to an old friend at York. "When this sad News reached York, a gloom overspread the Village, which lasted a length of Time and the remembrance of the Melancholy fate of the Passengers, Captain & Seamen, will not be forgotten by the surviving friends and Contemporaries of the Sufferers."[11] Stuart was twenty-eight years old in 1804. His words reflect not only the huge loss of life for the community but, more specifically, the loss of a good friend, in Thomas Cochran. We should not doubt that he held these memories closely until he passed away just two years after writing this letter.

Soon after the news broke at York, two of the wealthiest and most influential men in Upper Canada communicated by letter, lamenting the loss of the *Speedy* in their own way. Robert Hamilton[12] of Queenston, in the Niagara District, wrote to his long-time friend and associate, John Askin,[13] of Sandwich, across the river from Detroit. After recounting what he knew of the event, he added this comment: "Such Men as we have on this Occasion lost, will not soon be replaced; and it makes a sad Blank in the Society, particularly at York. The Absence of the Chief Justice also, who is gone this Season on a Visit to England, will render this more sincerely felt, and will most probably prevent much Business of any Kind, being done there this winter."[14] Aside from the disaster of the *Speedy*, Hamilton continues pleasantly, "In other respects, we have but little new here. A very wet season has hindered much the sowing of wheat; and we fear the Crop of next Season, will be short in Proportion."[15]

Another old hand at York would hear the terrible news at a much greater distance. David William Smith[16] had been appointed Surveyor General of Upper Canada in 1792, but he moved back to England ten years later. On November 11, 1804, an old business acquaintance in Montreal wrote Smith, recounting the depressing details. He begins with "I have now to relate a very melancholy loss . . . "[17] and goes on to list the individuals on board the *Speedy* that Smith would know. To summarize, "Scott writes me there is a stop to all business at York. The loss is dreadful — and will throw a damp for a long time on such a small place."[18] But, he is not done. "Many blame Gen'l Hunter for exposing people in such a vessel, ye Swift is condemned, and then its said ye Toronto is unserviceable."[19]

Here we see evidence of the state of affairs regarding the Provincial Marine and conditions that had been allowed to develop regarding the sailing ships on the lakes. Many people knew about the poor condition of the ships and had direct experience sailing on the lakes in a storm. Of course, personal bantering often missed practical realities. Few people would know about the work going on at Kingston to repair both *Swift*[20] and *Toronto Yacht*[21] and that both would be ready for the 1805 sailing season. Most folks would also be unaware of efforts to use salt[22] to retard the deterioration of timber in the newest ship being built at that time. In fact, efforts were being made to improve the ships.

The idea of blame would make the rounds in York and beyond. Lt.-Gov. Hunter was generally disliked for his cold, unfriendly demeanour, and the strong authoritarian approach he took to governing. In official circles, you must mind your words; but in private conversation, emotions took over. It was well-known that Captain Paxton had sailed under orders and could not be blamed, but the man who gave the order was fair game. Many folks, both in and out of government, would not disagree with the charge of carelessness directed at the lieutenant-governor in the months after the disaster.

On a different note, John Craigie,[23] an army officer in Quebec, sent a letter to Hunter, commiserating about the loss of the *Speedy*. "The melancholy loss of the speedy has been severely felt even by us who are at a distance and strangers, more or less, to the sufferers. What then must be the case with your neighbourhood who have been almost spectators of the catastrophe & to whom the vacuum of so many characters in your society must daily renew in your minds the sad events."[24]

Craigie goes on to address a practical matter. "I hope the General may be inclined to do something for the widow Paxton & the poor family who I am informed are left extremely destitute by the death of Lt. Paxton."[25] He then suggests a specific method by which financial support might be provided. He was able to do this because he was commissary general, head of the organization that handled procurement for material, supplies, clothing, weapons, ships, and all the things the army needed to perform its duties in Upper and Lower Canada.

For the wider community, the most complete contemporary report of the events around the *Speedy* came in a newspaper article published in the *Upper Canada Gazette*, under The Oracle, on November 3, 1804.[26] John Bennett was editor of the *Gazette*. He had been able to collect the best intelligence available in early November, only two weeks or so after the loss of the *Speedy* was officially confirmed. He mentioned the articles found on the American side of the lake, avoiding the skeptics by writing that the items were "known to have belonged to the vessel."[27]

The *Gazette*'s list of the important men lost on the *Speedy* is similar to those in other accounts. Bennett even refers to the servants and the two small children who were thought to have been on board. The total number of twenty is consistent with subsequent attempts to identify the passengers. In addition to the details, the editor provides several interesting perspectives. First, he comments on the rare occurrence of so many "persons of respectability"[28] sailing on the same ship, leaving the community open to such a disaster. He also counts nine widows resulting from the event, but he does not count the children.

THE ORACLE.

YORK —SATURDAY, NOVEMBER 1.

LOSS OF THE SPEEDY.

The following is an accurate account of the loss of the schooner Speedy, in his Majesty's service on Lake Ontario, as we have been able to collect :—

The *Upper Canada Gazette* published an article on November 3, 1804, to provide the first public notice of the loss of the *Speedy*. The full content of the article is available in Appendix B.

It is the article's last paragraph, however, that is the most tantalizing. After providing the facts of the story as he knew them, Bennett added an editorial opinion regarding a possible underlying cause of the disaster. Citing several recent marine accidents "of a similar nature,"[29] he suggested that there should be an investigation into the methods of shipbuilding practiced by the Provincial Marine. To the modern reader, his choice of words must seem very moderate but, in authoritarian Upper Canada in 1804, any kind of criticism of the government, and, in particular, the military, was considered seditious. (See the full article in Appendix B.)

John Bennett had changed the publishing business in York in the previous years with his introduction of The Oracle, which was printed as a separate column in the *Upper Canada Gazette* and had a distinctly different objective. In his original announcement, Bennett said "The Oracle [*Upper Canada Gazette*] will comprehend all domestic intelligence, as also such productions as may conduce to improve the mind without injuring the morals; but licentious writings and personal invective will be carefully avoided and constantly rejected."[30]

The term "domestic intelligence" is important here, because it represents an evolution of the newspaper from being strictly a source of "foreign intelligence," meaning news of Britain and the international world. In addition to this, The Oracle would provide much more of what we would call local news. Many conservative folks thought this was dangerous, but it was most welcome in the general public. There would be an uneasy balance between this and the *Gazette*'s first purpose, as a mouthpiece for the government.[31]

The Oracle was deliberately outside that official role. The number of people in Upper Canada who could read was still quite small, but The Oracle was designed to provide that growing group with access to news and commentary about local, national, and international events. Bennett knew he was playing both sides against the middle in this pursuit, which explains his very careful language. The simple fact that he would raise the issue of an investigation into the Provincial Marine, which was run by the British Army, was rather bold. The lieutenant-governor may have raised his eyebrows when his secretary set this paper in front of him. Yes, it was a tragedy, of course, but there would be no investigation into the loss of the *Speedy*. Although we might imagine a suggestion was made to the secretary that a little talk with Mr. Bennett was in order.

Despite what the lieutenant-governor might have wished, Bennett was not the only person in Upper Canada with vivid memories of previous shipwrecks. One occurred less than a year before and was announced in The Oracle on November 26, 1803. "It is currently reported and we are sorry to add, with every appearance of foundation, that the Sloop Lady Washington, commanded by Captain Murray, was lately lost in a gale of wind near Oswego, on her passage to Niagara."[32] An earlier loss was reported in the *Gazette* on December 21, 1799. "We hear from very good authority that the schooner York, Capt. Murray, has foundered and is cast upon the American shore about fifty miles from Niagara, where the captain and men are encamped. . . . This happened in November, 1799, at The Devil's Nose, about twenty miles west of Genesee River, which enters Lake Ontario seven miles north of Rochester."[33]

Of course, folks who had lived in Upper Canada for any length of time were also aware of the greatest disaster on Lake Ontario when the British warship HMS *Ontario* was lost in November 1780. "Six short months after His Majesty's 22-Gun Brig was christened Ontario, the valuable vessel, en route from Fort Niagara to Oswego and Fort Haldimand, was hit by a sudden onslaught of rain, wild winds and pounding waves that caused the ship to founder and find the deep on All Hollow's Eve, 1780. The cause of the catastrophe was an autumn nor'easter, spawned by the residue of a tornado that originated some 3000 miles away in the Caribbean Sea."[34]

The loss of life on HMS *Ontario* numbered around 130 people, mostly British soldiers but some American prisoners of war as well. Miraculously, in 2008, the wreck of HMS *Ontario* was found in almost perfect condition and was celebrated in magazine articles, photographs, and videos. Most ships broke up to some degree when they sank, and two centuries of pounding waves finished the job; but, in the case of HMS *Ontario*, the features of the ship were clear and provided historians and archaeologists with a major windfall.[35]

Bennett was likely voicing the opinion of many people in the community who were stunned at the extreme loss of life in the *Speedy* disaster. While important people were more inclined to see the loss in terms of the high-ranking individuals on board, regular folk wanted safer transportation on the lakes. In fact, it would be many decades before sailing on the lakes was made safe for passengers.

CHAPTER 15

WIDOW PAXTON

After alternating between hope and despair for several weeks, Jane Paxton sat in her parlour and sobbed as a family friend read the article from the *Gazette*, confirming, without any doubt, that her husband was dead. The most appropriate words in the newspaper might have been "A more distressing and melancholy event has not occurred to this place for many years."[1] Jane Paxton would agree.

We can only imagine the anguish and grief of Mrs. Paxton, her children, and their friends and associates in Kingston. This was a military and naval town, so the loss of sailors and soldiers in the course of their duties was not unusual. However, Captain Paxton was very well-liked in the community, and his family was a fixture in the growing town. They had a pew in St. George's Anglican Church[2] and several of the children had been baptized there.[3] The captain would be missed by many.

Jane had been well aware of the storm that had pounded the area around the same time her husband was sailing from York to Newcastle. As a sailor's wife, she worried about her husband's safety all the time, but she coped with the anxiety. In Upper Canada at this time, the steady income of a ship captain put his family in the comfortable middle class. It provided the family with a good home and a better life than many of their contemporaries. There was also a good deal of prestige in being the wife of a ship captain. The community respected her husband for his skill and dedication, and that counted for a lot.

The Paxton home was a substantial structure, ideal for a large, growing family. It was not far from the shoreline, which, in this area, was a squat peninsula that was still owned by Michael Grass,[4] one of the founders of the town of Kingston. By 1809, this land would be purchased by Henry Murney,[5] who would build ships there, establishing the name Murney Point. In modern terms, the location of the Paxton home can be described as Barrie Street, north of Murney Tower, across from City Park.

Mrs. Paxton took comfort in the proximity of Reverend John Stuart[6] and his family, in particular their welcoming farmhouse, which was a place she could always find help when her husband was away. The Paxtons and their neighbours were some distance from the centre of Kingston, so they relied on each other for support. Rev. Stuart was the first Anglican Church minister in Upper Canada. He had settled at Cataraqui in 1785 and was instrumental in the building of the original St. George's church in Kingston, which opened in 1792.[7]

In Kingston's dockyards at Point Frederick, the sailors, soldiers, carpenters, and commissary workers were shocked by the loss of someone they considered a friend. And it was not just Captain Paxton they mourned. The loss of John Cameron and Francis Labard also left gaping holes in the community. Sailors would grit their teeth and come aboard for the next trip, because it was their job, but they might say a prayer for their old friends as they set sail.

Jane Paxton probably did not know about John Craigie's suggestion to the lieutenant-governor about providing her with a pension, but she would have been appreciative. Arranging for a pension for a widow in those days was very much an ad hoc process, based on lobbying the right people. Captain Thomas Paxton had served the Provincial Marine diligently for more than two decades and, in spite of the occasional conflict, was considered by most to be a good man who served well.

It was well-known that he had young children and financial support would be crucial for his widow.

In fact, Jane Paxton made an official request for assistance in 1808. Documents show that she knew very well how to work the system for the benefit of her family. She sent a petition to the lieutenant-governor of Upper Canada in York and then waited for the document to work its way up the chain of command. The petition itself is dated October 20, 1808, and was probably written by a barrister or an office-holder who supported her, but it has Jane Paxton's signature at the bottom.

It begins by stating "That your Petitioner's late husband, Thomas Paxton, was a Lieutenant in His Majesty's Naval Armament upon the Rivers and Lakes of the Province of Upper Canada, as appears by Commissions in your Petitioner's custody, copies of which are hereto annexed."[8] (There are copies of these two commissions[9,10] in the archives with the letter and the petition.) Next, the tragic event is explained. The critical point, of course, is the condition of the Paxton family as a result of losing the breadwinner. "Leaving his widow and seven small children, the oldest only fourteen years, unprovided for and without anything to subsist upon, so that your Petitioner and her family are reduced to poverty and must inevitably want, if not relieved by your Excellency's bounty."[11] Governors had a lot of petitions to read, so brevity was required. It ends with a plea: "Your Petitioner therefore humbly prays that your Excellency will be pleased to grant her such allowance as is usually allowed to officers widows, or otherwise relieve her as your Excellency, out of your abundant goodness, shall think fit."[12]

Near the end of the process of accepting the widow's petition, one governor said to another that her husband was "a most visionary officer and bore an exemplary character. The widow and children are in great distress, and I take the liberty of recommending them, as objects of your Excellency's consideration."[13]

We have several hints about the pension Jane received. *The Parish Register of Kingston* includes notes about the Paxton family and the loss of the *Speedy* and says "The widow of Capt. Paxton was left with a large dependent family at Kingston. The widow drew a small pension of $100 per annum during her life, which continued till within a few years since."[14] That would certainly help.

A petition by her son, Thomas Paxton Jr., in 1827, stated "That by the unfortunate death of your petitioner's father, his mother and seven helpless children, were left unprovided for, there being no fund out of which she was of right entitled to receive any assistance — but some years afterwards His Late Majesty was most graciously pleased to bestow on her a pension of twenty five pounds currency of the Province (about twenty three pounds sterling) on which she has since existed, and brought up her family the best way she could."[15] It might be that her son, decades after the events, would be less aware of the details of his mother's pension. In spite of variations in the different stories, it would seem that Jane Paxton's petition bore fruit and that possibly Craigie's efforts were helpful, at least in the long run.

In 1817, Jane Paxton and the lawyers were still working to clean up her husband's estate. The *Kingston Gazette* provides this item: "All those having demands against the Estate of the late Captain Thomas Paxton, of this place, will please to render their accounts, properly authenticated, on or before the 1st of May next, to the subscriber, who is authorized to liquidate them; and all those who are indebted to the Estate, are requested to call and settle the same. JANE PAXTON, Kingston, Nov. 25, 1817."[16]

It would not be until 1830 that the widow Paxton put the house and lot near Murney Point up for sale for a final time. The *Kingston Chronicle* of September 11, 1830, has this item, "To be sold. - A town lot in Kingston, commonly called the Paxton Lot immediately adjoining Archdeacon Stuart's and within a few minutes walk of Mississauga Point. It has the advantage of fronting two Streets, and two or more additional dwelling houses could be erected on the same, without inconvenience to the present dwelling which is large and roomy."[17]

In the meantime, the Paxton children grew up and began their own lives. The greatest amount of documentation exists for John,[18] the oldest son, who would head to Montreal as a teenager and then become part of a group who settled at the west end of Lake Erie in the years just before the War of 1812 began. The new village near the mouth of the Raisin River would be called Frenchtown, as a result of those first settlers.[19]

John Paxton not only left home early, which is not surprising considering the loss of his father, but he also appears to have become an American very quickly. He participated in military action under General Clay, accompanying Leslie Coombs on a long and dangerous trek to take information to General Harrison. He participated in more than one encounter with British troops, was wounded and taken prisoner, but managed to escape and survive to fight another day.[20]

Luckily, he was occupied elsewhere on October 23, 1813, when his compatriots took a serious drubbing at the Battle of Frenchtown, where the death toll was over four hundred.[21] Young John Paxton would survive the war and settle in the area that would later become the town of Monroe, in Monroe County, Michigan. He conducted different businesses over time and served as sheriff of Monroe County from 1826 to 1828. He married and had a family of ten, all at Monroe, where he died in 1859.[22]

Both of the other Paxton sons, Henry and Thomas, Jr., took up residence in Amherstburg, Ontario, and their mother moved there to be near her family. Jane Paxton died in Windsor on March 5, 1843, and was buried in Our Lady of the Assumption Cemetery, Windsor.[23]

The family of Captain Paxton suffered greatly from his early death, but Jane Paxton showed her mettle by managing the practical affairs and keeping the household together. Many families around Upper Canada would suffer a similar anguish as they moved on to meet the future.

CHAPTER 16

LIFE GOES ON

For many months after the loss of HMS *Speedy*, York was subdued. In a town of less than five hundred people, the sudden absence of twenty souls had an impact across the board. The Solicitor General of Upper Canada was gone. A respected judge of the Court of King's Bench had vanished. Two productive barristers and members of the House of Assembly left gaping holes in the legislature. The Surveyor General's Office was suddenly without one of their best men, and the Indian Department lost a seasoned interpreter's years of experience. The void was everywhere and would be felt keenly for decades.

In response, Lieutenant-Governor Peter Hunter quickly turned his focus to practical matters. On November 12, 1804, he wrote two letters that clearly demonstrate his priorities. The most important was to Lord Camden,[1] Secretary of State for War and the Colonies, in London. This was a formal dispatch to his boss regarding the difficulties arising from the loss of the *Speedy*. He began with a brief description of the missing personnel[2] then got to the main point of his letter, which was to procure individuals of the proper type to fill the vacancies.[3] Hunter wanted men who were born and raised in England to fill these important jobs. "It is hardly necessary for me to suggest, that the situation of His Majesty's Subjects in this Province requires, not only a Gentleman in that office of Legal Abilities sufficient to discharge the Duties of a Judge, but also, of such manners and conduct, as to improve and instruct Society in private Life."[4] In effect, he wanted good English gentlemen, not Canadians.

The second letter was to his ex-chief justice, Henry Allcock, who was on his way to England.[5] Hunter informed Allcock of his request to Lord Camden and urged him to use any influence he might have in England to make sure the right kind of men were selected for the open positions. Hunter believed, for example, that only British-born and -trained lawyers were qualified, which was probably technically true, since legal training in Upper Canada was in its infancy. But there was also a strong feeling among the English upper classes that anyone born in the colonies could not be trusted. Republican tendencies from the United States were too pervasive, they thought; and, besides, most young men born in Upper or Lower Canada did not possess the kind of bloodline or wealth that was assumed necessary for public service. It came down to the English cultural reality that can be summed up in the word "privilege." For decades to come, office-seekers in Upper Canada would have an advantage if they came from the old country.

It is also apparent from Hunter's letter to Allcock that he wanted to present a unified front to the decision-makers in London. More missives would be sent from Upper Canada to support Allcock's lobbying of the authorities.[6] Little more than a month after HMS *Speedy* had disappeared beneath the waves of Lake Ontario, Lt.-Gov. Hunter was back to business.

The Provincial Marine would carry on as well, addressing the poor condition of ships, such as the *Toronto Yacht*, which was favoured by the higher officials at York but had been built with uncured timber, just like the *Speedy*. Captain Earle reported from Kingston on December 23, 1804, "I arrived here with the Toronto the 14th Nov. at 1 am . . . Hawled her into the yard; she is in a very bad state, her timbers very rotten, her plank equally so – her timbering is nearly completed and two thirds new."[7]

The legislature would also move forward quickly. Two men lost on HMS *Speedy* held seats in the House of Assembly: Robert Gray was a member for Stormont and Russell, and Angus Macdonell for the counties of Durham and Simcoe as well as the East Riding of York. The Macdonell seat was particularly important because it included the town of York, which had the greatest concentration of population, wealth, and influence in the province. There had been an election only a few months earlier, in June 1804, in which the sitting member, Angus Macdonell, had won handily over the challenger, William Weekes.[8]

Now that the seat was vacant, Weekes, who had returned safely from his ride to Newcastle in October, would take another run at being elected. His opponent was John Cameron,[9] who had a shop near the garrison. He had come to York around 1801 and was active in local projects, such as building a hall for the new fire engine that Lt.-Gov. Hunter had donated to the town.[10] While Cameron had little chance against the aggressive and experienced Weekes, he delivered an appropriate speech, considering events of the previous fall.

It began: "The much to be lamented, and truly affecting loss sustained by the Public, in the premature fates of so many valuable Citizens, is a calamity of melancholy magnitude and distressing operation; and is to the interests as well as the feelings of this small Community, a wound bordering upon vital; a wound which will long remain unhealed, and a disaster of which the effects will be painfully felt by the Bench, the Bar, Society, the Legislature and the Country."[11] The rest of Cameron's address concerned policies and he used moderate terms, which was his normal practice.

In response, Weekes gave a speech on January 24, which did not mention Macdonell's death but used terms such as "Charter of English liberty" and "Habeas Corpus."[12] If nothing else, Weekes could command attention, which is probably the main reason he won the election.[13] However, he revelled in his new-found success for only about a year before it came to an abrupt halt when he was killed in a duel.[14]

It may be shocking to modern sensibilities to learn that such an ancient form of combat was still practiced in York at this time. Technically, duels were against the law, but, in the minds of proud men, a duel was still considered an effective way to protect personal honour. As a result of this one last ill-conceived episode in the tumultuous life of William Weekes, an important seat in the House of Assembly would become vacant for the second time in two years. Another election would be held.

Duels notwithstanding, the machinery of government took on new business and tried to clean up loose ends from the *Speedy* disaster. David MacGregor Rogers,[15] a member of the House of Assembly for Hastings and Northumberland, was concerned that the copies of the *Statutes of Upper Canada* destined for Newcastle had been lost with the ship. On February 18, 1805, Rogers moved that a warrant be issued to allocate the funds needed to reprint them. The official record includes the comment that the previous copies had been "lost in His Majesty's Schooner 'Speedy.'"[16] Two days later, the lieutenant-governor approved the expense of sixteen pounds, five shillings for this purpose,[17] and the districts eventually received the statutes.

The wealthier people who were lost on the *Speedy* left many legal and financial problems to be addressed by their survivors. Solicitor General Robert Gray, for example, had lived extravagantly and accumulated significant debt. The following item appeared in the *Gazette*, under The Oracle, on April 13, 1805: "Gray, one of those drowned in the 'Speedy,' left some property which was ordered to be sold by auction on Monday, the 22nd inst., at the house of the late Chief Justice Elmsley, the property of the late I. D. Gray, Esq., deceased, consisting of household furniture, wearing apparel and farming utensils."[18]

The furniture and household goods would help in addressing the debt, but that was just a small part of the Solicitor General's legacy. As the son of a United Empire Loyalist and an important office-holder in the judiciary of Upper Canada, Gray had received grants and bought land as an investment. In addition, although Gray was single, his position required him to have a significant house. John Baker, who was a brother of Simon Baker and also a servant in Gray's house, recalled much later, "I lived two years in Toronto, or little York, in a large white house north of the boat landing."[19]

Gray had also been involved in wheeling-and-dealing for the park lots north of Lot Street, which is now Queen Street. These were properties where wealthy folks would build large homes and enjoy country living, outside the mud and filth of York. They were in high demand and were often used as assets in business deals.[20] Also, Robert Gray held at least four hundred acres of land in Whitby Township, near the farm of Moody Farewell at Annis Creek. John Baker would inherit Lot 11 on Concession 2 in Whitby Township as a result of Gray's will. Today, this is the land in Oshawa north of King Street between Simcoe Street North and Ritson Road North.[21]

Jacob Herkimer died intestate, and for decades his file occupied the Court of Probate. Many documents would be generated as his wife, Margaret, and older brother, Lawrence, tried to clean up the mess.[22] Lawrence Herkimer continued in the fur trade business, but the shock of losing his brother would last a lifetime.

Angus Macdonell operated on a much more modest scale but had been actively loaning small amounts of money around York for several years. At his death, the ledger came out on the negative side because most of his promissory notes were uncollectable.[23]

Over at the Surveyor General's Office, the loss of John Stegmann was disastrous. A survey of the Township of Uxbridge had been on Stegmann's calendar for later in November, and now they had to scramble to find a surveyor. His protege, Samuel Street Wilmot,[24] who was thirty-one at the time, was stunned at the loss of his boss and father-in-law,[25] but he wanted to carry on with the work, which meant doing the Uxbridge survey. There was a problem, however. Wilmot was not yet a deputy surveyor, so, by law, could not handle the survey himself. The authorities were in a bind. The Uxbridge survey was critical because settlers were coming and the land must be ready for them. If the survey was delayed, potential buyers might go elsewhere. The bureaucracy kicked into high gear. Within two weeks, Samuel Wilmot was sworn in as a deputy surveyor.[26] Soon after, the order for the Uxbridge survey was issued[27] and an illustrious career began. Wilmot's later assignments would include Toronto Township[28] and, in 1816, Cartwright Township,[29] where he would document the northern area of Lake Scugog, extending the 1804 survey he had helped John Stegmann conduct.

Outside York, there was a very different kind of distress. Only a few months after the loss of HMS *Speedy*, a group of citizens from Newcastle District presented the Legislative Assembly of Upper Canada with a petition stating that the site of the existing courthouse and jail was "inconvenient"[30] and should be moved to a more central location. The long list of signatures made it clear that there was wide agreement on the matter. An act was passed revoking the county town status of Newcastle and establishing a two-year period for concerned citizens to donate a parcel of land for a new courthouse and jail in a better location. In fact, it stipulated that the new location must be in Haldimand or Hamilton townships.[31] (See full text of both the petition and the act in Appendix E.)

After two years, Asa Burnham[32] offered some of his land in Amherst, a small village that would later be merged into the city of Cobourg. The first courthouse and jail there was built north of Elgin, on the east side of Burnham Street.[33] That building was replaced in 1831 by an impressive structure across Burnham Street, near today's Golden Plough Lodge seniors' residence. In 1861, the court and jail moved to the even more impressive Victoria Hall on King Street.[34] To this day, Cobourg is the county seat for Northumberland County, and the current county office is near the historic corner of Elgin and Burnham streets.

In the town of Newcastle, the story was not nearly so positive. Residents were stunned by the quick action of the government to revoke the status of county town. In addition to the tragic loss of their good friend Thomas Paxton, the Sellecks would lose their jobs as custodians of the courthouse and jail building. Charles Selleck would continue working with his father-in-law, George Gibson, delivering cargo around the lakes, but losing his primary position brought on tough times.

The impact on the entire town was deep and wide. Property values evaporated overnight and growth stopped. It is not an exaggeration to say Newcastle became a backwater. The War of 1812 generated some excitement, especially when a boat being built there was burned by pirates,[35] but this disturbing event highlighted the general feeling that the people who remained on Presqu'ile Point were isolated and vulnerable. Residents began to accept the futility of maintaining their small community on the point. Settlement on the mainland was increasing and authorities had improved the Kingston Road, along the north shore of Lake Ontario. Since there was no effective access to Newcastle except by water, the townsfolk were outside the mainstream and felt as if they were being left behind.

During the early 1820s, there were petitions and surveys[36] and, finally, with the support of the government, the town of Newcastle was moved across Presqu'ile Bay to a small peninsula on the mainland.[37] Not everyone was happy with this change, of course. The loss of the courthouse and jail would rankle Brightonians for decades. The prevailing attitude in Brighton for a long time was that wealthy, powerful forces in the west end of Newcastle District had wrestled county town status away from the folks at the east end, all with malicious intent. The reality is far less dramatic and much more practical.

Almost a year after the loss of HMS *Speedy*, Lieutenant-Governor Peter Hunter died suddenly at Quebec. The man who had ordered Captain Paxton to sail the *Speedy* to Newcastle was sixty years of age and had been suffering from various illnesses for some time. Even before he came to Upper Canada, his biography states, "By 1799 he was suffering from stomach ailments characterized by dysentery and biliousness. In addition, he was plagued by gout."[38] This was not uncommon in soldiers with long careers, especially those who spent time in places like Minorca and the West Indies.

On September 14, 1805, The Oracle republished the original report from Quebec: "August 22nd, 1805. Yesterday at four o'clock died His Excellency Lieut.-General Peter Hunter, Lieut.-Governor of Upper Canada, and Commanding in Chief of His Majesty's forces in both the Canadas. As an officer his character was high and unsullied; and at this present moment his death may be considered a great public loss. As Lieut.-Governor of Upper Canada, his loss will be severely felt, for by his unremitting attention and exertions, he has, in the course of a few years, brought that infant colony to an unparalleled state of prosperity."[39]

The funeral of a governor is always elaborate, and this one was no exception. The entire military establishment at Quebec was involved, including Lieutenant Colonel Isaac Brock, who was preparing to go back to England. Regiments marched and cannons roared. "During the procession, minute guns were fired, first one from the Grand Battery and afterwards continued by two guns from the cavalier battery at the Citadel. The body was received by the troops and militia, when they shouldered and presented arms, the music and drums playing the Dead March."[40]

The death of the lieutenant-governor left another void in the political life of the province, adding to the upheaval of the previous year. Certainly, a proper replacement would have to be found in England, but, in the meantime, someone had to be in charge. The executive council appointed Alexander Grant[41] as administrator of Upper Canada for the time being. It made this decision because, at age seventy-one, Grant was a respected senior figure in the government, and the appointment was appropriate based on seniority. In addition, the previous governor's abrasive style was well-known. As his biography says, "Certainly, Hunter's autocratic manner was more suited to a regiment or even a large family business. His brusqueness was probably temperamental; however, it was no doubt exacerbated by poor health."[42] The people of Upper Canada were tired of the drama and ready for some relief. Grant swiftly made an announcement to set everyone at ease. No jobs would be lost, and the policies of the government would continue as before.

Grant was a calm, genial fellow who would use his unassuming, down-home style to make people comfortable. He said it plainly, "Tho my late good worthy predecessor was Sensible & Clever, he latterly dealt very harsh with most of the people that had any business with him."[43] On the political front, Grant would not rock the boat. He would carry on with Hunter's policies, for the most part, trying to act as a benign placeholder until a new lieutenant-governor could be selected and sent to the province.

The next lieutenant-governor of Upper Canada was Sir Francis Gore,[44] who took over on August 25, 1806. While Gore had been in the army for many years, he also had some experience with administration of colonies, having served in Bermuda before coming to Upper Canada. He would arrive as a peacemaker and, over his eleven years in the post, would maintain the basic tenets of colonial rule but would do it with soft words and a smiling face. It would be a time of turmoil as the colony grew and evolved, but at least the harshness of Peter Hunter was in the past.

In the English culture of the time, an event became legend when a poem was written about it. The *Kingston Gazette* of June 18, 1811,[45] printed the poem "Elegy" under the column name Reckoner. It was a common habit for anonymous contributors to write pieces using catchy pseudonyms, and readers of the *Gazette* looked forward to seeing what the Reckoner had to say in each issue. In fact, most folks knew this columnist to be Reverend John Strachan, who ran a grammar school in Cornwall and would, much later, become Bishop of York.

"Elegy" consists of twenty-two four-line stanzas, presenting an emotional tribute to the people who were lost on the *Speedy*. The language is emotive and touching, with lines like "The adverse tempest backs the shaking sail" and "O cruel lake! Must thy insatiate jaws demand with rig'rous haste an annual prey?" It mentions "reluctant Gray" and "determined Cochrane" [sic] as well as the "smiling housewife."

The theme is fully expressed with "the province mourns a public woe." (See the full text of the poem in Appendix C.)

In light of this elaborate and emotional work of social mourning, we might notice that one of the twenty souls who was lost on the *Speedy* had no commemoration in poetry or prose. That would be the accused, Ogetonicut.

CHAPTER 17

NO POEM FOR OGETONICUT

In the years that followed the loss of HMS *Speedy*, Chief Wabbekisheco's fears of further encroachment by the English were realized. Moody Farewell and Eleazer Lockwood's new farms were only two examples of the slow, steady increase in settlement south of Lake Scugog. The policy of the government to maintain good relations with the Indigenous people continued for the next decade and would bear fruit in a big way. The War of 1812 saw farm boys from across Upper Canada join the militia and fight with British regulars to prevent an American invasion of Upper Canada. Many groups of Indigenous warriors fought bravely in support of their allies throughout the war.

Reverend Peter Jones[1] wrote that "During the war of 1812 between England and America, all the Indians in Canada, and many of the western tribes, rallied round the British standard; and it is generally believed, that had it not been for their efficient and timely aid, Canada would have been wrested from the crown of Great Britain."[2] Jones was born near Burlington in 1802, a son of surveyor Augustus Jones and a Mississauga chief's daughter. He was educated in the Wesleyan Methodist Church and became a revered minister and mentor who wrote extensively about the history and culture of the Mississauga community. In trying to protect his people, Jones was persistently pro-British. His words, which were published posthumously in 1861, demonstrate that the lieutenant-governor's plan to keep the Indigenous people as allies for the next fight with the British had worked well, at least for the British side.

Unfortunately for the Mississauga people, after the conflict with the United States ended in 1814, the need for military allies also ended. The priority for government officials became the settlement of more English farmers. This was a critical turning point in the relationship between Indigenous communities and the newcomers in Upper Canada. With a dwindling population and no demand for their services in war, Indigenous people began to be treated as wards of the state. For the long-time residents of the land around Lake Scugog, the changes were ominous.

Rice Lake Treaty No. 20, which was signed November 5, 1818,[3] is an example of the shifting times. The treaty covered the greater part of the Lake Scugog area. The western boundary was the line between Home and Newcastle districts, extended to the northeast corner of Lake Simcoe. The northern boundary went from Lake Simcoe to the top of Rawdon Township in Hastings County. The southern boundary was the top line of Darlington Township, and along the tops of the townships to the east, all the way to the Trent River. The Mississauga people ceded this enormous swath of land for "yearly, and every year, forever, the said sum of seven hundred and forty pounds currency in goods at the Montreal price."[4]

This might seem a middling price for such a huge property, but the chiefs and elders of the Mississauga people, and other Indigenous groups in Upper Canada, could see the writing on the wall. They expected, as more and more settlers arrived, that game would continue to abandon their hunting grounds. The treaty would ensure that the people would receive the food, clothing, tools, and weapons that they needed every year. Their villages and families were disintegrating before their eyes due to disease and drink, and it was becoming more difficult to maintain their traditional cultural practices. The leaders thought they must accept some sort of arrangement and get the best deal they could at the time. The offer might not be available at a later date. They were now bargaining from a position of weakness, and they knew it.

Settlers started to arrive in the area around Lake Scugog in the early 1820s.[5] The Mississauga people watched as farmers cut and burned trees to free up land for growing wheat. Deer and other game, which they required for food, retreated farther and farther north. Still, the original inhabitants persisted in their traditional practices as best they could. They needed to eat, so they maintained fishing weirs at the mouth of Annis Creek. John Henry had settled near the lakeshore in 1816, and his son, John Henry, Jr., recalled seeing "a large number of Indians camped in their wigwams on his father's farm, overlooking the mouth of the creek."[6] Since there were no wharfs at this time, this was a good launching place, and "The Indians found this marsh a safe place to bring their fleet of canoes."[7]

The settlers also became familiar with the leader of the local Mississauga community. Samuel Pedlar would later collect information and stories about the early settlers of Oshawa, and one item refers to the old chief: "Daniel Hinkson being asked if he ever met the old chief Wab-bok-ish-ego replied that he remembered seeing him quite frequently. When he saw him last his hair which were tinged with grey fell in masses over his back and shoulders, while his features wore a pinched wrinkled expression. A man of medium figure but exceedingly active for his age."[8]

The revered chief was gone by 1830 when the Mississauga people of Lake Scugog encountered their worst nightmare. Far downstream, where the town of Lindsay now straddles the Scugog River, an enterprising fellow named William Purdy[9] built a dam across the river. He had been granted four hundred acres in Ops Township on condition that he set up saw and grist mills to serve the settlers in the area. Purdy's biography states "Despite difficulties with spring floods and fever, he had made good progress by September 1830."[10] He had planted part of the five or six acres he had cleared and, at the site of present-day Lindsay, had "quarried out of a Rock on the Bank of the [Scugog] River, a place sufficient to set my saw Mill and for the [flume], and have erected a good and Substantial frame, with a good Solid frame of dam."[11] A visitor to Purdy's installation in 1833 gushed that it was "the largest mill-dam in the world."[12]

The authorities in York were anxious to encourage entrepreneurs like William Purdy. They needed individuals who were willing to invest their own time, energy, and money to create facilities that would not only support the current settlers but also be great advertising for more. It was men like Purdy who founded communities all around Upper Canada, very much out of their own grit and determination. Lindsay would grow into a thriving town based on the developments Purdy implemented.

His dam, however, created a huge problem. The water in the Scugog River kept rising until it was more than six feet higher than it had been.[13] The modest creek, which normally allowed wagons to cross in many places, became a navigable river. Loud complaints came from the few settlers who had established farms along its banks. Significant parts of their land were now submerged. Large swaths of low-lying tamarack forest were flooded. "The stagnant waters grew miasmic and a plague of fever and ague killed off scores of settlers."[14] The extensive marshlands, along with miles of wild rice fields, were destroyed. Lake Scugog would never be the same.

In response to loud and persistent complaints from settlers, Purdy doubled down by asking the government to provide a deed to the land, stipulating that he would be exempt from liability for damage caused by the flooding. The authorities still wanted to encourage this type of development, so Purdy's request was granted in May 1834.[15] Another factor they considered was that a navigable waterway in this area would compensate for the lack of roads. They knew navigation was critical to settlement and development.

The government eventually began to listen to angry settlers, not least because of an ugly incident when a mob went to Purdy's property and attacked the dam.[16] Civil engineer Nicol Hugh Baird[17] was asked to investigate.[18] Baird felt that the benefits of higher water levels far outweighed the negative impacts. He suggested the government build a dam of its own, at a height of only five feet. This would be enough to make the waterways navigable but also bring down the water level, helping the people who had lost property. William Purdy agreed to co-operate, and the dam was built.[19] Not long afterward, Purdy retired, leaving his enterprise in the hands of his sons.

Throughout all of this, no one considered the impact on the Mississauga people. For them, the flooding was a terrible disaster. The wild rice they relied on to supply a major part of their food during the winter was gone. So were the ducks and geese that had called the marshlands home, further reducing their food supply. One can imagine the elders standing on the shoreline, watching the water rise, knowing this was an existential threat to their families and their community as a whole. They would have to move.

At least, that was the government's solution. The authorities insisted that the Mississauga people in the Lake Scugog area leave their traditional home and find another place to live. They were less concerned about diminished living conditions due to the flooding than the rush of settlers coming to Upper Canada. It was a practical matter for them. The fewer Indigenous people taking up valuable farmland, the better. In hindsight, we can see the ugly hand of racial prejudice at work.

Jacob Crane was chief of the Lake Scugog Mississauga people during this difficult time.[20] Some of his group went to Lake Simcoe and settled on the reserve that had been set up at Coldwater.[21] Chief Crane went with the rest to Chemong Lake (also called Mud Lake), where they had friends and relatives. In 1836, the chief moved his band on to Balsam Lake.[22] Soon, they would move again.

These trials are explained on the website of the Mississaugas of Scugog Island First Nation:

> But by 1843, with non-native settlement increasing and game populations declining, the government was encouraging native people to take up subsistence farming to supply their food needs. Owing to the unproductive rocky soil at Balsam Lake, Chief Crane's people sought better land, and they chose to move back to the Scugog area. With increasing settlement at Scugog, the only land available was an 800-acre (320-hectare) landlocked parcel on Scugog Island. Despite the thousands of acres west of Lake Scugog earlier taken from them, the Mississauga people were required to purchase these 800 acres with their own money.[23]

Successes are also proudly described:

> Over the century and a half that followed, the people tried subsistence farming, but this didn't prove viable; fur trapping, hunting and basket-making supplied a meager income. Later, off-reserve jobs in the cities to the south were resorted to, but times were never bountiful. In spite of heavy enlistment for the great wars, and the recent history of Residential Schools, the "60's Scoop," and a dwindling member population, the Mississauga people survived and rebuilt their community. After much forward-thinking and hard work, the Mississaugas opened their community economic development project in 1997, the Great Blue Heron Casino. With the advent of the casino also came the Baagwating Community Association; Baagwating is run by members of the Mississaugas of Scugog Island First Nation and is the charitable arm of the Great Blue Heron. Through building community networks, the Mississaugas of Scugog Island First Nation have built

relationships of trust and respect with the Scugog Township, the Durham Region, and the local townspeople.[24]

More than two centuries after Ogetonicut perished in the hold of HMS *Speedy*, his people have demonstrated their resilience and determination. Their story is an integral part of Canadian history, and it continues.

PART II

CHAPTER 18

SEARCHING FOR HMS *SPEEDY*

Ed Burtt gazed across the blue waters of Lake Ontario. The summer of 1989 was providing some very good weather for diving. On this sunny July day, he was on his boat over Dobbs Bank, conducting training exercises with Ontario Provincial Police divers. They were about seven kilometres southeast of Presqu'ile Point, over the shallowest spot on the north side of this large underwater plateau.

Suddenly, there was a splash at the side of the boat. One of the divers emerged above the waves, pushed his mask to the top of his head, and shouted "Look what I found!" Burtt could see a coin between the thumb and forefinger of the diver's extended hand, and he motioned for him to come closer. Placing the coin in Burtt's palm, the diver said he had found it on the lake bottom. Then he put his mask back in place and disappeared beneath the waves.[1]

Burtt stared at the coin, turning it over to study both sides. He could tell it was extremely old just by its worn and faded appearance. Later that day, using a magnifying glass, it became apparent that the coin was Spanish. He could see the date 1732 and, on the reverse side, the English words, "Piece of Eight."[2]

The Spanish coin found on Dobbs Bank in 1989 was donated by Ed Burtt to the Mariners Park Museum, in Prince Edward County. This coin is a commercially reproduced replica of an original Spanish Piece of Eight minted in Mexico in 1732. Coin collectors say that the third line on the reverse side, which says "Piece of Eight" in English, shows it is not an original. This coin could have been in the pocket of one of the passengers on the ill-fated *Speedy* when it was lost in 1804.

This was a fascinating find for a fellow who had dedicated his life to underwater discovery. Ed Burtt[3] was born in Kirkland Lake in 1939 and moved with his family to Belleville as a youngster. He soon developed a love for scuba diving and was a fixture at diving clubs around Belleville and Trenton in his teen years. After obtaining a degree in engineering at the University of Ottawa, he launched a successful career in the volatile business of underwater search and salvage. By 1989, Burtt's company, Ocean Scan Systems[4] of Belleville, was engaged in many different types of underwater work, from locating small aircraft that crashed into remote lakes, to recovering boats and cars that ended up in the water. Contracts for training OPP divers represented an important revenue source for the company and added to the variety of the work.

Just a few weeks after finding the piece of eight, Burtt and his crew were back out on Lake Ontario, in the same general area south of Presqu'ile Point. His company was an agent for a marine exploration company in Florida headed by Mel Fisher,[5] the legendary treasure hunter who had found the Spanish galleon *Atocha* in 1985. On this day, they were testing a new model of underwater video camera.[6] For several hours they towed the camera under the boat, recording video onto a VHS tape as they went.

Reviewing the tape a couple of days later, Burtt saw intriguing objects and shapes that looked like pieces of wood or metal, often with jagged edges. Some items reminded him of very old shipwrecks he had studied and seen over the course of his diving career. One in particular came to mind. He recalled reading that HMS *Speedy* had been lost in this area in 1804 and the wreck was never found. Together, the coin and the video conjured the possibility of an important historic shipwreck not far from home. Resources were available and, as a professional diver, Ed Burtt had plenty of motivation. It was like waving a red flag in front of a bull. The explorer in him could not resist.

In September, Burtt contacted Ken Cassavoy, a professional marine archaeologist who worked with the Ontario Ministry of Culture and Communications.[7] Cassavoy saw the video and was impressed. While the resolution of the images was low, diminishing their quality, he agreed that several suggested a very early shipwreck. In particular, he cited a clay pipe and spectacles clearly shown in one part of the video.[8]

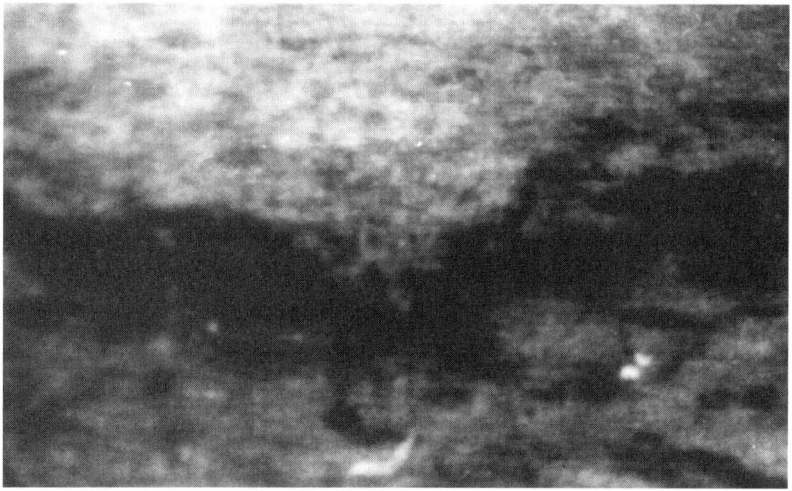

Archaeologists associated with the *Speedy* project agreed that a clay pipe and pair of spectacles shown in the 1989 video may be important artifacts. Both are personal items that evoke the time of the *Speedy*.

In the following months, Cassavoy applied to the Ontario government for a marine archaeology survey licence for the HMS *Speedy* project,[9] which would give Burtt and his crew exclusive rights to conduct underwater surveys at the site. An application for funding was also submitted. On another front, Burtt applied for articles of incorporation for the H.M.S. Speedy Foundation,[10] a non-profit organization designed to promote the underwater project and do fundraising. Hopes ran high for finding the remains of a historic ship like HMS *Speedy*.

The licence and funding applications bore fruit in April 1990[11] as preparations were underway to make sure the equipment and crew were ready to take advantage of the first good weather. Unfortunately, Mother Nature was not co-operative,[12] and so the crew's first day on the lake was not until the middle of June.[13] They began their survey work with the objective of locating the items shown on the video.

Glen Rover was a 24-foot steel hull vessel powered with two 75-horsepower outboard engines. It was the primary boat used for surveying the *Speedy* site during 1990. The *Avon* was a 20-foot inflatable boat owned by Ocean Scan Systems, used as a diving platform. This picture, taken July 26, 1990, shows Ed Burtt sitting in the *Avon*, looking out to the diver who is taking the picture. It was sunny and calm on the lake that day.

Between June and October that year, Burtt and his crew spent nineteen days out on the lake. Terry Coons,[14] Burtt's childhood friend and a professional diver who acquired his training with the US Navy,[15] was the chief diver for the project as well as a director in the H.M.S. Speedy Foundation.[16] Coons was responsible for managing the dives and the divers, and he did the bulk of the diving himself. A remotely operated tow video camera would record images onto tape and, when items of interest were identified, the divers went down to find the item and take close-up underwater photographs.

Ed Burtt was an agent in Canada for JW Fishers, a company in Florida who sold the Sea Otter ROV video camera. Ed and his crew used this equipment extensively to survey the ground in the *Speedy* debris field. It was towed under the boat and video came to a display terminal and VHS recorder on the boat as it moved along. When an unusual shape appeared in the video, a diver might be sent below with a 35mm camera to take close-up pictures of the item.

Of course, while this was going on, safety was top of mind for everyone. Diving in the rough and cloudy waters of Lake Ontario could be dangerous, but these experienced divers had the right equipment and lots of experience, which sometimes meant that you abort the dive in the face of high waves and gusting wind. Everything was based on the weather.

For the divers, it was gruelling work. In periods of good weather, when there were successive days of diving, fatigue could be a problem that needed to be managed. The best weather in 1990 was later in July and through August. During this time, Coons shed body weight at an alarming rate, due to the intense and constant diving.[17] Some days, he was called upon a dozen or more times to go down and check out interesting shapes that had been captured on video. It was exciting to dive on a potentially historic wreck, but there were also tedious days that bore no positive results. Such is the life of a professional diver.

Despite the spring's high hopes, as fall approached, nothing related to the *Speedy* had been found. Where were all those shapes from the previous year's video? A grid layout kept the work organized,[18] ensuring they did not search the same area by mistake. While the results they sought were not appearing, the survey continued.

Adding to their frustration, the crew learned early in the project that radar readings were not reliable in the area south of Presqu'ile Point. Readings mysteriously changed, often from hour to hour, which meant they had to constantly take new readings.[19] As a fallback, they used a compass, keying on trees, houses, silos, and barns within sight on the closest land, to establish their relative position. A lot of time and energy was wasted until GPS was introduced later in the project, which improved location finding significantly.

As October began, Burtt was still hoping for a breakthrough. On the eighth, while they were about a mile east of the entrance to Presqu'ile Bay, the tow video showed a large object below. The divers investigated and found that they had indeed located a shipwreck, but it was not the *Speedy*. It was the *Minnie Slausson*,[20] a freighter that sunk in 1877. This ship had three masts and was largely intact, sitting up in the water, as if inviting visitors. Burtt and the crew recorded the location and would come back another day to take more video.

The high point of 1990 came at the very end of the season, on October 14.[21] They had moved to another square on the grid and, in very short order, were seeing familiar shapes from the first video. There was an anchor, pieces of timber and chain, cannonballs, pulleys, and more.[22] Finally, they had located the debris field, a term Burtt would use from this point forward. They were able to go out again on October 20, and they saw more of the same things in the same general area.[23] This was the last of the diving for 1990, and Ed Burtt was very relieved to have something to show for a summer of intense work. He was even more excited about what they might find next year. (See details of the search in Appendix A.)

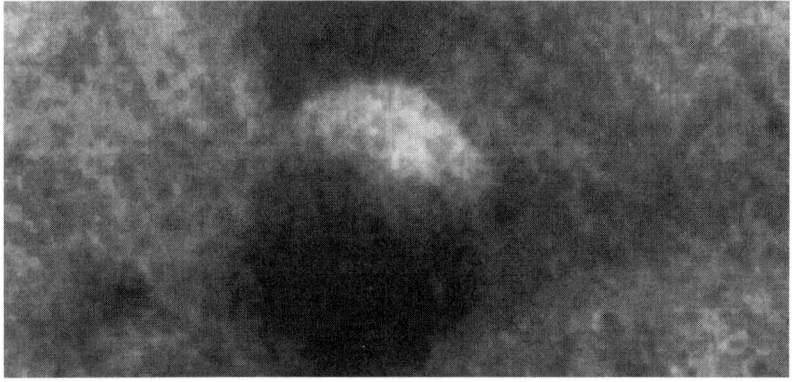

The *Speedy* was a gunboat, which means it had at least one small cannon onboard, and therefore some cannonballs. These cannonballs were found spread over the debris field and they were fairly easy to identify in pictures and video. The size and shape of the cannonballs found were all the same, resembling the type that would have been on the *Speedy*.

Ken Cassavoy had been the supervising marine archaeologist for the project during the 1990 season. He completed his responsibilities by writing a report outlining the genesis of the project and the activity that took place that season.[24] He also submitted an article for the *Ontario Archaeological Report* in 1991, which said that the results of the 1990 season had been inconclusive. He added, however, that promising sightings had occurred very late in the season and, given the historical importance of the *Speedy*, work should continue.[25]

Cassavoy did not return to the project in 1991 because of the many demands on his time and his belief that he had not seen enough evidence to support the theory that Burtt and his crew had found the remains of HMS *Speedy*. He indicated he would be happy to return if more definitive evidence was found, but, in the meantime, there were other projects to work on.[26] This would have significant consequences. It would cause a change in the terms of the archaeological licences issued by the ministry for the *Speedy* project. The rules for handling underwater artifacts take into consideration the experience and expertise of the licensee. With a professional marine archaeologist as the licensee in 1990, the licence said they were allowed to retrieve a limited number of artifacts for the purpose of identifying the ship.[27] Unfortunately, the debris field was not located until the end of the season, so retrieving artifacts to identify the ship was not yet possible, even if the licence allowed for it.

The licence for 1991 was taken out by Ed Burtt, who was not a certified archaeologist. As a result, the Underwater Survey clause in the licence read "Retrieval of artifacts from underwater sites is not covered under this license."[28] The practical impact of this was to prevent Ed and his crew from retrieving any artifacts, even if they found items that would be useful in identifying the ship. These restrictions were designed to protect underwater artifacts from destruction by careless divers and treasure hunters. In this case, however, they had the effect of putting the *Speedy* project in an impossible situation. If the identity of the ship was not yet confirmed, the professional archaeologists would not be inclined to pursue the project. On the other hand, if artifacts could not be retrieved, then the ship would not likely be identified. It was a classic catch-22.

To fill the void created by Cassavoy's departure, Phil Wright[29] came into the project as consulting archaeologist. Recently retired from the Ministry of Culture and Communications, where he had been the senior marine archaeologist, Wright had seen the original video and, like Cassavoy, considered the spectacles and clay pipe to be important artifacts.

One of Burtt's off-season jobs was to solicit expert opinions about what he had found from others in the world of underwater exploration. He sent the 1989 video to Louis E. Cook of Underwater Observation Services in Plymouth, Massachusetts. Cook wrote back listing nineteen different items he had identified in the video, including "pulleys, cannons and cannonballs, black bottles, square-head nails, masts and fittings, hand tools, eye glasses, dead eye."[30] The last part of his letter said: "From my experience with the work that we have done and are continuing to do on LaMagnifique in Boston, this shipwreck is very similar. The video work that has been done on this site definitely proves that this is a wooden sailing vessel from the early 1800 period."[31] Burtt thought so too.

The 1991 survey season opened with a lot of optimism. They went back to the debris field that was located in October and were rewarded with sightings of even more items of interest. Ed was particularly fascinated by the many small, shiny objects[32] that lay scattered around, sometimes in clusters. When visibility was good and the sun reached down to the lake bottom, the items glinted in the eyes of the divers. Burtt thought they were made of brass and, after seeing them on several survey days, he was confident enough to say they were brass buttons,[33] like those found on the uniforms of officers in the Provincial Marine.[34] But, according to his licence restrictions, none of them could be retrieved.

Later in June, they came across the clay pipe and spectacles seen in the 1989 video.[35] Terry Coons visited this location several times and took photographs at close range. It was clear to him that the spectacles and pipe were very old, although the job of dating them would fall to a professional marine archaeologist. Less visible in his pictures, but very obvious to the diver in the same immediate area, were a cannonball and a black bottle.[36] A few days later, not far from the spectacles and pipe, two long wooden objects were spotted. Initially, they looked like logs; however, on closer examination by the diver, they were identified as masts. Both were exactly the same length and girth, crafted in the same manner, including the dramatic taper at the bottom end, as was common in British gunboats in the late 1790s.[37]

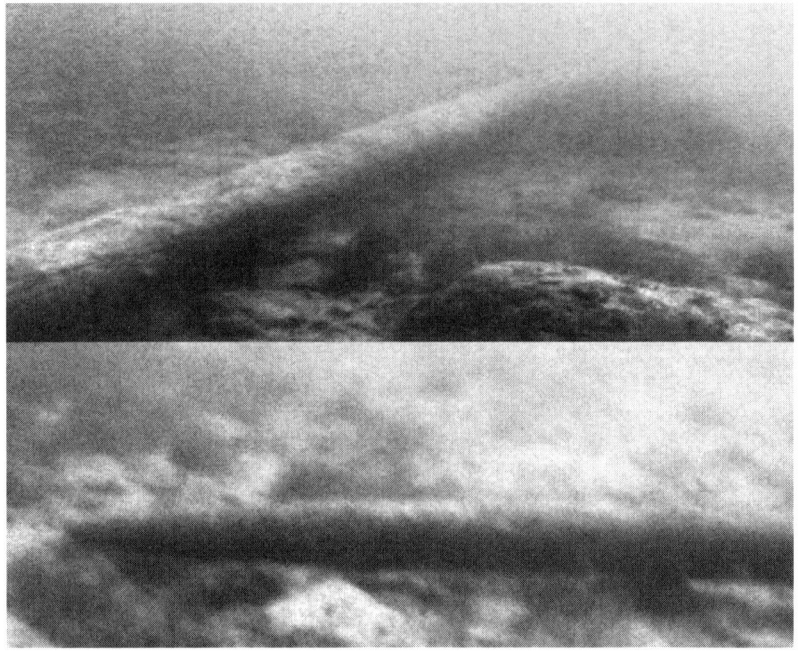

One day video presented images of what appeared to be two logs. Divers found two identical masts, not far from each other. The length, girth and workmanship suggest a ship from the early 1800s. Clearly visible is the taper at the end of the mast that was inserted into the deck.

The survey also turned up items that Burtt identified as deadeyes,[38] which would be part of the rigging of any early sailing ship. Various pulleys and pieces of chain were also found, in some cases still connected to nearby items. Black glass bottles with corks[39] were spotted as well as several examples of a style of bottle that was normally used to carry ginger beer,[40] a popular drink among sailors around 1800.

Much of the survey work in 1991 focused on documenting the debris field.[41] The crew wanted to determine how large it was, what its boundaries were, and whether there were clusters of items in some areas. The hope was that this information might shed light on how the objects ended up where they were. In this process, many grid squares were searched. In some, nothing was found; but in others, more artifacts were seen. Photographs were taken and location information recorded so they could return to the same spot if need be.

One discovery was particularly exciting. A dark, rectangular form appeared in the video they had just recorded. The divers went down to have a look and ventured close enough to get a decent picture, in spite of poor visibility. On closer scrutiny, they could see that it was a small chest,[42] just sitting there on the bottom, as if waiting for someone to walk by and carry it away. A large iron padlock secured the contents, showing little rust after more than two centuries in fresh water. The image seems odd to the modern eye because the ends of the chest are raised well over the lid. Burtt did some research and found that this design was common in the late 1700s.

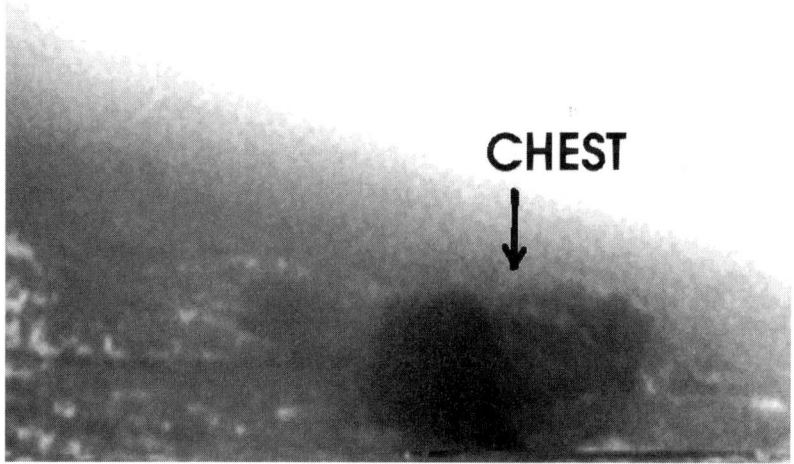

CHEST

Were the *Statutes of Upper Canada* in this chest? We may never know.

Terry Coons conducted several dives to the chest and observed that the landscape around it changed dramatically from day to day. Sometimes it was almost entirely covered by silt and sand, while other times the area had been swept clear and the chest stood on its limestone perch, proud and defiant of the elements. Close examination suggested the contents of the chest, whatever they may be, were very heavy.[43] As always, the artifact was not disturbed, but much discussion ensued on the boat each time this unique item was seen.

Ed Burtt knew from the historical record that six copies of the *Statutes of Upper Canada* had been on board HMS *Speedy*,[44] and he thought it likely that this chest contained those important papers. If that were the case, after almost two centuries in the water, it is probable that the documents would be nothing but mush. In any case, the chest still sits there.

Another important artifact discovered during the 1991 season was thought to be the ship's bell. Terry Coons encountered it on a dive, nestled between some rocks and completely covered in long, flowing moss. He could clearly see the ring at the top and could easily make out the familiar shape of a bell, even under the thick moss. It was tantalizing to think that a few swipes of a knife might reveal the name of the ship on the side of the bell. But, no! That was against the rules and could jeopardize the whole project. Terry wonders about it to this day.[45]

One of the objectives for the 1991 season had been to locate the ship's hull.[46] This was the most critical artifact to find because it might help identify the ship. The materials used, as well as methods of construction, can provide clues that place a ship in a particular time period or identify its specific type. While they did not discover the hull that year, a closer review of one of the survey videos revealed pieces of timber with protrusions that might be the stubs of broken ribs.[47] Visibility was very poor in the video, so they could not be sure it was part of the hull, but anticipation was high about returning to this location the following year to confirm the theory.

In the spring of 1992, Burtt and his crew were ready to resume the *Speedy* project, but the weather would not co-operate. On many days, high winds and waves made surveying over the debris field impossible.[48] Sometimes, they reverted to the second-best option and explored near the shore, where the water was calmer. One day, as they were surveying east of Dobbs Bank, closer to Wellers Bay, they located the remains of a World War I torpedo bomber. It was twisted and bent, but they were able to identify the aircraft as a Blackburn Shark biplane.[49] The sandspit that divides Wellers Bay from Lake Ontario was used as a bombing range during both world wars, so this find, while intriguing, was not a big surprise.

Later in the season, while taking another weather break from Dobbs Bank, Burtt and the crew made a return visit to the wreck of the *Minnie Slausson*,[50] which they had originally located two years earlier. They were able to shoot some video and enjoy the pleasures of diving for fun, so the day was not a total loss.

Before the 1992 season ended, the crew saw shapes that might be a hull, and Terry Coons went down to have a look. The result was interesting but disappointing. There was a collection of timbers buried in silt and sand, covered in moss. On one side, there were large jagged stubs that indicated ribs of a ship had been broken off. Nearby, he found a large, oddly shaped piece of wood beside several square wooden pegs, suggesting a piece of rib and some connecting parts.[51] These pieces were as close as they would come to finding the hull.

As the scattered nature of the debris field became evident, the crew's thoughts naturally moved to an explanation. They talked about the kind of extremely violent event that would create the many small, broken pieces they had seen. Initially Burtt floated a theory that gunpowder in the hold may have exploded in a storm,[52] but later he began to think that the ship may have hit something very solid and disintegrated on impact. It was mostly speculation, but a theme was emerging.

The 1993 diving season began with a difficult family situation for Ed Burtt and, as a result, no survey work was done on the *Speedy* project that year.[53] However, he was not totally inactive. During the summer, work was done to search for test models of the Avro Arrow off Point Petre, along the south shore of Prince Edward County. There are no documents in his files about this work, but there are numerous pictures. There was also a page about the search on the Ocean Scan Systems website.[54]

As it turned out, after three years of effort, the search for the remains of HMS *Speedy* was over. There were attempts to continue the work, but never again was there a boat on the water with divers going below. The last cheque from the Ontario Heritage Foundation had arrived in late 1992,[55] so Ed Burtt was now on his own in supporting any further work. He had a company to run and needed to pursue projects that would generate revenue.

CHAPTER 19

99.99% SURE

With the *Speedy* project confined to dry land in 1994, Ed Burtt engaged in ongoing research about early marine ship construction. His burgeoning collection of documents from the archives included diagrams of vessels built at Kingston in the same time period as HMS *Speedy*, as well as letters directly related to the construction of *Speedy* and its working life. He also consulted experts who could assist in providing historical context for the project.

On such person was Burtt's friend Ian Morgan,[1] an expert in early ship design and construction on the Great Lakes. Morgan was enthused about the project and provided a wealth of knowledge and experience. He talked to Burtt about the design of British gunboats at the time of the *Speedy* and responded to survey images with ideas of the function of certain components of the ship. His primary advice was to focus on the hull, which is the most critical part in identifying a ship.[2]

Over time, all the information Burtt had collected came together for him and formed a solid belief that he had located the *Speedy*. After the survey phase was over, the project became a marketing program, so a slogan was required. Based on all Burtt knew, it was easy for him to say, with emphasis, that he was "99.99% sure" he had found the remains of HMS *Speedy*. He couldn't say he was 100% sure, because it had not been scientifically proven, but a little exaggeration would go a long way when dealing with the public. The term "99.99% sure" would be repeated over and over again in interviews[3] and discussions over the next two decades.

With the *Speedy* project on hold, Burtt's company became involved in several contracts that would generate revenue while providing his inner treasure hunter with the experiences of a lifetime. In 1994, underwater exploration equipment was shipped to Ecuador to be used in a venture to find the Spanish galleon *La Capitana*, which sank off the coast in 1654.[4] The contact on this project was Walter Zacharchuk,[5] a Canadian marine archaeologist who has been called "the father of marine archaeology in Canada."[6] Zacharchuk had also been a member of the team that worked on the site of the Spanish galleon *Atocha*, which Mel Fisher had found.[7]

Walter Zacharchuk was Canada's first professional marine archaeologist, and Ed Burtt ran a marine salvage business. Both men were enthusiastic divers who loved discovering historical artifacts in the water. The prevailing caricatures of their two professions by this time was that the salvage divers wanted to pull everything out of the water and cash in, while the archaeologists wanted to perform endless analyses and leave the artifacts in the water until they rotted away. Of course, neither of these two extremes was true in practice. Zacharchuk, in his role as an archaeologist, was a proponent of collaboration between the scientists and divers.[8] Ed Burtt was a diver and salvage operator who was anxious to follow the rules that were set out for him but desperately wanted to show the public what he had found. Unfortunately, discussions around these issues, whether across the boardroom table or over a cold beer, often reverted to the extremes.

The most important work for Ocean Scan Systems outside the country in the 1990s was in Cuba. A *Toronto Star* article on February 27, 1998, was headed "Spoils of Havana harbour await new explorers."[9] Ed Burtt was vice-president of operations for the project. At fifty-eight, he was anxious to expand his horizons and make some serious money. This was a high-stakes enterprise that was expected to bring in a fortune in gold and artifacts.[10] Millions were invested in an effort to locate the remains of Spanish galleons sunk in the 1500s in hurricanes along the north shore of Cuba. There was widespread press coverage, including in Burtt's hometown. The *Belleville Intelligencer* said, "A salvage operator, who recently created a stir among historical circles for his alleged discovery of the HMS Speedy in Lake Ontario, has struck a potential mother lode."[11]

Ed Burtt supervised the outfitting of *Explorad'oro* in Kingston and had it shipped to Cuba. He was vice-president of operations for the project that hoped to find treasure from Spanish galleons on the north coast of Cuba.

One of Burtt's first jobs in this project was to have a customized exploration boat outfitted at Kingston and shipped to Cuba. He was very proud of the result, which was called *Explorad'oro*[12], so named because they were looking for gold, which is "oro" in Spanish. In Cuba, Burtt was like a kid in a candy shop, running a large and well-funded exploration project, searching for real sunken treasure. When asked whether he thought they would find anything, he responded, "I wish I'd never fallen in love with chasing shipwrecks. The truth is, I really don't know. But it's an incredible adventure."[13]

Late in 2000, however, the promising project came to an end. New investors were brought in to the project, and the emphasis changed from doing good archaeology to announcing big finds. The new situation was not to his liking, so he pulled out.[14] Ed Burtt headed back to Belleville.

In 2006, Burtt was involved in exploration work in the British Virgin Islands,[15] looking for shipwrecks from the 1700s. Later, he worked for the Bahamian government and a travel company.[16] All these projects were far from Presqu'ile Point, but the debris field south of Dobbs Bank was never far from his mind.

When he wasn't treasure hunting, Burtt was involved in constant promotion of the *Speedy* story. There were many newspaper interviews and some speaking engagements where he told his story. He was convinced that once people heard that the remains of HMS *Speedy* may have been found, investors and supporters would line up to help him pursue the project.

Burtt continued to apply for archaeological survey licences for the *Speedy* site every year, even though there was no survey work being done. On the other hand, he showed very little interest in writing the annual reports required by the ministry. The purpose of annual submissions was to provide the ministry with details of each season's survey work, but Ed was not paying attention. In 2005, the ministry cracked down, making it very clear that he would get no more licences if the reports were not completed.[17] He was provided with a list of all the reports that had not been submitted, along with instructions for coming back into compliance with the rules.

Sensing an opportunity, Burtt used the demand for a 1997 project report to provide the complete story of the *Speedy*, as he wanted it to be presented. The result was a 120-page document that included a lengthy description of what he believed had happened to the *Speedy* in 1804, along with many pictures from the surveys of 1990 through 1992.[18] The most important section is a nautical chart that shows the estimated route of the ship before its demise.[19] Burtt used this in his presentations because it demonstrates his version of the story. A line shows the course of HMS *Speedy* coming to Newcastle, pressed hard by a westerly storm. Captain Paxton was not able to turn into Presqu'ile Bay and sailed east, to Wellers Bay, to ride out the storm. Then, the nor'easter hit and drove the ship back out into the lake.

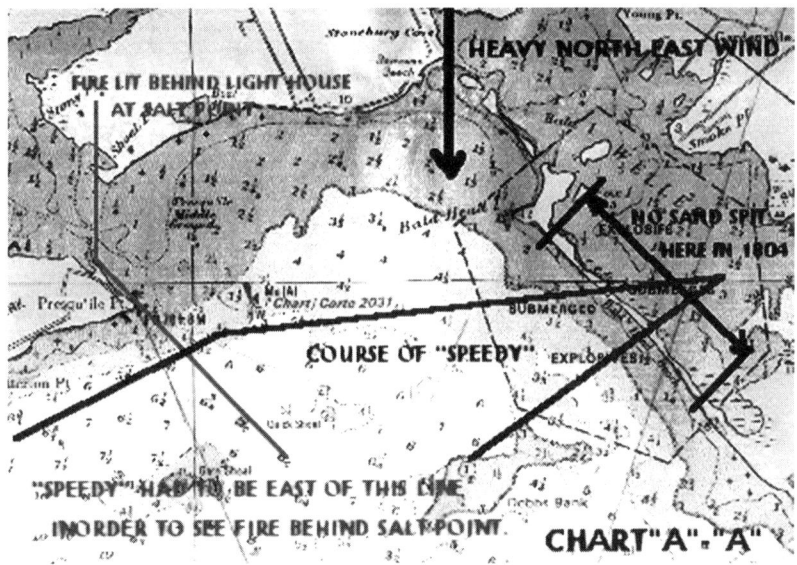

Ed Burtt created this nautical chart to demonstrate what may have happened to HMS *Speedy*. It was his way to explain why he had found a debris field and not a shipwreck.

At this point, Burtt gets creative. He explains how the geological phenomenon called the Sophiasburgh Triangle[20] contributed to Captain Paxton's problems by messing with his compass readings. Burtt and his crew had encountered the inconsistent nature of readings in the area until they became equipped with GPS, so it made sense to Burtt that, at this critical point in the *Speedy*'s voyage, its captain had experienced the same thing. Certainly, it adds a dramatic twist.

The next twist is even more dramatic. Burtt knew there was a very shallow spot on the north edge of Dobbs Bank, since he had conducted diving exercises there in previous years. For marketing purposes, a catchy name was applied to this landform. He called it "the Devil's horse block,"[21] referring to the shape of Dobbs Bank, which some say resembles a horse's head. The idea also comes from the practice of deliverymen in England tying their horse to a block, so it would not run away during the delivery.

Burtt had also read the words of Isaac M. Wellington,[22] a Brighton historian, who wrote about the pinnacle rock that had been identified south of Presqu'ile Point before the *Speedy* sailed. It was said to be only a few inches below the surface of the water, extremely dangerous for anyone sailing in the area. Wellington's account goes on to say that the rock could not be found after the *Speedy* was lost.[23] This story might be dismissed by modern readers, but Wellington was very close to the events of the *Speedy*. He was born in 1821 at Presqu'ile to Elizabeth Gibson, widow of Charles Selleck. He had heard this story from the day he was old enough to listen.

Burtt's story of the *Speedy* reaches a climax when the mix of elements erupts into a violent and tragic event. According to that story, by an extreme stroke of bad luck, the ship was driven by the nor'easter directly into the pinnacle rock. The impact tore the ship apart, scattering pieces of hull, decking, masts, and people into the water south of Dobbs Bank. In the process, the top of the rock was broken off.[24] The intent of this elaborate presentation is obvious. Burtt wanted to remove any doubt that the items he and his crew had seen and documented in the years 1990 through 1992 were from HMS *Speedy*. In order to do that, he needed to explain the destruction and sinking of the ship from the point of view of the artifacts he had seen on the floor of the lake. We might call it reverse engineering.

In the 1997 project report, each point is demonstrated very clearly, with coordinates and measurements,[25] supported by side scan sonar printouts,[26] all neatly labelled. There are lots of pictures, including the masts,[27] cannonballs,[28] the chest,[29] and, of course, the pipe and eye glasses.[30] Drag marks from both the hull[31] and the anchors[32] feature prominently as evidence of how the artifacts ended up in their current locations. Burtt's belief in every little point, as well as the entire elaborate picture he paints, is compelling.

His confidence in the story and his desire to promote it, led to the idea that artifacts from the debris field should be taken out of the water and located in a marine museum in the area. The objective was a line-up of local residents, anxiously waiting for their chance to experience history in a very tangible way. Burtt felt that Presqu'ile Provincial Park was the obvious place for this museum, and he was happy to expound on ideas for the expansion of the Lighthouse Interpretive Centre at the eastern end of Presqu'ile Point.[33] There were discussions as well with Mariners Park Museum in Prince Edward County, regarding the possibility of locating artifacts there.[34] For a time, it was suggested that a museum could be built at Gosport or near the entrance to Presqu'ile Park.[35]

In reality, Ed Burtt's plan to recover artifacts from the debris field ran directly counter to the prevailing practices in marine archaeology. There was a lot of discussion about this, and the conversation came to a head with an email from the ministry. It stated emphatically that the policy regarding underwater artifacts was to leave them in the water. In most cases, they should not be disturbed at all.[36] It could not be any simpler, but Burtt was not buying it. He kept a copy of the email and persisted in his story and promotions.

Even if it was possible to recover artifacts, it would be virtually impossible to comply with the strict regulations regarding preservation and storage of metal or wood items that had been in the water for two centuries.[37] From his point of view, Burtt felt confident he could bring things out of the water, coat them with a preservative, and everything would be fine. But in fact, the process is elaborate and scientifically complex, requiring large amounts of expertise and money. It was not remotely feasible in this case.

On another side of the issue, it was obvious that no organization or individual was going to spend bundles of money on a marine museum in a small town or rural area. The accounting just did not work. Sure, thousands of visitors come to Presqu'ile each year, but the cost of providing a facility would be in the millions, and that was not available from either the public or private sector.

In spite of this, the media campaign continued. There was an article in the *Belleville Intelligencer* on August 23, 2004,[38] with a photograph of Ed Burtt holding one of the cannonballs he had manufactured at his foundry in Belleville in order to promote the *Speedy* project. Two years later, there was a rumour that Burtt had removed cannonballs from the debris field, which everyone knew was illegal. The solicitor for the H.M.S. Speedy Foundation pounced on this hard, writing a sharp letter to the ministry, denying anything of the sort had happened.[39]

Around the same time, an article in the *Toronto Sun* included Burtt's comment that the remains of HMS *Speedy* were like "A Spanish galleon in my own backyard."[40] This was a cute turn of phrase, but it had the unintended consequence of supporting the idea that Burtt was just another treasure hunter looking to make money off a local history story. Numerous articles about his treasure hunting in Cuba and else-where had contributed to this perception, and here, in one phrase, Ed seemed to be confirming it himself. It did not help.

In spite of this, promotion continued. In 2012, Burtt refreshed the H.M.S. Speedy Foundation with a new set of directors.[41] The intent was to create a new wave of publicity for the *Speedy* story and take another run at the plan to recover artifacts and display them in a museum. A new set of ears listened to the same old story and saw the same fuzzy pictures. The same questions were asked of the folks at the ministry, and the same polices were confirmed. Nothing had changed.

I was one of the new directors in 2012.[42] As a historian from Brighton, my involvement was due to the importance of the *Speedy* story as a main component of the heritage landscape of the com-munity. In fact, it was a great opportunity to learn more about the history behind the story, including the work of Ed Burtt. At one of our meetings, someone asked Burtt what motivated him to be involved in underwater exploration. He thought for a second and then responded that his greatest thrill was to be the first person to see something that had been under the water for centuries. He had experienced the emo-tional rush of discovery many times in his long diving career, including the day he viewed the video of the debris field south of Dobbs Bank.

Several times, Burtt and I collaborated on speaking engagements. I prepared the presentation and supplied the computer equipment, and Burtt did the talking. As an old salt with tales to tell, Burtt was engaging, and the audiences were charmed. One such event was at the PROBUS Club of Brighton on March 2014,[43] and there were more to come.

One very tangible result of the work of the H.M.S. Speedy Foundation was a large storyboard,[44] which was installed just inside the front door of the Lighthouse Interpretive Centre in Presqu'ile Provincial Park. This display complements the dramatic video in the small theatre nearby, which envelops visitors in darkness and brings them into the disaster along with the residents of Newcastle.

Outside the Interpretive Centre, near the shore, stands an historical plaque entitled "The Loss of the Speedy."[45] If you glance out onto Lake Ontario from there, the remains of HMS *Speedy* are about seven kilometres away, under the water. At least, Ed Burtt was 99.99% sure they are. Burtt was still persistently promoting his version of the story when he passed away at Belleville General Hospital on November 11, 2017.[46]

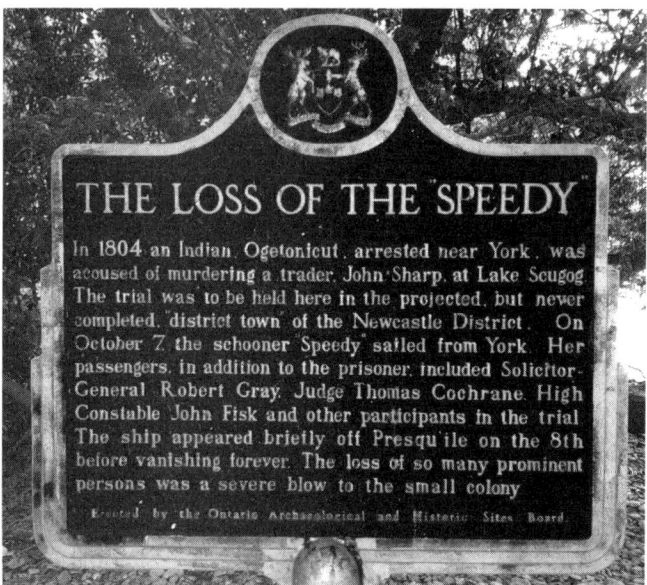

An historical plaque stands at the east end of Presqu'ile Point, to commemorate the loss of the *Speedy*.

EPILOGUE

THE MYSTERY OF HMS *SPEEDY*

Why was Ed Burtt 99.99% sure he had found the remains of HMS *Speedy*?

The historical record tells us that the HMS *Speedy* was seen by Moody Farewell and Eleazer Lockwood near Port Hope on the evening of October 8, 1804, heading eastward to Newcastle. A terrible nor'easter hit soon afterward and ravaged Lake Ontario for two days. The *Speedy* was not seen again. A week later, a binnacle lantern with the name "Paxton" on it washed ashore about forty miles east of Fort George, on the south shore of Lake Ontario.

From this information, we can estimate that HMS *Speedy* came to its end in the Presqu'ile area. The storm hit hard and fast, before Captain Paxton had a chance to accomplish the tricky manoeuvre of entering the channel into Presqu'ile Bay. The fact that no wreckage was found along the shores of Presqu'ile Point and Wellers Bay suggests that strong winds drove the ship southwest of the point where it first encountered the nor'easter.

Today, the information that Ed Burtt collected in the early 1990s represents the best information available regarding the final resting place of HMS *Speedy*. There are thirty-five survey sheets that show the

items that were identified and their exact locations. Annual reports
to the ministry included summaries of survey activity, explanations
of problems encountered, as well as many pictures of artifacts and
charts illustrating the debris field. Many of the pictures included in Ed
Burtt's private collection are from the 1989 video, which produced low-
resolution images, hampered by poor underwater visibility. On the
other hand, divers took hundreds of 35-mm pictures of artifacts they
found. Unfortunately, the 35-mm pictures, which would be much
better than those from the video, were not part of the collection of documents reviewed by the author. Even so, the existing images represent
real things that cannot be discounted out of hand.

All this information does not constitute a thorough review by
professional marine archaeologists, but it is extensive evidence of an
unusual set of artifacts from a very early time, sitting on the floor of the
lake in clusters. Are these items from a ship other than the *Speedy*? If
so, which ship are they from? Consistently, the items appear to be from
a very old ship, and there is no historical record of any other early ship
being lost in this area. Research shows that all ships on Lake Ontario
in 1804 are accounted for in other places and times. The *Speedy* is the
only one not accounted for. If we look at the information in total, the
arrows all point in the same direction. The artifacts south of Dobbs
Bank may well be from HMS *Speedy*.

Ed Burtt was not an archaeologist, and it's certainly fair to say that
reporting to the Ontario government was not his strong suit. However,
that does not negate the potential value of the collection of documents
he created and the underwater artifacts he described. The evidence
suggests that there is enough to warrant serious consideration of a second phase of survey work on the site. Of course, this time, professional
marine archaeologists must participate in the diving and the analysis
of the artifacts.

It would be an important "brick in the wall" for Canadian history
if we could determine whether or not the remains of HMS *Speedy* rest

south of Dobbs Bank. In the absence of a full archaeological survey, we will have to rely on the best information we have.

For this author, it is a moot point. In spite of the uncertainty, nothing prevents us from studying the history of HMS *Speedy* and telling the story in a full-throated way. Artifacts are helpful, but not necessary. Without them, we can use the best information available, along with a bit of imagination, to tell the story effectively. In fact, the sources we have at our fingertips today provide a rich and fascinating glimpse into that particular time in our past. The story of HMS *Speedy* is engaging and informative, all by itself, without the assistance of artifacts in a museum.

Ed Burtt may have found the remains of HMS *Speedy*. We might never know for sure. That's just fine with me.

ACKNOWLEDGEMENTS

The gift of Ed Burtt's documents by Kirsten Musclow in the fall of 2018 is the primary reason that this book exists today. Until then, the *Speedy* story was in the back of my mind while I did a lot of other things. However, once I had the documents about the search and Ed's correspondence regarding the *Speedy* project, I knew I had to do a book. Thank you, Kirsten! Oh yes, and please pass on my thanks to your mother as well.

The British Military and Naval Records on the website of Library and Archives Canada is a wonderful resource for the early history of Upper Canada. My desire to tell history stories through documents of the time was satisfied in this project, and I thank the Archives of Canada. Many of these documents deal directly with HMS *Speedy*, the mundane details of daily operations and maintenance, along with wonderful insights into the roles of different people.

With the technology of today, my approach to research is to scour the internet with all sorts of different keywords, names, and phrases. I've learned to be persistent by repeating the same search but drilling down into different links. You never know what will come up. I am constantly amazed at the documents that come up in searches and are available in PDF form. The scanners of the world have been working overtime (the Notes section of this book will make that perfectly clear).

This is especially true regarding the Archives of Ontario. I don't plan a trip to the wonderful new facilities on the York University campus until I have exhausted the search tools and am sure that the documents I need are only available on microfilm or in physical form. That list shrinks every day. Make no mistake, when documents of our history are more readily accessible to us, producing historical work is easier to do, less expensive, and therefore more likely to be done.

When I go into a library, I think of a computer and all the bits of information flashing around, being transferred from where they are to where they are needed. If you sit for a moment, you can almost hear the buzz of knowledge moving around, helping people. Libraries are important to our communities, and my research took me to several for specific documents and information. The Brighton Public Library was under renovation through much of the work for this book, but the staff were helpful, and the renovated library is terrific. Visits to the libraries at Cobourg, Port Hope, Whitby, Oshawa, and Bowmanville proved fruitful and enjoyable due to helpful support staff.

The Toronto Reference Library is a major source of information, especially rare and very early documents. During my research, I pursued specific documents that were in the Special Collections section and was rewarded for my curiosity and persistence. Staff was helpful and pleasant, and the facility is delightful.

I want to thank Paul Arculus, President of the Lake Scugog Historical Society, for permission to use the plan from John Stegmann's survey in 1804. This amazing document was not with the surveyor's diary in the Archives of Ontario, as one might expect, but was located by Mr. Arculus, in the Ontario Legislative Building, while browsing through a collection of maps. Thanks for your history sleuthing, Paul!

Much useful information was provided regarding the Lake Scugog area by Grant Karcich, author of *Scugog Carrying Place* and *Legacy of Vanished Trails*. Grant was generous with his knowledge, which allowed me to understand the context of the Farewell trading post in the upper reaches of Lake Scugog in the first years of the 1800s. Thanks for these useful books, Grant.

The *Speedy* story includes an important component of Indigenous history and I want to thank J.R. Miller for his encouragement in dealing with that topic in the context of this book. I have learned a lot about the move toward reconciliation between the Indigenous and non-Indigenous people of Canada, and my hope is that this treatment of Ogetonicut and his people supports the basic theme of that movement. We need to tell our history fairly and objectively, using all the players and elements.

Unfortunately, there is sparse information available about the Mississauga people of Lake Scugog in the time of HMS *Speedy*. I want to thank Donald B. Smith, author of *Sacred Feathers* the biography of Reverend Peter Jones, for his encouragement to look at the work of Indigenous authors a few decades later than 1804, in order to understand the stresses and conflicts being experienced by Ogetonicut and his family at that time.

This book would not have materialized as it is without the efforts of my friend and associate, Beth Bruder. Publishing is complex and confusing, but Beth used her extensive experience in the industry to find the right resources for editing, publishing, distribution, and promotion. It never hurts to have a professional in your corner. Thanks, Beth!

The editor who handled the developmental edit for the book was Sylvia Barrett of Touchplate (www.touchplate.ca). This author learned a lot through the editing process, and the result is a clear testament to the experience and knowledge of the editor. Thanks, Sylvia!

The publisher of the book is Milner & Associates Inc. (www.milnerassociates.ca), owned and operated by Karen Milner. Karen approached this project with energy and organization, and the results speak volumes for her skill and dedication to publishing. Thank you, Karen.

Distribution and promotion for the book was handled by Rob Dawson of Georgetown Publications (www.georgetownpublications.com). This author has never enjoyed such support and encouragement, and I want to thank Rob and his folks for giving this book a great opportunity for success.

APPENDIX A

DETAILS OF
THE *SPEEDY* PROJECT

Three years of survey work resulted in many documents and lots of details about the day-to-day diving activity, the problems the divers encountered, and the things they found, as well as the days they found nothing. The following table shows the identifiable events in this process, leading up to and including the diving, and highlights from later years. Please note that information taken from survey sheets is paraphrased and presented without more specific details such as location coordinates, due to regulations governing marine archaeology sites.

DATE	DESCRIPTION
Jul. 1989	A diver found a piece of eight on the floor of Lake Ontario on the shallowest part of Dobbs Bank, southeast of Presqu'ile.
Aug. 1989	Video of the floor of the lake south of Dobbs Bank was taken during testing of an ROV camera. On reviewing the tapes, Ed Burtt saw images he thought might be part of an old shipwreck.
Sep. 1989	Ed showed the video to Ken Cassavoy, a professional marine archaeologist, who agreed that some images in the video may be the remains of a shipwreck.

Oct. 1989   Ed Burtt formed the H.M.S. Speedy Foundation, to support himself and other interested parties who would work to further the project of searching for the remains of the *Speedy*.

Nov. 1989   Applications were prepared for the Ministry of Culture and Communications regarding a licence to explore the *Speedy* site and funding to support the survey work.

Jan. 17, 1990   A meeting was held in Toronto at the ministry to discuss the project, in particular to arrange for protection around the site.

Apr. 3, 1990   Licence No. 90-067 was issued with Ken Cassavoy as the licensee and with the stipulation that a limited number of items can be recovered for the purpose of identifying the wreck. This licence expired December 31, 1990, so was only valid for this one survey season.

Apr. 26, 1990   A news conference was held in Toronto announcing the project and the protection that was now in place around the site.

May 22, 1990   The ministry issued formal authorization for the H.M.S. Speedy Foundation to implement protection measures on the site, along with the Canadian Coast Guard, including a radar system and the deployment of marked buoys around a triangular area south of Dobbs Bank.

May 28, 1990   An article appeared in the *Trentonian* that included an interview with Ed Burtt about the *Speedy* project. He said they had not been out yet, as they were waiting for good weather.

Jun. 16, 1990   The first survey work was done on June 16 when they ran video camera in a zigzag pattern over a selected square in the grid Mr. Cassavoy had created. Nothing found.

Jun. 25, 1990   Further work in the same grid square as was done on the 16th, focusing on an area 100 metres by 100 metres. Nothing found.

Jun. 26, 1990   Fifteen boating restriction buoys were installed around the sides and at corners of the protected area.

Jul. 1, 1990   On the second run of the day, the drop video hit two rock pillars and stopped functioning. On examination, they saw the housing was cracked and the video camera destroyed. Work continued with an older drop video device. Although the survey sheet says no material was located on this day, a picture of a cannonball was dated July 1, 1990.

Jul. 2, 1990   Surveying in the same area, two aircraft engine valves were located, inspected by divers but not pursued. Nothing regarding *Speedy* found.

Jul. 6, 1990   Weights were installed on some of the protective buoys to keep them in place. Survey work continued in same area as earlier days, but work aborted early due to high winds. Nothing found.

Jul. 7, 1990   Six survey runs at approximately 300 metre spacings. Smoke bomb detected but not pursued. Nothing found.

Jul. 24, 1990   Possible material sighted and marker placed, but anchor line fouled; lost anchor and position of marker.

Jul. 25, 1990   Back on same site as day before. Could not find anchor; low visibility, surface choppy.

Jul. 26, 1990   Proton magnetometer launched but malfunctioned, immediately recovered. Possible metal objects detected, inspection by divers finds nothing except a bottle cap. Nothing found. Photos of boat and Ed taken—beautiful sunny day.

Jul. 28, 1990   More magnetometer readings suggest possible metal objects, not considered significant.

Jul. 29, 1990   ROV spot checks around an area. Nothing found.

Aug. 12, 1990   Machine gun shell located. ROV motor seizes up. Nothing regarding *Speedy* found.

Aug. 18, 1990   Drop video possible sighting; divers thought they saw round item like a wheel or barrel, but not confirmed. Wind increasing, forced to abort.

Aug. 19, 1990   Proton magnetometer survey showed metal objects while running east side of *Speedy* area. Divers found numerous machine gun shell casings, some larger .40 calibre shell casings. Nothing regarding *Speedy* found.

Sep. 12, 1990   Magnetometer runs found no anomalies.

Oct. 3, 1990   H.M.S. Speedy Foundation incorporated with directors Kenneth Cassavoy, Peterborough; Edward Burtt, Belleville; William P.H. Procter, Belleville; Terry Coons, Belleville; Gary MacDonald, Belleville.

Oct. 8, 1990   *Minnie Slausson* found one mile east of entrance to Presqu'ile Bay. This is a known wreck from 1877, a sizable three-mast steamer, largely intact. Great diving spot.

Oct. 14, 1990   Ed recorded these items: Tow camera ran into debris field:
Anchor, cannonball, wheel, hull, cannonball, chain, hull
wreckage, wheel, boards, pulley, chain, wreckage, wreckage,
wreckage, cannonball, wreckage, chain & pulley (these items
seen successively on Run 1 and Run 2, in depths from 40 to
47 ft.) Work Notes: Run 3: Wreckage, more wreckage, chain,
wreckage, wreckage, cannonball, wreckage. Run 4: Marker
buoy placed in water in debris field.

Oct. 20, 1990   More runs on debris field that had been found on the
14th. Special attention to LORAN readings of site. Readings
change several times a day—not reliable for locating items.
Very curious about this radar problem—much time spent
testing. No solution!

Feb. 18, 1991   *HMS Speedy Project Report* issued by Ken Cassavoy,
outlining activity for the year.

May 11, 1991   Started same place as October 1990 finds. Conditions
perfect, material found right away. Cannon and numerous
small shiny objects seen. Thought to be brass. Numerous
other things not defined. More evidence of LORAN
problems. Great day!!

May 20, 1991   Bright, sunny, light winds, 40 degrees, lots of wreckage
seen, now sure the shiny things are brass buttons. Cannon,
pulleys, deadeye, rope, chain. Lots of material.

May 29, 1991   Start same place; extend out. More material found:
deadeyes, pulleys.

Jun. 2, 1991   Weather threatening, wind increasing, moved to safer area
near shore, saw shells. Nothing regarding *Speedy* found.

Jun. 25, 1991   Hot, muggy, low visibility, back to western part of main
area. Sighted timbers, bottles, deadeyes, large round item
unclear. Also list pipe, shiny boards, other wreckage.

Jul. 1, 1991   High wind, waves, went out anyway, low visibility in water.
Cannonballs, odd shapes. Aborted early due to increasing
winds.

Jul. 6, 1991   Good weather, 11.5 hrs on site. Extending area where
debris field found. Saw possible mast. Cannonball, bottles,
jug, bright objects. Many pieces of timber and planking.
Mention of a skull seen this day.

Jul. 14, 1991   More in this area, many items not identified, more
cannonballs, chain, bottles.

Jul. 16, 1991   Licence No. 91-94 for *Speedy* project in 1991 was issued with this date. Ed Burtt is the licensee in this case. Restrictions tightened—cannot remove any items at all.

Jul. 26, 1991   High winds. Arrangements had been made to test McQuest Marine side scan sonar equipment and Ed did not want to abort. They ran the system using long runs west to east, then retrieved the equipment and returned to the west side for another run the same way. Not efficient, but all the weather allowed. They saw something that was shaped like an airplane wing. Nothing regarding *Speedy*. Near end of day, an SOS sent rescue choppers and boats to save five men in the water near Scotch Bonnet. Gladly, they were all OK.

Jul. 28, 1991   Weather better, but previous day's bad weather had stirred up sediment so underwater visibility was impossible. Early abort. Found nothing.

Aug. 4, 1991   High winds, terrible underwater visibility. Early abort. Nothing found.

Aug. 24, 1991   Weather still unsettled, high winds. Water visibility still impossible. Early abort.

Sep. 2, 1991   Wind and waves too high, underwater visibility still bad.

Sep. 7, 1991   Weather better, but everything underwater covered in silt and visibility poor. Lots of readings, but nothing found. Wildcat strike closed Murray Canal and canal would be closed for the week.

Sep. 20, 1991   Wind and waves high. Only 2.5 hrs. on site. Early abort. Nothing found.

Sep. 21, 1991   Waves past Presqu'ile 8 feet. Early abort. Nothing found.

Oct. 13, 1991   Better weather and underwater visibility, 10 hours on site, sighted bottles, deadeyes, buttons.

Oct. 20, 1991   Sunny with small rollers, survey showed wheel, pulley, deadeye, many shapes not defined. Wind picked up so early abort. Last day—freeze next week.

Mar. 22, 1992   *HMS Speedy Project Report* for 1991 issued by Ed Burtt.

Jun. 23, 1992   Article in the *Brighton Independent* regarding the *Speedy* project.

Jul. 5, 1992   Magnetometer readings were pursued by divers and they found timber that looked like it was part of a deck. Broken stubs suggest ribs of hull broken off, one lying in the sand. Major find!!

Jul. 20, 1992   Last cheque received for funding from Ontario Heritage Foundation. Books closed.

Jul. 25, 1992   Warm, hazy day, good visibility, worked 6 a.m. to 2 p.m. Sudden temp drop caused abort. Barely made it back—extremely thick fog chased them to Murray Canal and home. No report of survey results.

Aug. 1, 1992   High winds from east, decided to work along shore line east of *Speedy* site. Tow camera found airplane wreckage & divers confirmed. It was a Shark, a WWI torpedo bomber. Sandspit was a test range for both wars.

Sep. 1992   Article in *Search Team News*, JW Fishers newsletter, regarding Ed Burtt finding the Shark WWI bomber aircraft using Sea Otter ROV from JW Fishers. It was called Ed's third major find.

Oct. 31, 1992   Cold and overcast, high winds. Decided to go back to *Minnie Slausson* to get some video. Report says could not take pictures due to winds and poor underwater visibility. Ed's video has a 20-minute section of his crew diving on the *Minnie Slausson*. Not sure when, exactly, that was recorded.

Jun. 6, 1993   Ed reported in the 1993 project report that he was preparing to go to the site on this day when his mother had a heart attack, and he did not go out onto the lake all that season.

Jul. 1993   Later documents would show that Ed was searching for models of the Avro Arrow in 1993. There is a picture of Ed with Larry Scott beside a wing from one of the models that Ed found during their search. That, apparently, is all they found.

Jan. 26, 1994   Licence No. 94-007 was taken out by Ed Burtt.

Apr. 1994   *HMS Speedy Project Report* is issued by Ed Burtt. This report has little on the *Speedy* work; is mostly a collection of the historical documents Ed had collected regarding the loss of the *Speedy*.

Oct. 19, 1994   Ocean Scan Systems shipped equipment to Ecuador for a project involving Walter Zacharchuck, a famous Canadian marine archaeologist. They were working on the project to find *La Capitana*, a Spanish galleon lost off the coast of Ecuador in the 1500s.

Mar. 14, 1995   Letter from the ministry complaining of non-compliance with regard to reports not provided. Outstanding reports must be done if any more licences to be issued.

Apr. 11, 1995   *HMS Speedy Project Report* for 1992. This report is largely about non-*Speedy* items found and the radar anomalies. Little about the *Speedy* work.

Apr. 21, 1995   Licence No. 95-061 is issued for the 1995 survey season. No evidence this was used.

1997   Licence No. 97-092 was issued to H.M.S. Speedy Foundation.

Apr. 5, 1997   AP News article announcing the discovery of *La Capitana* off Ecuador coast. Ed's equipment may have been involved in this.

1997   *HMS Speedy Project Report* for 1997. The date on this document is March 24, 2005, which is when it was completed. It has nothing about actual survey work for any year, per se, but is a full-throated presentation of Ed's story of the *Speedy*. All the sub-plots are here: the Devil's horse block, the Sophiasburgh Triangle, and the draglines. It's really more of a magazine article than a technical report. Lots of pics. This illustrates very clearly what Ed was thinking.

Feb. 27, 1998   Article in *Toronto Star* about the Visa Gold project in Cuba and Ed Burtt as the vice-president of operations. Early days, lots of excitement.

Aug. 31, 1998   Letter from the ministry complaining that reports have not been provided. If not, no licences will be issued.

Dec. 21, 1998   Article in the *Brighton Independent* reports that residents turned down the idea of marine museum at Gosport.

Oct. 21, 1999   Article in the *Globe and Mail* regarding Ed Burtt's role as vice-president of operations for Visa Gold Explorations Inc., which would begin searching for sunken Spanish galleons in Cuba.

Nov. 10, 1999   Visa Gold Explorations Inc. published a detailed article in
the *Globe and Mail*, Silicon Investor, on November 10,
1999, which includes more information about Ed Burtt, the
vice-president of operations:

"Mr. Burtt is a seaman with first-class credentials. He says
gold runs through his veins, having been born in Kirkland
Lake, Ont., home of one the earliest Canadian gold mines.
He trained as an [*sic*] metalurgical [*sic*] engineer and runs
a metal-products business in Belleville, Ont., when he's not
in the Caribbean hunting treasure. He has also worked
for the FBI, hauling up drug boats and with the Canadian
government, looking for bodies, shipwrecks and planes in
Canadian waters.

"But his passion for chasing shipwrecks was born in his
search for the H.M.S. *Speedy*, a British vessel that sank in
Lake Ontario in [1804]. It took him 18 years—working on
and off—to find it, but he's never looked back. His first
brush with the ancient Spanish galleons was off the coast of
Florida, working alongside Mel Fischer [*sic*] in his hunt for the
Atocha. Two weeks before Mr. Fischer [*sic*] hit the jackpot,
Mr. Burtt was scooping up gold coins from the bottom of
the ocean. He wasn't there for the big find, but his appetite
for treasure-hunting was whetted. Mr. Burtt says it's the
intellectual drama that fuels his passion for the hunt."

Jan. 2001   Visa Gold project changes and Ed Burtt and Doug Lewis
resign and leave Cuba. Later, there would be fraud charges
laid against several stockbrokers in Canada. The project did
not continue.

Mar. 24, 2005   This is the date on the *HMS Speedy Project Report* for
1997.

Apr. 8, 2005   Email from ministry staff insists that policy regarding
handling artifacts in marine archaeology sites is to leave
them in the water.

Sep. 21, 2005   Licence No. 2005-017 issued to Ed Burtt, Ocean Scan
Systems. This appears to be for Avro Arrow survey work.

Feb. 25, 2006   Letter from H.M.S. Speedy Foundation to the ministry
regarding accusations for removing items from *Speedy*
site. Cannonballs were mentioned. There was a rumour
prompted by someone seeing the cannonballs Ed was having
made at his foundry as promotion items for the Foundation.

Apr. 10, 2006   Licence No. 2006-006 issued to Ed Burtt, regarding *Speedy*, no recovery included.

Dec. 2006   Ed goes to Tortola, British Virgin Islands, for some exploration work and takes his friend Kirsten with him.

Jan. 2007   Ed goes to the Bahamas, working for the Bahamian government and a travel company.

Jan. 23, 2013   Ed Burtt refreshes H.M.S. Speedy Foundation with Directors Ed Burtt, Norm Forman, Dan Buchanan, and Phil Spencer.

Apr. 10, 2013   Licence No. 2013-001 for *Speedy* survey work. Also, Licence No. 2013-002 for Avro Arrow survey work.

Apr. 23, 2013   Notice of non-compliance regarding incorporation of H.M.S. Speedy Foundation.

Jan. 23, 2014   Notice to Dissolve H.M.S. Speedy Foundation.

Mar. 13, 2014   Ed Burtt and Dan Buchanan speak at Brighton PROBUS Club.

Nov. 11, 2017   Ed Burtt passed away in Belleville.

Nov. 17, 2017   Visitation for Ed Burtt. Dan Buchanan spoke to Kirsten Musclow, Ed's close friend and Reeann Burtt, one of Ed's daughters.

Sep. 27 2018   Ed Burtt's documents were delivered to Dan Buchanan by Kirsten Musclow.

Sep. 9, 2019   A meeting took place between Dan Buchanan and Kirsten Musclow regarding the book being planned. Very positive, supportive.

Dec. 17, 2019   A meeting took place between Dan Buchanan and Terry Coons, the chief diver in Ed Burtt's crew searching for the remains of HMS *Speedy*. Great info! Interesting guy!

APPENDIX B

"LOSS OF THE SPEEDY"

The first full account of the disaster of HMS *Speedy* appeared in the *Upper Canada Gazette* on November 3, 1804. It is under The Oracle, the local news part of the *Gazette*, and it was probably written by John Bennett, who was editor of the *Gazette* and Printer to the King.

The following transcription of that article comes from *Landmarks of Toronto*, Volume 6, Chapter XXXIV, "Gazettes of Upper Canada," page 318. The only difference from the original newspaper article is that topic headings have been added for *Landmarks of Toronto*.

The Oracle; York – Saturday, November 3

LOSS OF THE SPEEDY

The following is as accurate an account of the loss of the schooner Speedy, in His Majesty's service on the Lake Ontario, as we have been able to collect: -

The Speedy, Captain Paxton, left this port on Sunday evening, the 7th of October last, with a moderate breeze from the N.W., for Presque Isle, and was descried off that island on the Monday following before dark, where preparations were made for the reception of the passengers; but the wind coming

round from the N. E. blew with such violence as to render it
impossible for her to enter the harbour, and very shortly after
she disappeared. A large fire was then kindled on shore, as a
guide to the vessel during the night; but she has not been seen
or heard of, and it is with the most painful sensations we have
to say we fear she is totally lost. Enquiry, we understand, has
been made at almost every port on the Lake, but without effect, and no intelligence respecting the fate of this unfortunate
vessel could be obtained. It is therefore generally concluded
that she has either upset or foundered. It is also reported by
respectable authority, that several articles, such as the compass box, hencoop and mast, known to have belonged to this
vessel, have been picked up on the opposite side of the Lake.

LIST OF PASSENGERS

The passengers on board the ill-fated Speedy, as near as we
can recollect, were Mr. Judge Cochrane [*sic*], Robert I.D. Gray,
Esq., Solicitor-General, and member of the House of Assembly;
Angus McDonell [*sic*], Esq., advocate, also a member of the
House of Assembly; Mr. Jacob Herchmer, merchant; Mr. John
Stegman [*sic*], surveyor; Mr. George Cowan, Indian interpreter; James Ruggles, Esq.; Mr. Anderson, student in the law; Mr.
John Fisk, high constable, all of this place. The above named
gentlemen were proceeding to the district of Newcastle, in
order to hold the Circuit and for the trial of an Indian (also
on board) indicted for the murder of John Sharp, late of the
Queen's Rangers. It is also reported, but we cannot vouch for
its authenticity, that exclusive of the above passengers, there
were on board two other persons, one in the service of Mr.
Justice Cochrane, and the other in that of the Solicitor-General;
as also two children of parents whose indigent circumstances
necessitated than to travel by land.

STRENGTH OF THE CREW

The crew of the Speedy it is said, consisted of five seamen, (three of whom have left large families) exclusive of Capt. Paxton, who also had a very large family. The total number of souls on board the Speedy is computed to be about twenty. A more distressing and melancholy event has not occurred to this place for many years; nor does it often happen that such a number of persons of respectability are collected in the same vessel. Not less than nine widows and we know not how many children, have to lament the loss of their husbands and fathers who, alas have perhaps in the course of a few minutes met with a watery grave.

It is somewhat remarkable, that this is the third or fourth accident of a similar nature within these few years, the cause of which appears worthy the attention and investigation of persons conversant in the art of shipbuilding.

APPENDIX C

"ELEGY"

"Elegy" is a poem that appeared in the *Kingston Gazette* on Tuesday, June 18, 1811. The overarching title of the section is "Original Miscellany" and the column is called Reckoner. The first sentence of the introduction says "SIR—If you admit of poetry, you will please some of your admirers by inserting the following verses in your paper, commemorating a melancholy event, which filled the whole province with the most poignant sorrow." Then it goes on to recount the well-known facts of the *Speedy* story, before breaking into verse.

Reckoner is the column written by an anonymous scribe who often contributed to the *Gazette*. It is most likely that Reverend John Strachan was the author of Reckoner at this time. His good friend and mentor, Reverend John Stuart, had been known as the author of Reckoner for some time but was now close to death, so the younger man, who was running his grammar school in Cornwall, was most likely the writer of "Elegy."

This is a very emotional, heartfelt expression of the shock and grief of the community of Upper Canada at the loss of the *Speedy* in 1804. Today, we may roll our eyes at the sumptuous language and extreme emotion displayed in these lines, but what else is poetry for? In those days before modern media, writing poetry to express oneself was an expected pastime for members of society who had education and leisure time. In effect, a work like this was considered to be a public service for the benefit of the whole community.

ELEGY

O! what avails distinction's splendid crown!
Blest years in view with smiling prospects fair,
For swept away by fate's terrific frown,
We know them now as only things that were.

Affliction's poison'd arrows sternly flew
Our trembling hearts that man must often mourn;
At morn abroad with golden hopes we go,
But cruel death arrests our wish'd return.

Yet sweet's the mem'ry of departed worth,
That dims our eyes and melts our swelling hearts,
Calls all the force of dear affection forth,
And grateful sorrow to the soul imparts.

With hasty steps the luckless ship they throng,
Unhappy Gray reluctant looks behind;
As York withdraws the sailors pensive song
With tremor shakes determin'd Cochrane's mind.

Newcastle bleak appears in open view,
The destin'd port at which they wish to land,
They gladly bid the surly lake adieu,
And jump in fond idea on the strand.

Alas the redd'ning sun's departing beam
Sheds on the fading woods a chequer'd light,
The hollow blasts a rising storm proclaim,
And thick'ning clouds obscure the face of night.

The adverse tempest backs the shaking sail.
About the ship! the watchful boatswain cries,
    The feeble bark, by ancient service frail.
Before the storm with dreadful crashing flies.

    The raging billows dash her op'ning sides,
    Pale fear appals the lately jovial train;
    His secret grief the friendly captain hides,
    And keenly tries the nautic art in vain.

    O cruel Lake! must thy insatiate jaws
Demand with rig'rous haste an annual prey?
    Asunder burst kind nature's dearest laws,
    And blast the finest gems we can display?

    The weeping mother mourns her darling son,
    The brightest hope of all her lovely race;
Scarce had the youth his virtuous course begun,
When barb'rous death obtrudes his loath'd embrace.

    The smiling housewife tells her children dear,
    As round her chair in boistrous mirth they fly,
"Peace—peace my loves—papa will soon be here"
    Just as he heaves with life's departing sigh.

    Perhaps she trembles at the dreadful storm,
    And dark foreboding feels, yet knowns not why,
She clasps her laughing babe, of beauteous form,
    While crystal drops land glistening in her eye.

    These terrors gone, & lock'd in gentle sleep,
    Her husband meets her with the smiles of love,
    She fondly tells his dangers make her weep,
    But present joys her hasty fears remove.

Dream on thou fair! in sweet delusion blest,
The mournful tale too soon shall meet thine ear,
Why dissipate the pleasure-giving mill,
Or draw with baneful haste the burning tear?

These private griefs a gen'ral notice crave,
In them the province mourns a public woe,
Oh! to bedew with tears the sacred grave
Where Cochrane mild & lib'ral Gray lie low.

Struck as their worth in full meridian shone,
Their baleful lot a weeping tomb denies,
Where friendship's hallow'd voice might oft bemoan
The loss of pleasures never more to rise.

Ah! little thought their aged, anxious fires,
Who saw with joy their rip'ning minds expand,
That early deaths would crush their living fires,
When strewing blessings o'er a favor'd land.

They cheer'd with joyful hope their setting days,
That when deliver'd from this varying scene,
The sons they left deserv'd the brightest praise,
More worthy still than they themselves had been.

Cold are the hands that loos'd the captive's chain,
And stills the heart that cherish'd honor bright.
Lock'd is the tongue that sooth'd the ear of pain,
And pale the illumin'd face that spread delight.

But hark! A voice from yonder cloud proclaims,
The hallowed friends of virtue never die,
Wash'd pure, and cloth'd in bright seraphic flames,
They join their kindred spirits in the sky.

Life's never short but lasting pleasure knows,
If pious deeds its diff'rent portions date,
Th' attending angel budding palms bestows,
For holy triumphs in this mortal state.

No more in sighs your happy friends lament,
Go, rather seek with care the way they trod,
On pious resignation rest content,
That leads the ardent Christian straight to God.

APPENDIX D

RECOLLECTIONS OF MARY WARREN BRECKENRIDGE

Ogetonicut murdered John Sharp at the Farewell trading post in revenge for the murder of his brother, Whistling Duck, a year before. While we know little about that earlier event, the following text describes an event that happened later in 1803 at the home of Robert Baldwin, in Clark Township, near today's Newcastle. It sheds light on the earlier death as well as the conditions around the John Sharp event.

Mary Warren Baldwin (1791–1871) was the youngest daughter of Robert Baldwin (1741–1816), who had immigrated from Ireland in 1798. She married John Breckenridge in 1816 and her daughter, Maria, wrote down this story in 1859, using her mother's words. A grandson of the original settler was Honourable Robert Baldwin, the lawyer and politician who spearheaded reforms to establish responsible government in Canada in the 1840s.

This text is found in *Recollections of Mary Warren Breckenridge of Clarke Township*, by Catherine F. Leroy, read before the Women's Canadian Society of Toronto and published by the Ontario Historical Society, Papers and Records, Vol. III, Toronto, 1901, page 112 & 113.

Here is what Mary said and Maria wrote:

One Sunday he (my grandfather) had gone to see his neighbor, Mr. Cozens, when soon after he had gone several Indians came, bringing furs and asking for whiskey. My mother and aunt refused them. The Indians became so urgent and insolent and so constantly increasing in number that they became terrified and sent the French girl to beg my grandfather to return. She came back in a few minutes more frightened than ever, saying that as she passed the camp, she saw the squaws hiding away all the knives, as they always do when the Indians are drunken, and that they chased her back. Some of the Indians were intoxicated before they came to the house, and their threats were awful. They had collected to the number of forty, and those poor girls still held out stoutly in refusing the whiskey, which was kept beneath a trapdoor in the kitchen, in a sort of little cellar. At length my aunt thought of the large, handsome family Bible, in two volumes, in which they had been reading, and opened them and pointed out the pictures to try and attract their attention, while my mother knelt down at the other end of the table and prayed to God loudly and earnestly.

In this position my grandfather found them, and fearful was the shock to him. He brought Cozens with him. No sooner did the Indians see him than one man drew his knife and showed it to my mother, saying, 'Cozens kill my brother, I kill Cozens.' Then my grandfather, to divert that idea, was obliged to get them the whiskey. Nothing else probably saved their lives.

Notes:

"My grandfather" refers to Robert Baldwin, who was sixty-one years old at this time.

"Mr. Cozens" refers to Samuel D. Cozens, who had a farm near the Baldwins. He had recently moved there from York. His father, Daniel Cozens, was well-known as one of the earliest residents of York, coming with Lieutenant-Governor John Graves Simcoe in 1794. He was a devoted Loyalist and had lost much wealth and property as a result of the War of Independence. His sons acquired a good deal of property from grants and inheritances.

"Cozens kill my brother": This suggests very strongly that the fellow with the knife is Ogetonicut. We can't tell for sure, since the word "brother" was used rather loosely, but it seems to be the case. This story demonstrates the simmering anger that existed as a result of no justice for the death of Whistling Duck. The Mississauga people were not impressed with the finding of self-defence in Whistling Duck's death and still wanted something in return. By the next spring, they got nothing, and Ogetonicut had waited long enough. Thus, the murder of John Sharp.

APPENDIX E

NEWCASTLE COUNTY TOWN STATUS: PETITION AND LEGISLATION

PETITION

The town of Newcastle, on Presqu'ile Point, had been established with a survey in 1797, based on the excellent protected harbour of Presqu'ile Bay and the demand for lots by various land speculators. Then, in 1802, Newcastle was assigned the status of county town, resulting in the building of the courthouse and jail for Newcastle District. The trial of Ogetonicut was scheduled to take place there on October 10, 1804, as part of the fall assizes. HMS *Speedy* never made it to Newcastle, and the extreme distress of the loss caused existing conflicts to surface.

Only a few months after the *Speedy* was lost, the House of Assembly addressed the problem. A petition was presented on February 5, 1805, by the inhabitants of Newcastle District. We find the original petition as well as developing versions of the legislation in the *Journals of the Legislative Assembly of Upper Canada* for the year 1805, located in the Archives of Ontario.

Here is the petition, found on page 10:

To the Honorable the Legislative Council and House of Assembly of the Province of Upper Canada in Parliament assembled.

The Petition of the Inhabitants of the District of Newcastle, Humbly Showeth,

That the place appointed by Law for building a Gaol and Court House in the District of Newcastle appears to Your Petitioners to be inconvenient.

Your Petitioners therefore pray that so much of an Act entitled "An Act to provide for the Administration of Justice within the District of Newcastle" as directs that a Gaol and Court House should be built in the Town of Newcastle may be repealed, and that it may he lawful for Your Petitioners to cause a Gaol and Court House to be built in some part near the centre of the said District. And as in duty bound they will ever pray.

Signed by Robert Baldwin, Lieut, of the County of Durham, John Spenser, Leonard Soper, Joseph Keeler, Elias Jones, Elias Smith, Senior, Benjamin Marsh, Asa Burnham, Joel Merriman, John Peters, Sheriff, Timothy Porter, Coroner, D. McG. Rogers, Clerk of the Peace, and one hundred and twenty-three others.

Signatories from the above list, with notes from the author:

Robert Baldwin: Lieutenant of the County of Durham, lived in Clarke Township

Leonard Soper: Lived in Port Hope, married to Mary Marsh, daughter of Col. Wm Marsh

Joseph Keeler: Old Joe, of Lakeport, Justice of the Peace for Newcastle District

Elias Jones: Lived in Hamilton Township, on today's King St., Cobourg

Elias Smith: Senior, Founder of Port Hope

Benjamin Marsh: Lived at Port Hope

Asa Burnham: Magistrate, lived at Amherst, would two years later
give land for new court house and jail

Joel Merriman: Lived on Concession 1 Lot 24, Cramahe Township

John Peters: Sheriff, Cramahe Township, owned land on Presqu'ile
Point, married to sister of David M. Rogers

Timothy Porter: Coroner, lived in Murray Township

David McGregor Rogers: Clerk of the Peace, Member of House
of Assembly, Hastings & Northumberland Counties, lived in
Cramahe Township, moved to Haldimand 1806

LEGISLATION

After several weeks of legislative procedure, the final act was passed
on March 2, 1805, revoking the status of county town from Newcastle,
and establishing a new procedure for selecting a new location for the
county town of Newcastle District. Here is the text of the act as it appeared in the *Upper Canada Gazette*, May 4, 1805.

An ACT to alter certain parts of an Act, passed in the forty
second year of his Majesty's reign, intituled "An Act to provide
for the administration of justice in the District of Newcastle."
[Passed 2nd March, 1805]

Whereas the place appointed by law, for building a Gaol
and Court House, in the District of Newcastle, is inconvenient
for the inhabitants of the said district; Be it therefore Enacted
by the King's most excellent Majesty, by and with the advice
and consent of the Legislative Council and Assembly of the
Province of Upper Canada, constituted and assembled by virtue of, and under the authority of an Act passed in Parliament

of Great Britain, intituled, "an Act to repeal certain parts of an Act, passed in the fourteenth year of His Majesty's reign, intituled, "An Act for making more effectual provision for the government of the Province of Quebec, in North America, and to make further provision for the government of the said Province," and by the authority of the same, That so much of an Act, passed in the forty-second year of his Majesty's reign, intituled, "An Act to provide for the administration of justice in the district of Newcastle," as directs, that a Gaol and Court House shall be built in the town of Newcastle, shall be repealed," and that it shall and may be lawful, for his Majesty's Justices of the Peace, in and for the said district of Newcastle, or the greater part of them, in the first General Quarter Sessions, after the passing of this Act assembled, to appoint some fit and proper place, in either of the townships of Haldimand, or Hamilton, within the said district of Newcastle, where a Gaol and Court House may be built, in the same manner that a Gaol and Court House is at present directed to be built within the said town of Newcastle, any law to the contrary notwithstanding.

II. Provided, That nothing in this Act, shall extend, or be construed to extend, to authorize the said Justices of the Peace, to fix the place for building the said Gaol and Court House, on any reserve of the Crown or Clergy, or on land belonging to any person, or persons, without permission first obtained, from the Government, or from the owner, or owners of said land.

III. Provided always, and be it further Enacted by the Authority aforesaid, That unless such Gaol and Court House shall be built, and finished, within two years, from the passing of this Act, so that prisoners may be confined in the one, and the different Courts of Justice be properly accommodated in the other, then, and in such case, this Act shall be, and the same is hereby declared to be null and void.

Note: After the full two years stipulated, Asa Burnham of Amherst (later Cobourg) would offer some land and the new courthouse and jail would be built on the east side of Burnham Street, above Elgin Street. By 1831, that building was getting old, so they built a much bigger courthouse and jail building across Burnham Street, around where the parking lot of the Golden Plough Lodge seniors' residence is today. The court and jail would move from there to Victoria Hall in 1861, not long after the sensational trial and hanging of Dr. William Henry King.

APPENDIX F

STATUTES OF UPPER CANADA

Six copies of the *Statutes of Upper Canada* were on HMS *Speedy* when it left York on October 7, 1804, bound for Newcastle. These documents had been published only a few weeks before, and the authorities were sending copies to the various districts for the use of the magistrates, judges, and members of the House of Assembly.

The front page of the document is shown below. This can be seen at the Archives of Ontario and a PDF copy can be downloaded online from HathiTrust.org.

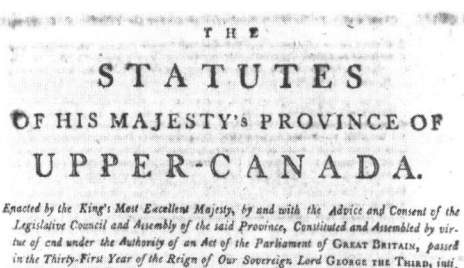

APPENDIX G

MORE INFORMATION

Readers who are interested in more information regarding the HMS *Speedy* story can use the following resources:

www.danbuchananhistoryguy.com
My main website includes a "Books" section, and under the "Speedy" option there is a menu to many different pieces of information regarding the story and my research for this book. There are many pictures and more detailed text to support the content of the book.

www.treesbydan.com
This is my genealogy website that has been growing since 2004 and now contains lots of detail regarding many of the people who are mentioned in my books. If readers are interested in the family context for a person in the *Speedy* story, it might be found there, along with historical information presented in the context of that person's life and times.

Email: danbuchanan@cogeco.ca
Readers are encouraged to ask questions and send information to me via email. Please provide as much detail as possible and give me some time to respond. Here's a hint: The more detail I get, the more likely I am to respond quickly. I love detail because it helps move my work ahead.

NOTES

PART I

Chapter 1: Death at the Trading Post

1. *Samuel Pedlar Manuscript*, Frame 182, downloaded from Oshawa Library http://images.ourontario.ca/Partners/oshawa/OshPL0035787871T.PDF.

2. Walker, Glenn, *The Changing Face of the Kawarthas: Land Use and Environment in Nineteenth Century Ontario*, Department of History and Classical Studies, McGill University, December 2012, page 50.

3. *Samuel Pedlar Manuscript*, Frame 175

4. *Samuel Pedlar Manuscript*, Frame 31.

5. *Samuel Pedlar Manuscript*, Frame 182.

6. *Samuel Pedlar Manuscript*, Frame 183.

7. William Farewell (1779–1845), genealogy website of Dan Buchanan, http://www.treesbydan.com.

8. Acheus Moody Farewell (1782–1869), genealogy website of Dan Buchanan, http://www.treesbydan.com.

Chapter 2: Over the Scugog Carrying Place

1. Karcich, Grant, *Scugog Carrying Place: A Frontier Pathway*, Dundurn Press, Toronto, 2013, Chapter 1, "Early Description," page 20 & 21.

2. Beacon Marina, Caesarea, http://www.lakescugogmarinasailing.com/marina-history.php.

3. Jones, Rev. Peter, *History of the Ojebway Indians: With Especial Reference to Their Conversion to Christianity*, A.W. Bennett, London, 1861, Chapter IX, "Councils, General Councils," page 105.

4. Benjamin Wilson (1739–1821), genealogy website of Dan Buchanan, http://www.treesbydan.com.

5. *Samuel Pedlar Manuscript*, Frame 163.

6. Eleazer Lockwood (1774–1859), genealogy website of Dan Buchanan, http://www.treesbydan.com.

7. Charles Annis (1738–1804), genealogy website of Dan Buchanan, http://www.treesbydan.com.

8. *Samuel Pedlar Manuscript*, Frame 163.

9. Sabean, John W., "Chief Wabbekisheco of the Mississaugas," *Pathmaster*, page 7, Pickering Township Historical Society, Autumn Edition (1998), Volume 2, Number 1.

10. Karcich, Grant, *Scugog Carrying Place: A Frontier Pathway*, Dundurn Press, Toronto, 2013, Chapter 4, "Yankees on the Trail," page 72 & 73.

11. *Scugog Carrying Place*, Chapter 3, page 66.

12. Surtees, R., *Indian Land Surrenders in Ontario 1763–1867*, Canadian and Northern Affairs Canada, February 1984, page 60.

13. Smith, Donald B., *Sacred Feathers: The Reverend Peter Jones (Kahkewaquonaby) and the Mississauga Indians*, Second Edition, Kindle Version, University of Toronto Press, 2013, page 24 & 25.

14. Schmalz, Peter J., *The Ojibwa of Southern Ontario*, University of Toronto Press, 1991, Notes to pages 15–22, page 271.

15. *The Ojibwa of Southern Ontario*, page 93.

16. *Samuel Pedlar Manuscript*, Frame 183.

Chapter 3: Along the Shore to York

1. Karcich, Grant, *The Legacy of Vanished Trails*, self-published in 2017, produced by Red Handprint Publishing, page 24.

2. Buchanan, Dan, *38 Hours to Montreal: William Weller and the Governor General's Race of 1840*, self-published, 2018, produced by FriesenPress, page 63.

3. Mohr, Tom, "Was Duffin Really Up the Creek?," *Pathmaster*, Pickering Township Historical Society, Autumn Edition, Volume 16, Number 1 & 2, pages 1–9.

4. Graymont, Barbara, "THAYENDANEGEA," in the *Dictionary of Canadian Biography*, vol. 5, University of Toronto/Université Laval, 2003–. Accessed October 21, 2018, http://www.biographi.ca/en/bio/thayendanegea_5E.html.

5. Surtees, R., *Indian Land Surrenders in Ontario 1763-1867*, Canadian and Northern Affairs Canada, February 1984, page 20 & 26.

6. Letter from Hazelton Spencer, Commanding 2nd Batt., at Kingston, to Major Green, at York, regarding the launch of HMS *Speedy*, September 6, 1798, British Military and Naval Records, Volume 723, page 152.

7. Robertson, J. Ross, *Landmarks of Toronto*, Volume 6, Toronto, 1914, Chapter XXXIV, "Gazettes of Upper Canada," page 253.

8. *Landmarks of Toronto*, Volume 6, page 291.

9. Letter from Assistant Deputy Quartermaster General, Charles D. Shekleton, in Kingston, to Military Secretary, Major James Green, at York, December 9, 1801, British Military and Naval Records, Volume 725, page 108.

10. Karcich, Grant, *Scugog Carrying Place: A Frontier Pathway*, Dundurn Press, Toronto, 2013, Chapter 2, "Iroquois and Mississauga on the Trail," page 38.

11. Buchanan, Dan, *38 Hours to Montreal: William Weller and the Governor General's Race of 1840*, Chapter 9, "Highland Creek and the Rouge River," page 55.

12. Levy, Joel, "The History Scarborough Bluffs and Guild Park," July 4, 2013, *Toronto Guardian*, https://torontoguardian.com/2013/07/the-history-scarborough-bluffs-and-guild-park.

13. Simcoe, Mrs. John Graves, *The Diary of Mrs. John Graves Simcoe with Notes and Biography by John Ross Robertson*, Toronto, William Briggs, 1911, page 180.

14. Fairburn, M. Jane, *Along the Shore: Rediscovering Toronto's Waterfront Heritage*, ECW Press, 2013, Kindle Edition, Chapter 1, "The Nature of the Place," location 194.

15. "Map of South East part of York Township," *The Canadian County Atlas Digital Project*, York Township.

16. "1802 Chewett: Plan of 916 ¼ acres, in the Township of York in Upper Canada," *Historical Toronto Maps*, http://oldtorontomaps.blogspot.com/2013/02/1802-chewett-plan-of-916-14-acres-in.html.

Chapter 4: Muddy Little York

1. Schmalz, Peter S., *The Ojibwa of Southern Ontario*, University of Toronto Press, Toronto, 1991, Chapter 2, "Conquest," page 32.

2. Robert J. Hayward, "COLLINS, JOHN (d. 1795)," in *Dictionary of Canadian Biography*, vol. 4, University of Toronto/Université Laval, 2003–. Accessed October 21, 2018, http://www.biographi.ca/en/bio/collins_john_1795_4E.html.

3. Scadding, Dr. Henry, *Toronto of Old*, Introductory, page 16.

4. Guillet, Edwin C., M.A., *Early Life in Upper Canada*, University of Toronto Press, 1933, page 116.

5. Scadding, Dr. Henry, *Toronto of Old*, Chapter I, "Palace Street to the Market Place," page 35.

6. Firth, Edith G., (Editor), *The Town of York 1793-1815: A Collection of Documents of Early Toronto*, University of Toronto Press, 1962. Introduction, page xxxiv.

7. Scadding, Dr. Henry, *Toronto of Old*, Chapter I, "Palace Street to the Market Place," page 35.

8. *Toronto of Old.*

9. Robertson, J. Ross, *Landmarks of Toronto*, Volume 1, Toronto, 1894, Chapter CXXIV, "Two Plans of the Town," page 388.

10. *Landmarks of Toronto*, Volume 1, Chapter CXXXIX, "King and Bay Street Corner," page 439.

11. Scadding, Dr. Henry, *Toronto of Old*, Chapter XVI, "From Berkeley Street to the Bridge and Across It," page 223.

12. Robertson, J. Ross, *Landmarks of Toronto*, Volume 6, Toronto, 1914, Chapter XXXIV, "Gazettes of Upper Canada," page 262 & 263.

13. *Landmarks of Toronto*, Volume 6, page 263.

14. *Landmarks of Toronto*, Volume 6, page 263.

15. *Landmarks of Toronto*, Volume 6, page 263.

16. *Landmarks of Toronto*, Volume 1, Toronto, 1894, Chapter CXIV, "Houses of Parliament," page 354.

17. *Landmarks of Toronto*, Volume 1, page 354.

18. *Landmarks of Toronto*, Volume 1, page 352.

19. *Landmarks of Toronto*, Volume 1, page 352.

20. In collaboration, "HUNTER, PETER," in *Dictionary of Canadian Biography*, vol. 5, University of Toronto/Université Laval, 2003–. Accessed October 29, 2018, http://www.biographi.ca/en/bio/hunter_peter_5E.html.

21. Steppler, Glenn A., "GREEN, JAMES," in *Dictionary of Canadian Biography*, vol. 6, University of Toronto/Université Laval, 2003–. Accessed December 30, 2018, http://www.biographi.ca/en/bio/green_james_6E.html.

22. Letter from J.W. Steel, Point Frederick, to York, noted by Major Green, Military Secretary, November 11, 1803, British Military and Naval Records, Volume 726, page 102.

23. Letter from William Ross, Commander at Kingston, to York, noted by Lt. Col. Green, Military Secretary, May 8, 1804, British Military and Naval Records, Volume 726, page 151.

24. Armstrong, Frederick H., "ALLCOCK, HENRY," in *Dictionary of Canadian Biography*, vol. 5, University of Toronto/Université Laval, 2003–. Accessed April 6, 2019, http://www.biographi.ca/en/bio/allcock_henry_5E.html.

25. John Fisk (1752–1804), genealogy website of Dan Buchanan, http://www.treesbydan.com.

26. James Ruggles (1770–1804), genealogy website of Dan Buchanan, http://www.treesbydan.com.

27. "Timothy Ruggles," *Appleton's Cyclopedia of American Biography*, 1600-1889, Vol. V Pickering-Sumter, page 362 of 786. Accessed on Ancestry.ca.

28. Leslie, John F., "GIVINS, JAMES," in *Dictionary of Canadian Biography*, vol. 7, University of Toronto/Université Laval, 2003–. Accessed January 26, 2019, http://www.biographi.ca/en/bio/givins_james_7E.html.

29. Butts, Edward, *Line of Fire: Heroism, Tragedy, and Canada's Police*, Dundurn Press, 2009, page 15.

30. Letter from Peter Russell to Robert Prescott regarding the appointment of James Givins as an agent of the Indian Department, February 21, 1798, *The Russell Papers*, Volume 2, page 90 & 91.

31. Robertson, J. Ross, *Landmarks of Toronto*, Volume 1, Chapter I, "Toronto, 1894," page 2.

32. *Landmarks of Toronto*, Volume 1, page 1.

33. Gilmore, James, "The St. Lawrence River Canals Vessel, The Canals," *Maritime History of the Great Lakes*.

34. Edith G. Firth, "COOPER, WILLIAM (d. 1840)," in *Dictionary of Canadian Biography*, vol. 7, University of Toronto/Université Laval, 2003–. Accessed April 27, 2019, http://www.biographi.ca/en/bio/cooper_william_1840_7E.html.

35. Robertson, J. Ross, *Landmarks of Toronto*, Volume 1, Toronto, 1894, Chapter CLXX "Church and Cathedral," page 501.

36. *Landmarks of Toronto*, Volume 1, page 83.

37. *Landmarks of Toronto*, Volume 6, page 345.

38. *Landmarks of Toronto*, Volume 1, page 439.

39. William Knott's eldest child, William Jr., was probably born at the garrison in 1794, possibly the first white child to be born at York. He would play a role in the War of 1812, serving with General Brock at Queenston Heights. (*Landmarks of Toronto*, Volume 1, page 440.)

40. *Landmarks of Toronto*, Volume 1, page 83.

Chapter 5: A Critical Question

1. Robert J. Burns, "GRAY, ROBERT ISAAC DEY," in *Dictionary of Canadian Biography*, vol. 5, University of Toronto/Université Laval, 2003–. Accessed April 20, 2017, http://www.biographi.ca/en/bio/gray_robert_isaac_dey_5E.html.

2. Hamilton, James Cleland, *Osgoode Hall Reminiscences of the Bench and Bar*, Chapter VIII, page 130.

3. Firth, Edith G., (Editor), *The Town of York 1793-1815: A Collection of Documents of Early Toronto*, "Documents," page 227.

4. John Anderson (1784–1804), genealogy website of Dan Buchanan, http://www.treesbydan.com.

5. Edith G. Firth, "RUSSELL, PETER," in *Dictionary of Canadian Biography*, vol. 5, University of Toronto/Université Laval, 2003–. Accessed October 29, 2018, http://www.biographi.ca/en/bio/russell_peter_5E.html.

6. "Letter from John Graves Simcoe to the Duke of Portland," April 26, 1799, Russell, Peter, *The Russell Papers*, Ontario Historical Society, Toronto, 1936, Volume 3, page 184.

7. *The Russell Papers*, "Letter from Peter Russell to John King," September 22, 1799, page 298.

8. *The Russell Papers*, Introduction, page xxii.

9. *The Russell Papers*, Introduction, page xxii.

10. *The Russell Papers*, Introduction, page xxiii.

11. Pringle, J.F., *Lunenburg or the Old Eastern District*, Chapter XXXVI, page 321.

12. S.R. Mealing, "McGILL, JOHN," in *Dictionary of Canadian Biography*, vol. 6, University of Toronto/Université Laval, 2003–. Accessed February 19, 2019, http://www.biographi.ca/en/bio/mcgill_john_6E.html.

13. Letter from John McGill, in York, to David William Smith, in England, mentioning the threat of invasion, October 4, 1804, *David William Smith Papers*, Metro Reference Library, Toronto, Special Collections, (A10-1) page 86 & 87.

14. Letter from Peter Hunter to the Duke of Portland, November 19, 1800, *Peter Hunter Papers*, Heritage.canadiana.ca.

15. A note to self by Henry Allcock, May 31, 1804, Archives of Ontario, C1203, Volume 100, Pg. 181.

16. Allcock, note to self.

17. Allcock, note to self.

18. Allcock, note to self.

19. Allcock, note to self.

Chapter 6: The Survey

1. John Stegman (1760–1804), genealogy website of Dan Buchanan, http://www.treesbydan.com.

2. Merz, John, "The Sinking of the Speedy," *The Hessians*, http://freepages.rootsweb.com/ ~ amrevhessians/military/speedy.htm.

3. Correspondence from the Surveyor General's Office often used the initials SGO beside the date. Once John Stegmann became a deputy surveyor, he was in the habit of signing "Dy. Surveyor." (Letter from Surveyor General's Office to John Stegmann confirming that he was to sail to Newcastle for the trial, September 28, 1804, Archives of Ontario, U.C.L.P. S13, C-2814, Roll 265, page 92e.)

4. Letter from John Stegmann, Osnabruck, to the Surveyor General's Office in York, October 27, 1792, Archives of Ontario, MS 7434, Volume 36, page 2.

5. Letter from John Stegmann, Surveyor, to Chewett and Ridout, acting for the Surveyor General, regarding Elmsley survey, June 15, 1804, Archives of Ontario, MS 7434, Volume 36, page 314.

6. Letter from Stegmann, May 22, 1804, page 308.

7. Letter from Stegmann, June 15, 1804, page 310.

8. Letter from Stegmann, August 11, 1804, page 322.

9. Letter from Stegmann, August 11, 1804, page 322.

10. "John Stegmann, Diary of the Survey of Home/Newcastle Boundary," August 31, 1804, Archives of Ontario, MS 7438, Volume 46, page 214 & 215.

11. Letter from Chief Justice Henry Allcock to John Stegmann ordering the survey of the boundary between Home and Newcastle districts, August 15, 1804, Archives of Ontario, MS 7442, Volume 62, page 1909, bottom.

12. Elwood H. Jones, "WYATT, CHARLES BURTON," in *Dictionary of Canadian Biography*, vol. 7, University of Toronto/Université Laval, 2003–. Accessed April 16, 2019, http://www.biographi.ca/en/bio/wyatt_charles_burton_7E.html.

13. Richard J. Simpson, "CHEWETT, WILLIAM," in *Dictionary of Canadian Biography*, vol. 7, University of Toronto/Université Laval, 2003–. Accessed November 28, 2018, http://www.biographi.ca/en/bio/chewett_william_7E.html.

14. Robert J. Burns, "RIDOUT, THOMAS," in *Dictionary of Canadian Biography*, vol. 6, University of Toronto/Université Laval, 2003–. Accessed April 17, 2019, http://www.biographi.ca/en/bio/ridout_thomas_6E.html.

15. Letter from Chief Justice Henry Allcock to John Stegmann ordering the survey of the boundary between Home and Newcastle districts, August 15, 1804, Archives of Ontario, MS 7442, Volume 62, page 1909, bottom.

16. Letter from Allcock, page 1909.

17. Letter from John Allcock, page 1909.

18. Letter from John Stegmann, York, to the Surveyor General's Office, regarding the need for money, August 15, 1804, Archives of Ontario, MS 7434, Volume 36, page 328.

19. "Receipt for expenses of John Stegmann," August 6, 1804, page 330.

20. Diary of John Stegmann for survey of Home & Newcastle Boundary, Archives of Ontario, MS 924, Box 15, starts page 128.

21. Diary of John Stegmann.

22. The name Beobescugog is an Indigenous term that suggests a shallow, swampy body of water, which is exactly the right description for Lake Scugog. At that time, this name referred to the part of the lake on the west side of the large island we now call Scugog Island. Beg Bay was the name of the eastern part of Lake Scugog. (Diary of John Stegmann.)

23. Diary of John Stegmann.

24. Letter from John Stegmann, York, to the Surveyor General's Office, reporting on the survey of the Home/Newcastle boundary, August 28, 1804, Archives of Ontario, MS 7434, Volume 36, page 324.

25. Arculus, Paul, *Steamboats on Scugog*, 2000, page 6.

26. Samuel Wilmot conducted surveys for the north and south parts of Reach Township in 1810 and then Cartwright Township in 1816. (Karcich, Grant, *Scugog Carrying Place: A Frontier Pathway*, Chapter 5, "Preachers on the Trail," page 90.)

Chapter 7: Planning for a Trial

1. Allison, David, M.A., LL.D., *History of Nova Scotia*, Volume II, A. W. Bowen & Co., Halifax, 1916, Chapter XVIII "Educational," page 822.

2. Robertson, J. Ross, *Landmarks of Toronto*, Volume 6, Chapter XXXIV, "Gazettes of Upper Canada," The Oracle, *York Gazette*, October 9, 1802, No. 24, page 295.

3. Thomas Cochran, Sr. had recently passed away but was still a major presence in the family and community. He had been a prosperous merchant and a member of the Nova Scotia House of Assembly. Several siblings of his were very successful, so there was a good deal of motivation for Thomas, Jr. to show what he could do. (Allison, David, M.A., LL.D., *History of Nova Scotia*, Volume II, A. W. Bowen & Co., Halifax, 1916, Chapter XVIII Educational, page 822.)

4. O'Brien, Brendan, *Speedy Justice*, Dundurn Press, Toronto, 1992, Chapter 5, "The Speedy Sails," page 84.

5. J.F. Pringle, *Lunenburg or the Old Eastern District*, Chapter XXXVI, page 323.

6. Somerset v Stewart, https://eachother.org.uk/slavery-somerset-v-stewart-oldest-50-cases/.

7. Robertson, J. Ross, *Landmarks of Toronto*, Volume 1, Toronto, 1894, Chapter XLL, "A Sketch of Russell Abbey," page 123.

8. *Slave Trade Act of 1807*, http://www.esp.org/foundations/freedom/holdings/slave-trade-act-1807.pdf.

9. Pringle, J.F., *Lunenburg or the Old Eastern District*, Chapter XXXVI, page 323.

10. Scadding, Dr. Henry, *Toronto of Old*, Chapter XX, "Queen Street, from George Street to Yonge Street, Memories of the Old Court House," page 293.

11. Letter from Surveyor General's Office to John Stegmann confirming that he was to sail to Newcastle for the trial, September 28, 1804, Archives of Ontario, U.C.L.P. S13, C-2814, Roll 265, page 92e.

12. Merz, John, "The Sinking of the Speedy," *The Hessians*, http://freepages.rootsweb.com/ ~ amrevhessians/military/speedy.htm.

13. Allan J. MacDonald, "MACDONELL, ANGUS (Collachie)," in *Dictionary of Canadian Biography*, vol. 5, University of Toronto/Université Laval, 2003–, accessed February 12, 2020, http://www.biographi.ca/en/bio/macdonell_angus_5E.html.

14. J.M. Bumsted, "McDONELL (Collachie), ALEXANDER," in *Dictionary of Canadian Biography*, vol. 7, University of Toronto/Université Laval, 2003–, accessed August 5, 2019, http://www.biographi.ca/en/bio/mcdonnell_alexander_7E.html.

15. Constable John Fisk, York Regional Police Association, https://www.yrpa.ca/in-memory/john-fisk/.

16. Butts, Edward, *Line of Fire: Heroism, Tragedy, and Canada's Police*, Dundurn Press, 2009, page 13.

17. James Ruggles (1770–1804), genealogy website of Dan Buchanan, http://www.treesbydan.com.

18. Scadding, Dr. Henry, *Toronto of Old*, Chapter XXIII, "Queen Street, From Brock Street and Spadina Avenue to the Humber," page 370.

19. Firth, Edith G., (Editor), *The Town of York 1793-1815: A Collection of Documents of Early Toronto*, "Law and Order," page 97.

20. Letter from James Ruggles to the Surveyor General's Office, certifying that Lot 5, Concession 6, Markham Township is occupied, Archives of Ontario, MS 7442, Volume 61, page 1766.

21. Firth, Edith G., (Editor), *The Town of York 1793-1815: A Collection of Documents of Early Toronto*, "Life in York," page 250.

22. Matchedash Bay, https://taytownshipheritage.wordpress.com/2012/06/10/a-brief-history-of-waubaushene-2/.

23. Cowan's Chimneys Historic Site, https://www.ontarioabandonedplaces.com/upload/wiki.asp?entry = 2229.

24. Villemaire, Tom, "Local History: Long road, long history," *Orillia Packet and Times*, August 19, 2016.

25. Schmalz, Peter S., *The Ojibwa of Southern Ontario*, University of Toronto Press, 1991, Chapter 6, "The Surrenders," page 127 & 128.

26. *The Ojibwa of Southern Ontario*, page 127 & 128.

27. Letter from Peter Russell, Administer of Upper Canada, to George Cowan, Interpreter to the Indian Department at Matchedash Bay, regarding relations with the Indigenous people north of Lake Ontario, June 25, 1797, *The Russell Papers*, Volume I, page 232.

Chapter 8: The Ship and the Captain

1. Robertson, J. Ross, *Landmarks of Toronto*, Volume 1, Toronto, 1894, Chapter CXIV, "Houses of Parliament," page 354.

2. Russell, Peter, *The Russell Papers*, Volume III, 1798-1799, Introduction, page xxii.

3. Letter from Major Hazleton Spencer, at Kingston, to York, announcing the launching of the *Speedy*, September 6, 1798, British Military and Naval Records, Volume 723, page 152.

4. Letter from Jacques Calerant, Navy Point, Kingston, to Commodore Bouchette, regarding an estimate for adding two feet to the *Speedy* and *Swift*, January 23, 1798, British Military and Naval Records, Volume 723, page 139.

5. Canniff, William, *History of the Settlement of Upper Canada (Ontario)*, page 150.

6. Letter from Captain W.G. Edwards, Kingston, to York, respecting planned swap of sails between *Speedy* and *Swift*, September 27, 1804, British Military and Naval Records, Volume 726, page 162.

7. Letter from Will Ross, at Kingston, to Lt. Col. Green, at York, respecting the loading of peas on the *Speedy*, April 17, 1804, British Military and Naval Records, Volume 726, page 145.

8. Letter from Capt. McKenzie, at Kingston, to Major Green, at York, respecting the forwarding of corn on the *Speedy*, August 31, 1801, British Military and Naval Records, Volume 107, page 193.

9. Letter from Major D. Campbell, at Kingston, to Major Green, at York, respecting the loading of port on the *Speedy*, July 6, 1802, British Military and Naval Records, Volume 725, page 176.

10. C.P. Stacey, "BROCK, Sir ISAAC," in *Dictionary of Canadian Biography*, vol. 5, University of Toronto/Université Laval, 2003–, accessed February 12, 2020, http://www.biographi.ca/en/bio/brock_isaac_5E.html.

11. Letter from Lt. Col. Brock, at Fort George, to Major Green, at York, respecting the delay in sailing of the *Speedy*, October 1, 1803, British Military and Naval Records, Volume 547, page 87 & 88.

12. Letter from Brock to Major Green, October 1, 1803.

13. Thomas Paxton (1754–1804), genealogy website of Dan Buchanan, http://www.treesbydan.com.

14. Letter from Robert Prescott appointing Thomas Paxton Lieutenant, August 1, 1797, British Military and Naval Records, Volume 728, page 29.

15. "Board of Survey Report, Kingston, ordering a Board of Survey to examine the Mohawk, Lt. Paxton as one of the examiners," January 16, 1799, British Military and Naval Records, Volume 724, page 5.

16. Letter from Lt. Thomas Paxton and Lt. Earle, at Kingston, certifying that they had not received firewood and candles as expected, April 8, 1799, British Military and Naval Records, Volume 724, page 42.

17. Letter from Major D. Campbell, at Kingston, to Major Green, at York, respecting conduct of Captain Paxton, June 26, 1802, British Military and Naval Records, Volume 725, page 173.

18. Russell, Peter, *The Russell Papers*, Volume II, 1797-1798, page 279 & 280.

19. *The Russell Papers*, page 309.

20. W.A.B. Douglas, "BOUCHETTE, JEAN-BAPTISTE," in *Dictionary of Canadian Biography*, vol. 5, University of Toronto/Université Laval, 2003–. Accessed November 6, 2018, http://www.biographi.ca/en/bio/bouchette_jean_baptiste_5E.html.

21. G.P. Browne, "CARLETON, GUY, 1st Baron DORCHESTER," in *Dictionary of Canadian Biography*, vol. 5, University of Toronto/Université Laval, 2003–. Accessed August 7, 2019, http://www.biographi.ca/en/bio/carleton_guy_5E.html.

22. Report from Court of Inquiry regarding Captain Bouchette, by Robert H. Buston, Assistant Deputy Quartermaster General, Quebec, February 10, 1800, British Military and Naval Records, Volume 724, page 114.

23. Letter from Capt. Edwards, Kingston, to Lt. Col. Green, York, regarding plan to swap sails between *Speedy* and *Swift*, September 27, 1804, British Military and Naval Records, Volume 726, page 162.

24. Thomas Paxton, Jr. (1794-c.1875) genealogy website of Dan Buchanan, http://www.treesbydan.com.

25. Brush, Mark, "Fighting Island in the Detroit River no longer a wasteland," *Michigan Radio NPR*, June 12, 2013, https://www.michiganradio.org/post/fighting-island-detroit-river-no-longer-wasteland.

26. Petition of Thomas Paxton, Jr., of Amherstburg, regarding request for grant or purchase of Fighting Island, in the Detroit River, mentioning his militia service as well as his father's loss on the Speedy in 1804, November 12, 1827, Archives of Ontario, MS 691, R52.

27. Petition of Thomas Paxton, Jr.

Chapter 9: The Accused and the Law

1. Kaiser, T.E., *Historic Sketches of Oshawa*, The Reformer Printing and Publishing Co. Ltd., 1921, page 12 & 13.

2. Lefroy, Catherine, "Recollections of Mary Warren Breckenridge, of Clarke Township," read before the Women's Canadian Society of Toronto, published by the Ontario Historical Society, Papers and Records, Vol. III, Toronto, 1901, page 112 & 113.

3. Michael S. Cross and Robert Lochiel Fraser, "BALDWIN, ROBERT," in *Dictionary of Canadian Biography*, vol. 8, University of Toronto/Université Laval, 2003–. Accessed August 7, 2019, http://www.biographi.ca/en/bio/baldwin_robert_8E.html.

4. Canada, Loyalist Claims, 1776-1835, Daniel Cozens (1741–1801), A.O.12 /14, originally from National Archives of the UK, Kew, Surrey, England, American Loyalist Claims, Series I, Class AO 13, piece 014, found through family tree of Jill Hurley on Ancestry.ca.

5. Mary Warren Baldwin (1791–1871), genealogy website of Dan Buchanan, http://www.treesbydan.com.

6. Lefroy, Catherine, "Recollections of Mary Warren Breckenridge, of Clarke Township," read before the Women's Canadian Society of Toronto, published by the *Ontario Historical Society, Papers and Records*, Vol. III, Toronto, 1901, page 112 & 113.

7. Recollections, page 112 & 113.

8. Kaiser, T.E., *Historic Sketches of Oshawa*, page 13.

9. Miller, J.R., *Skyscrapers Hide the Heavens: A History of Native-Newcomer Relations in Canada*, Fourth Edition, University of Toronto Press, 2018, Introduction, page 10.

10. Schmalz, Peter S., *The Ojibwa of Southern Ontario*, University of Toronto Press, 1991, Chapter 4, "The Beaver War," page 82.

11. Schmalz, page 96.

12. Walker, Glenn, *The Changing Face of the Kawarthas*, McGill University, page 50.

13. Walker, page 51.

14. Donald B. Smith, "WABAKININE," in *Dictionary of Canadian Biography*, vol. 4, University of Toronto/Université Laval, 2003–. Accessed October 21, 2018, http://www.biographi.ca/en/bio/wabakinine_4E.html.

15. Firth, Edith G., (Editor), *The Town of York 1793-1815: A Collection of Documents of Early Toronto*, "Documents," page 84.

16. Russell, Peter, *The Russell Papers*, Volume I, 1796-1797, page 49.

Chapter 10: Preparations at Newcastle

1. Charles Selleck (1760–1809), genealogy website of Dan Buchanan, http://www.treesbydan.com.

2. "Charles Selleck birth record," *Connecticut Town Birth Records, pre-1870*, (Barbour Collection), Vol. 1, page 152, Stamford Vital Records, page 227, per family tree of sally Russell-Hubbard on Ancestry.ca.

3. Crown Land Petitions, transcription found on family tree of ruadhan on Ancestry.ca, who cited Library and Archives Canada, *Upper Canada Land Petitions (1763-1865)*, C-2806, pages 937–39, at www.collectionscanada.gc.ca.

4. "Weddings at Niagara, 1792," *Ontario Historical Society*, page 54.

5. Letter from George Gibson to John McGill, Commissariat of Stores at York, May 5, 1796. Transcription sent to me via email by Deborah Gibson, a researcher in Gibson history. She says, "I know there is a handwritten document in the Parliamentary Library."

6. Scadding, Dr. Henry, *Toronto of Old*, Chapter XXIX, "The Harbour: Its Marine, 1793–99," page 524.

7. *Toronto of Old*, page 523.

8. Wellington, Isaac M., "Presqu'isle," *Ontario Historical Society, Papers and Records*, Volume 5, 1905, page 63.

9. "Crown Grant to Charles Selleck for one acre of land at Presqu'ile if he builds a wharf." Digital copy of this document sent to me by Catherine Stutt, of the Brighton Digital Archive, after their members had digitized the original. Document was in collection of Bud and Jill Guertin, of Brighton, who donated it to the Municipality of Brighton, December 17, 2018.

10. Seguin, Marc, *For Want of a Lighthouse*, Part II, Lighthouses, Chapter 5, "Harbour Lights, Presqu'ile Lights (1851)," page 142 & 143.

11. Seguin, page 239.

12. Seguin, page 300.

13. Presqu'ile Point Lighthouse Preservation Society, 2018 Photos, https://pplps.wordpress.com/2018-11-lighthouse-photos/

Chapter 11: All Aboard

1. Robertson, J. Ross, *Landmarks of Toronto*, Volume 6, Toronto, 1914, Chapter XXXIV, "Gazettes of Upper Canada," Vol. XIV, The Oracle, Saturday, September 15, 1804, No. 21 Total No. 697, page 317.

2. *Landmarks of Toronto*, Chapter XXXIV, "Gazettes of Upper Canada," Vol. XII, The Oracle, June 5, 1802, No. 6 Total No. 577, page 290 & 291.

3. "49th Regiment of Foot – Grenadier Company," *War of 1812 Historical Re-enactment Group*, http://49thgrenadiers.com/?page_id = 6.

4. Ogetonicut may have noticed that there were a lot more stumps along the side of the street, indicating that the residents had been busy cutting trees. He would have been disgusted with this, angry at the wonton destruction. This emotion came directly out of his culture. "Because the Ojibwas lived close to nature, they did not envisage any great chasm separating them from the rest of creation. Everything around them was alive and had power. Humans had to stay on good terms with all objects, for they had the supernatural power to punish anyone who wasted them. The Mississauga elders, for instance, avoided cutting down living trees to save them from pain. When green trees were cut, the elders told Sacred Feathers, you could hear them wailing from the ax's blows." (Smith, Donald B., *Sacred Feathers: The Reverend Peter Jones (Kahkewaquonaby) and the Mississauga Indians*, Second Edition, page 11.)

5. Tobin, Brian, *The Upper Canada Gazette and Its Printers*, Ontario Legislative Library, Toronto, 1993, The Printers, John Bennett, page 12.

6. Robertson, J. Ross, *Landmarks of Toronto*, Volume 6, Toronto, 1914, Chapter XXXIV, "Gazettes of Upper Canada," Vol. XIV, The Oracle, Saturday, September 8, 1804, No. 20 Total No. 696, page 317.

7. Letter from Major Hazelton Spencer at Kingston to Major James Green at York, regarding an estimate for two hen coops for the *Mohawk*, May 10, 1800, British Military and Naval Records, Series C, Volume 724, page 128.

8. Langley, John G., *Canadian Confederate Cruiser*, Nimbus Publishing, 2018, Chapter 11, "An Important Gesture," page 129.

9. Pringle, J.F., *Lunenburg or the Old Eastern District*, Chapter XXXVI, "John Baker, the Last of Those Who Had Been Born in Slavery in Canada," page 321.

10. G.H. Patterson, "WEEKES, WILLIAM," in *Dictionary of Canadian Biography*, vol. 5, University of Toronto/Université Laval, 2003–. Accessed October 23, 2018, http://www.biographi.ca/en/bio/weekes_william_5E.html.

11. Merz, John, "The Sinking of the Speedy," *The Hessians*, 2005, http://freepages.rootsweb.com/ ~ amrevhessians/military/speedy.htm.

12. Elwood H. Jones, "WILLCOCKS, JOSEPH," in *Dictionary of Canadian Biography*, vol. 5, University of Toronto/Université Laval, 2003–. Accessed October 29, 2018, http://www.biographi.ca/en/bio/willcocks_joseph_5E.html.

13. Letter from Chief Justice Henry Allcock to Receiver General Peter Russell, regarding the fees associated with Joseph Willcocks being appointed Sheriff of Home District, Archives of Ontario, MS 75, Reel 5, 1804.

14. Robertson, J. Ross, *Landmarks of Toronto*, Volume 6, Toronto, 1914, Chapter XXXIV, "Gazettes of Upper Canada," Vol. XIV, The Oracle, Saturday, November 3, 1804, No. 28 Total No. 704, page 318.

Chapter 12: On the Way to Newcastle

1. Scadding, Dr. Henry, *Toronto of Old*, Introductory, page 17.

2. Frederick H. Armstrong, "AITKEN, ALEXANDER," in *Dictionary of Canadian Biography*, vol. 4, University of Toronto/Université Laval, 2003–. Accessed November 17, 2018, http://www.biographi.ca/en/bio/aitken_alexander_4E.html.

3. A.J. Anderson, "STUART, GEORGE OKILL (1776-1862)," in *Dictionary of Canadian Biography*, vol. 9, University of Toronto/Université Laval, 2003–. Accessed November 9, 2018, http://www.biographi.ca/en/bio/stuart_george_okill_1776_1862_9E.html.

4. Robert E. Saunders, "ROBINSON, Sir JOHN BEVERLEY," in *Dictionary of Canadian Biography*, vol. 9, University of Toronto/Université Laval, 2003–. Accessed August 12, 2019, http://www.biographi.ca/en/bio/robinson_john_beverley_9E.html.

5. Letter from Rev. George Okill Stuart, Kingston, to Sir John Beverley Robinson, Toronto, recalling the *Speedy* disaster, December 22, 1860, Archives of Ontario, *J.B. Robinson Papers*, MS 4, Reel 6, Index Item page 28.

6. Robertson, J. Ross, *Landmarks of Toronto*, Volume 6, Toronto, 1914, Chapter XXXIV, "Gazettes of Upper Canada," Vol. XIV, The Oracle, Saturday, November 3, 1804, No. 28 Total No. 704, Loss of the Speedy, page 318.

7. J.F. Pringle, *Lunenburg or the Old Eastern District*, Chapter XXXVI, page 322.

8. Letter from Rev. George Okill Stuart, Kingston, to Sir John Beverley Robinson, Toronto, recalling the *Speedy* disaster, December 22, 1860, Archives of Ontario, *J.B. Robinson Papers*, MS 4, Reel 6, Index Item page 28.

9. Garcia, Bob, "The Provincial Marine at Amherstburg 1796-1813," Access Heritage, War of 1812 Website, http://www.warof1812.ca/provmarine.htm.

10. Weld, Isaac, *Travels Through the States of North America, and the Provinces of Upper and Lower Canada, during the years 1795, 1796 and 1797*, Fourth Edition, Vol. II, Letter XXX, page 68.

11. Canniff, William, *History of the Settlement of Upper Canada, (Ontario)*, Chapter XIV, "The First Sailing Vessels," page 149.

12. Letter from J.W. Steel, at Kingston, to Major James Green at York, providing specifications for cabin stoves, September 28, 1804, British Military and Naval Records, Volume 726, page 165.

13. Berchem, F.R., *The Yonge Street Story 1793-1860: An Account from Letters, Diaries and Newspapers*. Chapter One, "The Simcoe Years (1791–96)," location 244 of 4479.

14. Scadding, Dr. Henry, *Toronto of Old*, Chapter XVI, "From Berkeley Street to the Bridge and Across It," page 215.

15. Robertson, J. Ross, *Landmarks of Toronto*, Volume 6, Chapter XXXIV, "Gazettes of Upper Canada," Vol. III, Wednesday, February 1, 1797, No. 15, Inoculation General, page 228.

16. Merz, John, "The Sinking of the Speedy," *The Hessians*, http://freepages.rootsweb.com/ ~ amrevhessians/military/speedy.htm.

17. The Danforth Highway had been built in 1799 and 1800 by Asa Danforth, under a contract with the government. The road went from York, east along the shore of Lake Ontario, then into Prince Edward County and across to Bath. Construction was hurried and the government objected to the route in many places, which simply kept to the high ground, allowing for quick completion. Long sections of the road would not be maintained at all because so few lots had been sold and lot owners were responsible for keeping the road open. By 1804, parts of the road would have been impassable. (Lillian F. Gates, "DANFORTH, ASA," in *Dictionary of Canadian Biography*, vol. 6, University of Toronto/Université Laval, 2003–. Accessed March 13, 2017, http://www.biographi.ca/en/bio/danforth_asa_6E.html.)

18. Buchanan, Dan, *38 Hours to Montreal*, Chapter 14, "Hope Township," page 78.

19. Kaiser, T.E., *Historic Sketches of Oshawa*, page 13 & 14.

20. Joel Dean (1731–1815), genealogy website of Dan Buchanan, http://www.treesbydan.com.

21. "Early Mill Streams of Cobourg, Ont." *2 Old Guys Walking*, March 29, 2017, https://2oldguyswalking.wordpress.com/2017/03/29/the-early-mill-streams-of-cobourg-ont/.

22. Kaiser, T.E., *Historic Sketches of Oshawa*, The Reformer Printing and Publication Co. Ltd., Oshawa, 1921, page 13 & 14.

Chapter 13: Beacon Fire

1. Letter from Captain Mosely in Kingston, to Major Green at York, regarding the leaky state of the *Speedy*, November 7, 1803, British Military and Naval Records, Volume 726, page 94.

2. Joseph Gibson (1788–1880), genealogy website of Dan Buchanan, http://www.treesbydan.com.

3. Nor'easter, https://www.weather.gov/safety/winter-noreaster.

4. Buchanan, Dan, *38 Hours to Montreal*, Chapter 14, "Hope Township," page 97.

5. *38 Hours*, page 105.

6. Presqu'ile Provincial Park website, https://www.ontarioparks.com/park/presquile.

7. Snider, C.H.J., "Passing Thro' the Devil's Nose," Schooner Days No. CMXLVII, *Toronto Telegram*, April 15, 1950, Maritime History of the Great Lakes, http://images.maritimehistoryofthegreatlakes.ca/120690/data.

Chapter 14: A Stop to All Business at York

1. Letter from William Ross in Kingston, to Lt. Col. Green in York, regarding the non-arrival of the *Speedy*, October 15, 1804, British Military and Naval Records, Volume 726, page 174.

2. Otte A. Rosenkrantz, "VINCENT, JOHN," in *Dictionary of Canadian Biography*, vol. 7, University of Toronto/Université Laval, 2003–. Accessed July 5, 2019, http://www.biographi.ca/en/bio/vincent_john_7E.html.

3. Letter from Lt. Col. Vincent at Fort George, to Lt. Col. Green at York, reporting articles from *Speedy* found on shore east of Newark, October 25, 1804, British Military and Naval Records, Volume 726, page 176.

4. British Military and Naval Records, Vol 726, page 176.

5. Carlton, Orleans County, New York, https://townofcarlton.org/town-history/.

6. Firth, Edith G., (Editor), *The Town of York 1793-1815: A Collection of Documents of Early Toronto*, "Documents," page 250.

7. Letter from Peter Russell to W.H. Clinton, regarding the loss of the *Speedy*, October 26, 1804, Archives of Ontario, Peter Russell Fonds (F46), MS 75, Reel 5.

8. Letter from J.W. Steel, at Fort George, to Major James Green at York, expressing regret regarding the loss of the *Speedy*, October 26, 1804, British Military and Naval Records, Volume 726, page 177.

9. Letter from John Stuart in Kingston to his son James Stuart in Quebec, November 10, 1804, Archives of Ontario, *Inventory and Calendar of the Stuart Family Papers*, June 1981, Prepared by Marion Beyea & William Ormsby, MS 606, MU 2923, page 201.

10. Letter from John Stuart to James Stuart, MS 606, MU 2923, page 201.

11. Letter from John Stuart to John Beverley Robinson, December 22, 1860, *J.B. Robinson Papers*, Archives of Ontario, MS 4, Reel 6.

12. Bruce G. Wilson, "HAMILTON, ROBERT," in *Dictionary of Canadian Biography*, vol. 5, University of Toronto/Université Laval, 2003–. Accessed November 6, 2018, http://www.biographi.ca/en/bio/hamilton_robert_5E.html.

13. David R. Farrell, "ASKIN, JOHN," in *Dictionary of Canadian Biography*, vol. 5, University of Toronto/Université Laval, 2003–. Accessed October 29, 2018, http://www.biographi.ca/en/bio/askin_john_5E.html.

14. Letter from Robert Hamilton, Queenston, to John Askin, Sandwich, November 8, 1804, *The John Askin Papers*, Volume II: 1796–1820, Chapter V, "Letters and Paper 1802-1804," pages 441–3.

15. *John Askin Papers*, pages 441–3.

16. S.R. Mealing, "SMITH, Sir DAVID WILLIAM," in *Dictionary of Canadian Biography*, vol. 7, University of Toronto/Université Laval, 2003–. Accessed April 4, 2019, http://www.biographi.ca/en/bio/smith_david_william_7E.html.

17. Letter from Alexander Auldjo of Quebec to David William Smith in England, November 11, 1804, Toronto Public Library, Metro Reference Library, Special Collections, *David William Smith Papers*, S126, B4, Accounts with Auldjo, Maitland and Co., John McGill. (This letter is the only non-accounts item in this folder, probably misfiled.)

18. *David William Smith Papers*, S126, B4.

19. *David William Smith Papers*, S126, B4.

20. Letter from Captain W.G. Edwards, Kingston, to York, respecting planned swap of sails between *Speedy* and *Swift*, September 27, 1804, British Military and Naval Records, Volume 726, page 162.

21. Letter from Hugh Earle at Kingston, to Col. Green at York, regarding the repairs to *Toronto Yacht*, December 23, 1804, British Military and Naval Records, Volume 726, page 186.

22. Letter from Will Ross at Kingston, to Col. Green at York, regarding immediate procurement of salt for preserving the timbers of the new vessel, October 22, 1804, British Military and Naval Records, Volume 726, page 175.

23. Christian Rioux, "CRAIGIE, JOHN," in *Dictionary of Canadian Biography*, vol. 5, University of Toronto/Université Laval, 2003–. Accessed January 21, 2019, http://www.biographi.ca/en/bio/craigie_john_5E.html.

24. Letter from John Craigie, Commissary General in Quebec, to Col. Green at York, regarding the loss of the *Speedy* and possible ways to help the widow Paxton, November 12, 1804, British Military and Naval Records, Volume 726, page 182 & 183.

25. British Military and Naval Records, Vol. 726, page 182 & 183.

26. Robertson, J. Ross, *Landmarks of Toronto*, Volume 6, Toronto, 1914, Chapter XXXIV, "Gazettes of Upper Canada," Vol. XIV, The Oracle, Saturday, November 3, 1804, No. 28, Total No. 704, "Loss of the Speedy," page 318 & 319. (The full text of the article "The Loss of the Speedy" is provided in Appendix B.)

27. *Landmarks of Toronto*, page 318 & 319.

28. *Landmarks of Toronto*, page 318 & 319.

29. *Landmarks of Toronto*, page 318 & 319.

30. Tobin, Brian, *The Upper Canada Gazette and Its Printers, 1793-1849*, The Printers, John Bennett, page 12.

31. Tobin, Foreword, page v.

32. Scadding, Dr. Henry, *Toronto of Old*, Chapter XXX, "The Harbour – Its Marine, 1800-1814," page 527.

33. Robertson, J. Ross, *Landmarks of Toronto*, Volume 6, Toronto, 1914, Chapter XXXIV, "Gazettes of Upper Canada," Vol. VIII, No. 36 – York, Saturday, Dec. 21st, 1799, Total No. 451, Loss of a York Schooner, page 257.

34. "HMS *Ontario*," *Historical Narratives of Early Canada*, page 6 of 10, http://www.uppercanadahistory.ca/uel/uel8.html.

35. Kennard, Jim, "Shipwreck Explorers Discover HMS Ontario - 1780 British Warship in Lake Ontario," June 13, 2008, Shipwreck World, http://www.shipwreckworld. com/articles/shipwreck-explorers-discover-1780-british-warship-in-lake-ontario.

Chapter 15: Widow Paxton

1. Robertson, J. Ross, *Landmarks of Toronto*, Volume 6, Toronto, 1914, Chapter XXXIV, "Gazettes of Upper Canada," Vol. XIV, The Oracle, Saturday, Nov. 3, 1804, No. 28, Total No. 704, Loss of the Speedy, page 318 & 319.

2. "Sales of Pews in St. George's Church," December 6, 1802, *The Parish Register of Kingston Upper Canada 1785-1811*, Part 1, page 59.

3. *Parish Register*, Part 2, page 5, Baptism of James S. Paxton.

4. Larry Turner, "GRASS, MICHAEL," in *Dictionary of Canadian Biography*, vol. 5, University of Toronto/Université Laval, 2003–. Accessed December 3, 2019, http://www.biographi.ca/en/bio/grass_michael_5E.html.

5. McLeod, Susanna, "Murney a towering figure of early Kingston," *The Kingston Whig-Standard*, https://www.thewhig.com/2013/03/19/murney-a-towering-figure-of-early-kingston/wcm/9d85d0e8-5676-a97f-faca-3db1efe5b417.

6. T.R. Millman, "STUART, JOHN (1740/41-1811)," in *Dictionary of Canadian Biography*, vol. 5, University of Toronto/Université Laval, 2003–. Accessed January 8, 2019, http://www.biographi.ca/en/bio/stuart_john_1740_41_1811_5E.html.

7. "Timeline," History & Architecture, St. George's Cathedral, http://www.stgeorgescathedral.ca/index.cfm/history-architecture/ a-st-georgee28099s-cathedral-timeline/.

8. Letter from General James Craig, Commander of British Forces at Quebec, to Francis Gore, Lieutenant-Governor of Upper Canada, at York, regarding the petition of Jane Paxton, October 20, 1808, British Military and Naval Records, Volume 728, page 24.

9. Commission as Second Lieutenant for Thomas Paxton, signed by Lord Dorchester, August 7, 1791, British Military and Naval Records, Volume 728, page 28.

10. Commission as Lieutenant for Thomas Paxton, signed by Robert Prescott, August 1, 1797, British Military and Naval Records, Volume 728, page 29.

11. Petition of Jane Paxton to Lieutenant-Governor of Upper Canada, asking for assistance, October 20, 1808, British Military and Naval Records, Series C, Volume 728, page 26 & 27.

12. Petition of Jane Paxton to Lieutenant-Governor of Upper Canada, asking for assistance, October 20, 1808, British Military and Naval Records, Volume 728, page 26 & 27.

13. British Military and Naval Records, Vol. 728, page 24.

14. "Baptism of James S. Paxton," *The Parish Register of Kingston Upper Canada 1785-1811*, Part 2, page 5.

15. Petition of Thomas Paxton Jr. regarding use of Fighting Island, November 12, 1827, Archives of Ontario, MS 691, R52, (no page numbers).

16. "Notice of demands against estate of Thomas Paxton," *Kingston Gazette*, December 2, 1817, page 5, column 4, bottom, http://images.ourontario.ca/Partners/kfpl/KFPL000097001p0005f.pdf.

17. "Notice regarding the sale of the Paxton lot," *Kingston Chronicle*, September 11, 1830, page 3, column 3, http://images.ourontario.ca/Partners/kfpl/KFPL000097310p0003f.pdf.

18. John Paxton (1791–1859), genealogy website of Dan Buchanan, http://www.treesbydan.com.

19. Frenchtown, Monroe County, Michigan, https://frenchtowntownship.org/.

20. "Speech of General Leslie Combs," *General Leslie Combs: Incidents in the Early History of the Northwestern Territory*, Library of Congress.

21. "The American Attack at Frenchtown on the River Raisin, January 18, 1813," *Access Heritage, The War of 1812 Website*, http://warof1812.ca/frenchtown1.htm.

22. John Paxton, *Findagrave*, https://www.findagrave.com/memorial/67286463.

23. "Jane Paxton Death Record," *Parish Register*, Our Lady of Assumption Roman Catholic Church, Windsor, Ontario, Burial March 7, 1843, Diocese of London (Ontario), https://www.ancestry.ca/interactive/61505/ FS_004146625_00098?pid = 814144&treeid = &personid = &rc = &usePUB = true&_ phsrc = rEb4169&_phstart = successSource.

Chapter 16: Life Goes On

1. "John Pratt, 1st Marquess Camden," Biography, *Encyclopedia Britannica*, https://www.britannica.com/biography/Charles-Pratt-1st-Earl-Camden.

2. O'Brien, Brendan, *Speedy Justice*, Chapter 1, "The Scene," page 4. Quoting from a letter sent by Lt.-Gov. Peter Hunter to Lord Camden, Secretary of War for the Colonies, November 12, 1804. (Ref. AO, CO42, vol. 336 (Q Series 299): 125-6).

3. *Speedy Justice*, page 4.

4. *Speedy Justice*, page 4.

5. Letter from Lt.-Gov. Peter Hunter at York, to Henry Allcock, on his way to England, November 12, 1804, *Peter Hunter Papers*, Image 189.

6. *Peter Hunter Papers*, Nov. 12 1804.

7. Letter from Capt. Earle at Kingston, to Col. Green at York, regarding the repairs to *Toronto Yacht*, December 23, 1804, British Military and Naval Records, Volume 726, page 186.

8. Firth, Edith G., (Editor), *The Town of York 1793-1815: A Collection of Documents of Early Toronto*, Introduction, page lxvi & lxvii.

9. *The Town of York*, D. Commercial Development, page 133, footnote 41.

10. *The Town of York*, C. Law and Order, page 101.

11. *The Town of York*, F. Political Ferment, page 170.

12. *The Town of York*, F. Political Ferment, page 171.

13. *The Town of York*, H. Life in York, page 251.

14. Robertson, J. Ross, *Landmarks of Toronto*, Volume 6, Toronto, 1914, Chapter XXXIV, "Gazettes of Upper Canada," Vol. XVI, The Oracle, Saturday, October 18, 1806, No. 27, Total No. 807, Shot in a Duel, page 334.

15. Robert Lochiel Fraser, "ROGERS, DAVID McGREGOR," in *Dictionary of Canadian Biography*, vol. 6, University of Toronto/Université Laval, 2003–. Accessed April 28, 2019, http://www.biographi.ca/en/bio/rogers_david_mcgregor_6E.html.

16. *Journals of the Legislative Assembly of Upper Canada*, Volume Two, 1911, Archives of Ontario, (B97, Reel 124), page 28. (An image of the front page of the *Statutes* and a link to the full document are found in Appendix F.)

17. *Journals*, page 34.

18. Robertson, J. Ross, *Landmarks of Toronto*, Volume 6, Toronto, 1914, Chapter XXXIV, "Gazettes of Upper Canada," Vol. XIV, The Oracle, Saturday, April 13, 1805, No. 51, Total No. 727, God Save the King, page 323.

19. Hamilton, James Cleland, *Osgoode Hall Reminiscences of the Bench and Bar*, Chapter VIII, "Gowns, Wigs, Bags and Aethiops in Aulis," page 131.

20. "Simcoe's Gentry: Toronto Park Lots, Park Lot 27," Ontario Genealogy Society, Toronto Branch, https://torontofamilyhistory.org/simcoesgentry/27.

21. Kaiser, T.E., *Historical Sketches of Oshawa*, page 32 & 33.

22. "Bond for the due Administration of the Estate of Jacob Herkimer," Archives of Ontario, MS 638, Reel 51, (RG 22-155 Court Probate Estate Files), page 30.

23. "List of Promissory Notes Payable to the late Angus Macdonell," Archives of Ontario, MS 638, Reel 56, (RG 22-155 Court Probate Estate Files), McDonell, Angus, 1806, no page numbers.

24. A.B. McCullough, "WILMOT, SAMUEL," in *Dictionary of Canadian Biography*, vol. 12, University of Toronto/Université Laval, 2003–. Accessed April 19, 2019, http://www.biographi.ca/en/bio/wilmot_samuel_12E.html.

25. Samuel Street Wilmot (1773–1856), genealogy website of Dan Buchanan, http://www.treesbydan.com.

26. Letter from Lieutenant-Governor Peter Hunter to the Surveyor General's Office, November 6, 1804, Archives of Ontario, MS 7442, Vol. 61, page 1850.

27. Wilmot, Samuel, "Diary of the Survey of Uxbridge Township, from December 18, 1804 to April 8, 1805," Archives of Ontario, MS 7442, Vol. 61, page 216.

28. Hicks, Kathleen A., *Dixie: Orchards to Industry*, The Friends of the Mississauga Library System, Mississauga, 2006, Part One, 1805-1850, "Samuel Wilmot's Survey – 1805-1806," page 24, http://www.mississauga.ca/file/COM/9635_DixieBook_PartOne.pdf.

29. Karcich, Grant, *Scugog Carrying Place: A Frontier Pathway*, Chapter 5, "Preachers on the Trail," page 90.

30. *Journals of the Legislative Assembly of Upper Canada*, Volume Two, 1911, Archives of Ontario, Microfilm B97, Reel 124, 1911, 5th February, 1805, page 10. (The full text of both the petition and the legislation are found in Appendix E.)

31. "An Act to provide for the administration of justice in the District of Newcastle," *Upper Canada Gazette*, Toronto Public Library, Toronto (York) R. Stanton, Microform, *The Upper Canada Gazette* or *American Oracle*, Saturday, May 4, 1805, Volume XV, No. 2, copied from microfilm, which was obtained through interlibrary loan at Brighton Public Library.

32. Asa Burnham (1774–1813), genealogy website of Dan Buchanan, http://www.treesbydan.com.

33. Climo, Percy L., "Amherst, Now Part of Cobourg," *Cobourg History*, April 1987, https://www.cobourghistory.ca/histories/short-histories/9-amherst.

34. Guillet, Edwin C., *Cobourg 1797-1948*, The Building of Victoria Hall, pages 39-45.

35. Wellington, Isaac M., *The Tobey Book*, Chapter III, "1811-1820," page 56.

36. Petition to Sir Peregrine Maitland, *The Tobey Book*, Chapter IV, "1821-1830," page 78.

37. Map of Presqu'ile Bay regarding the survey of 1825 in preparation for the move of Newcastle to the north shore, *The Tobey Book*, Chapter I, "Before 1800," page 31.

38. In collaboration, "HUNTER, PETER," in *Dictionary of Canadian Biography*, vol. 5.

39. Robertson, J. Ross, *Landmarks of Toronto*, Volume 6, Toronto, 1914, Chapter XXXIV, "Gazettes of Upper Canada," Vol. XV, The Oracle, Saturday, September 14, 1805, No. 21, Total No. 740, pages 324-326.

40. *Landmarks of Toronto*, pages 324-26.

41. In collaboration with Carol Whitfield, "GRANT, ALEXANDER," in *Dictionary of Canadian Biography*, vol. 5, University of Toronto/Université Laval, 2003–. Accessed October 23, 2018, http://www.biographi.ca/en/bio/grant_alexander_5E.html.

42. In collaboration, "HUNTER, PETER," in *Dictionary of Canadian Biography*, vol. 5.

43. In collaboration with Carol Whitfield, "GRANT, ALEXANDER," in *Dictionary of Canadian Biography*, vol. 5.

44. S.R. Mealing, "GORE, FRANCIS," in *Dictionary of Canadian Biography*, vol. 8, University of Toronto/Université Laval, 2003–. Accessed May 22, 2019, http://www.biographi.ca/en/bio/gore_francis_8E.html.

45. "Elegy," *The Kingston Gazette*, Tuesday, June 18, 1811, No. 39, front page, Original Miscellany, Reckoner, Digital Kingston. ("Elegy" is provided in its entirety in Appendix C.)

Chapter 17: No Poem for Ogetonicut

1. Donald B. Smith, "JONES, PETER," in *Dictionary of Canadian Biography*, vol. 8, University of Toronto/Université Laval, 2003–. Accessed November 27, 2019, http://www.biographi.ca/en/bio/jones_peter_8E.html.

2. Jones, Rev. Peter, *History of the Ojebway Indians*, Chapter XVIII, "Opinion of the Indians Respecting the Sovereign and People of Great Britain," page 209.

3. "Rice Lake Treaty No. 20," *Treaty Texts – Upper Canada Land Surrenders*, https://www.aadnc-aandc.gc.ca/eng/1370372152585/1370372222012#ucls18.

4.   "Rice Lake Treaty No. 20."

5.   *Samuel Pedlar Manuscript*, Frame 225.

6.   *Samuel Pedlar Manuscript*, Frame 205.

7.   *Samuel Pedlar Manuscript*, Frame 205.

8.   *Samuel Pedlar Manuscript*, Frame 234.

9.   Elwood H. Jones, "PURDY, WILLIAM," in *Dictionary of Canadian Biography*, vol. 7, University of Toronto/Université Laval, 2003–. Accessed December 29, 2018, http://www.biographi.ca/en/bio/purdy_william_7E.html.

10. William Purdy BIO.

11. William Purdy BIO.

12. William Purdy BIO.

13. "Lake Scugog," Hvidsten, J. Peter, *Scugog Exposed*, 2004, Observer Publishing of Port Perry, page 14, https://scugogheritage.com/online_pdfs/exposed.pdf.

14. Hvidsten, page 14.

15. "Some Annals of the Scugog" Eastern Concessions, Victoria County, *Canadian Genealogy,* http://www.canadiangenealogy.net/ontario/victoriacounty/eastern_concessions.htm#Annals.

16. "Some Annals of Scugog."

17. John Witham, "BAIRD, NICOL HUGH," in *Dictionary of Canadian Biography*, vol. 7, University of Toronto/Université Laval, 2003–. Accessed August 19, 2019, http://www.biographi.ca/en/bio/baird_nicol_hugh_7E.html.

18. Baird was a very active and respected civil engineer at this time. He had been working on plans for dams and canals along the Trent River and had designed structures like the covered bridge at Trent Port (Trenton) and the Presqu'ile Point Lighthouse, near Brighton. (Buchanan, Dan, *38 Hours to Montreal*, Chapter 20, "Trent Port and Belleville," page 115.)

19. "Some Annals of the Scugog" Eastern Concessions, Victoria County, *Canadian Genealogy.* http://www.canadiangenealogy.net/ontario/victoriacounty/eastern_concessions.htm#Annals.

20. Jones, Rev. Peter, *Life and Journals of KAH-KE-WA-QUO-NA-BY (Rev. Peter Jones)*, *Wesleyan Missionary*, Chapter VI, page 197.

21. Riedner, Heidi, "History of Indigenous people residing along Lake Simcoe region," Muskokaregion.com, Community, June 7, 2017, https://www.yorkregion.com/community-story/7335943-history-of-indigenous-people-residing-along-lake-simcoe-region/.

22. "Mississaugas of Scugog Island First Nation," Origins & History, Mississaugas of Scugog Island First Nation, https://www.scugogfirstnation.com/Public/Origin-and-History.

23. "Mississaugas of Scugog Island First Nation."

24. "Mississaugas of Scugog Island First Nation."

PART II

Chapter 18: Searching for HMS *Speedy*

1. The story of the Spanish coin has been repeated many times. Recently, the event was confirmed in a discussion with Terry Coons, chief diver of the *Speedy* project and long-time friend of Ed Burtt. They were, in fact, training OPP divers and one of them brought up the Spanish coin. (Per Terry Coons, in conversation with the author, December 17, October 2019.)

2. The Spanish coin that a diver found on Dobbs Bank in 1989 was donated by Ed Burtt to the Mariners Park Museum, in Prince Edward County. This coin is a commercially reproduced replica of the original Spanish piece of eight minted in Mexico in 1732. Coin collectors say that the third line on the reverse side, which says "Piece of Eight" in English, is the proof it is a copy and not an original. These copies were printed after 1732 in various places in North and South America and were common currency in the United States and the colonies of British North American during the later 1700s. This coin could have been in the pocket of one of the passengers on the ill-fated *Speedy* when it was lost in 1804. (Coinsite, https://coinsite.com/1732-spanish-8-reales-pillar-dollar/.)

3. Edward Vernon "Ed" Burtt (1939–2017), genealogy website of Dan Buchanan, http://www.treesbydan.com.

4. The Ocean Scan Systems website (http://www.oceanscan.com/) contained information about the various explorations Ed Burtt had been involved with, including the HMS *Speedy* project. The author made copies of some pages of the site during involvement with the H.M.S. Speedy Foundation starting in 2012. The website is no longer active.

5. Mel Fisher's Treasures, https://www.melfisher.com/SalvageOperations/TributeToMel.asp.

6. Cassavoy, Ken, marine archaeologist, *Speedy Project Report for 1990*, Introduction, page 1, private collection of Ed Burtt.

7. "List of Archaeologists Licensed in Ontario," Ontario Ministry of Heritage, Sport, Tourism and Culture Industries, http://www.mtc.gov.on.ca/en/archaeology/licensed_archaeologists_list.shtml.

8. Cassavoy, Ken, *Speedy Project Report for 1990*, page 1, private collection of Ed Burtt.

9. Cassavoy, Ken, *Speedy Project Report for 1990*, Acknowledgements, page i, private collection of Ed Burtt.

10. "Application for Incorporation of a Corporation without Share Capital," Letters Patent, H.M.S. Speedy Foundation, Blue Box, 23 Blue Folder, page 2, private collection of Ed Burtt.

11. "Licence to Conduct Archaeological Exploration Survey or Field Work No. 90-067," Ministry of Culture and Communication, 02 Blue Box, 05 Green Binder, 08 Policy and Licence, page 12, private collection of Ed Burtt.

12. Le Blanc, Jack, "A 'Speedy' trip back in Time," *The Trentonian*, Monday, May 28, 1990, private collection of Ed Burtt, Loose Misc., page 21.

13. Cassavoy, Ken, Marine Archaeologist, *Speedy Project Report for 1990*, Project Survey, Survey Activity, page 40, private collection of Ed Burtt.

14. Burtt, Ed, "Survey Sheet," July 26, 1990, 01 Black Binder 2, page 38, private collection of Ed Burtt. (A detailed list of events and activities for the *Speedy* project is found in Appendix A.)

15. Terry Coons, in conversation with the author, December 17, 2019.

16. "Application for Incorporation of a Corporation without Share Capital," Letters Patent, H.M.S. Speedy Foundation, Blue Box, 23 Blue Folder, page 2, private collection of Ed Burtt.

17. Terry Coons, in conversation with the author, December 17, 2019.

18. Cassavoy, Ken, Marine Archaeologist. *Speedy Project Report for 1990*, Project Survey, Survey Activity, page 37, private collection of Ed Burtt.

19. Cassavoy, page 51.

20. Burtt, Ed, "Dive Sheet," Oct. 8, 1990, 01 Black Binder 2, pages 21-23, private collection of Ed Burtt.

21. Burtt, Ed, "Survey Sheet," Oct. 14, 1990, 01 Black Binder 2, page 17, private collection of Ed Burtt.

22. Survey Sheet, October 14, 1990.

23. Burtt, Ed, "Survey Sheet," Oct. 20, 1990, 01 Black Binder 2, page 12, private collection of Ed Burtt.

24. Cassavoy, Ken, Project Archaeologist. *Speedy Project Report for 1990*, Front Cover, private collection of Ed Burtt.

25. Cassavoy, Kenneth, "Underwater Surveys, HMS Speedy Project: The 1990 Fieldwork," Summary, page 129, *New Series Second Annual Archaeological Report, Ontario*, 1991, Toronto Reference Library, 971.301.A 1991, Humanities & Social Science Desk, 2nd Floor, requested and reviewed onsite.

26. Ken Cassavoy, in telephone conversation with the author, July 27, 2019.

27. "Licence to Conduct Archaeological Exploration Survey or Field Work No. 90-067," Ministry of Culture and Communication, 02 Blue Box, 05 Green Binder, 08 Policy and Licence, page 12, private collection of Ed Burtt.

28. "License to Conduct Archaeological Exploration Survey or Field Work No. 91-94, July 16, 1991, to Dec. 31, 1991," Ministry of Culture and Communications, 02 Blue Box, 05 Green Binder, 08 Policy and License, page 14, private collection of Ed Burtt.

29. Cassavoy, Ken, Project Archaeologist. *Speedy Project Report for 1990*, Site Protection, page 16, private collection of Ed Burtt.

30. Letter from Louis E. Cook to Ed Burtt responding to Ed sending the 1989 video, November 21, 1990, 01 Black Binder, page 170, private collection of Ed Burtt.

31. Cook letter.

32. Burtt, Ed, "Survey Sheet May 11, 1991," 02 Blue Box, 05 Green Binder, 05 Survey, page 44, private collection of Ed Burtt.

33. Burtt, Ed, "Survey Sheet, May 20, 1991," 02 Blue Box, 05 Green Binder, 05 Survey, page 48, private collection of Ed Burtt.

34. Garcia, Bob, "The Provincial Marine at Amherstburg 1796-1813, What They Wore," *Access Heritage, War of 1812 Website*, http://www.warof1812.ca/provmarine.htm.

35. Burtt, Ed, "Survey Sheet, June 25, 1991," 02 Blue Box, 05 Green Binder, 05 Survey, page 60, private collection of Ed Burtt.

36. Terry Coons in conversation with the author, December 17, 2019.

37. Burtt, Ed. "Survey Sheet, July 6, 1991," 02 Blue Box, 05 Green Binder, 05 Survey, page 65, private collection of Ed Burtt.

38. Burtt, Ed, "Survey Sheet, June 25, 1991," 02 Blue Box, 05 Green Binder, 05 Survey, page 60, private collection of Ed Burtt.

39. Burtt, Ed, *HMS Speedy Project Report for 1991*, March 11, 1992, Introduction, page 17, private collection of Ed Burtt.

40. Burtt, E.V., Project Technical Director. *HMS Speedy Project Report 1997*, March 24, 2005, Project Work, page 11 of 120, 02 Blue Box, 17 Project Report 1997, private collection of Ed Burtt.

41. Burtt, Ed, *HMS Speedy Project Report for 1991*, March 11, 1992, Introduction, page 1, private collection of Ed Burtt.

42. Burtt, E.V., Project Technical Director. *HMS Speedy Project Report 1997*, March 24, 2005, Project Work, page 61 of 120, 02 Blue Box, 17 Project Report 1997, private collection of Ed Burtt.

43. Terry Coons in conversation with the author, December 17, 2019.

44. *Journals of the Legislative Assembly of Upper Canada*, Volume Two, 1911, Archives of Ontario, 1911, B97, Reel 124, page 28.

45. Terry Coons in conversation with the author, December 17, 2019.

46. Burtt, Ed, *HMS Speedy Project Report for 1991*, March 11, 1992, Introduction, page 1, private collection of Ed Burtt.

47. Terry Coons in conversation with the author, December 17, 2019.

48. Burtt, E.V., Project Technical Director. *HMS Speedy Project Report 1992*, April 11, 1995, Project Work, page 9, private collection of Ed Burtt.

49. Burtt, page 10.

50. Burtt, Ed, "Dive Sheet, Oct. 8, 1990," 01 Black Binder 2, pages 21–23, private collection of Ed Burtt.

51. Terry Coons in conversation with the author, December 17, 2019.

52. Burtt, Ed, Letter to Stan Brown of Cosgrove/Meurer Productions, Burbank, California, regarding media exposure for *Speedy* story, April 16, 1992, 02 Blue Box, 21 Loose Misc., page 27 & 28, private collection of Ed Burtt.

53. Burtt, E.V., Project Technical Director. *HMS Speedy Project Report 1993*, Acknowledgements, page 1, private collection of Ed Burtt.

54. "Avro Project," Ocean Scan Systems, several pages on the website www.oceanscan.com which were copied in 2014, 02 Blue Box, 23 Blue Folder pages 34–36, private collection of Ed Burtt.

55. Letter from Gloria M. Tylor to Ed Burtt with last payment of funding,
     Administrator, Archaeology Committee, Ontario Heritage Foundation, letter to E.V.
     Burtt, HMS Speedy Project, July 20, 1992, 02 Blue Box, 32 File Folder 08, Ontario
     Heritage Foundation, page 1, private collection of Ed Burtt.

Chapter 19: 99.99% Sure

1.   Ian Morgan Biography, attached to News Release announcing the Heritage
     Hydrographic Launch Project, June 14, 1992, The Canadian Hydrographic
     Association, 02 Blue Box, 35 File Folder 11, pages 20–23, private collection of Ed
     Burtt.

2.   FAX from Ian Morgan of ROMOR Equipment, Mississauga, to Ed Burtt, Ocean
     Scan Systems, regarding the nature of the Speedy, July 15, 1993, 02 Blue Box, 35
     File Folder 11, page 15, private collection of Ed Burtt.

3.   Fralick, Rick, "'Speedy' Sunk by perfect storm of circumstances," *The Picton
     Gazette*, Wednesday, April 20, 2005, 02 Blue Box, 21 Loose Misc., pages 38-40,
     private collection of Ed Burtt.

4.   De Bry, John, "Identifying the Capitana Site off El Real, Ecuador," *Archaeological
     Report 1997*, http://www.treasurenet.com/forums/shipwrecks/66919-identifying-
     capitana-site-off-el-real-ecuador-1997-archaeological-report.html.

5.   Walter Zacharchuk was born in Poland, soon after his parents escaped
     persecution in the Soviet Union. As a youngster, he was forced to work in a Nazi
     labour camp before liberation in 1945. By chance, young Walter encountered
     some military frogmen emerging from the Mediterranean, and he was hooked on
     diving for life. His family soon moved to Montreal, where Walter could not afford
     diving gear, so he developed his own. Parks Canada would offer him a job in
     1964 and, from 1969 to 1972, he would focus on the wreck of the French frigate
     Machault in the Restigouche River, in the Gulf of St. Lawrence. This project would
     put Parks Canada on the map in the marine archaeology community. (Watson,
     Paul, *Ice Ghosts, The Epic Hunt for the Lost Franklin Expedition*, page 2.)

6.   Watson, pages 255–56.

7.   Shaughnessy, Carol, "Atocha's 'A Team', Consultants Agree to Help,"
     http://atochastory.com/AtochasATeam.htm. (Note: This article is no longer
     available through this link but can be accessed on the author's website at
     www.danbuchananhistoryguy.com/Books/Speedy.)

8.   Shaughnessy, Atocha's 'A Team.'

9.   Baldwin, Derek, "Spoil of Havana harbour await new explorers," *The Toronto
     Star*, February 27, 1998, 02 Blue Box, 21 Loose Misc., page 12, private collection
     of Ed Burtt.

10. Baldwin, "Spoil of Havana harbour."

11. Malette, Chris, "Salvage Operator hopes to find riches in Cuba," *The Belleville
     Intelligencer*, March 3, 1998, 02 Blue Box, 21 Loose Misc., page 14, private
     collection of Ed Burtt.

12. Bourette, Susan, "Castro's gold rush," *The Globe and Mail*, Silicon Investor,
     Wednesday, November 10, 1999, blog entry from T A P, VGLD News
     Article, Silicon Investor blog, https://www.siliconinvestor.com/readmsgs.
     aspx?subjectid = 30288&msgnum = 3&batchsize = 10&batchtype = Next.

13. Bourette, "Castro's gold rush."

14. Email from Doug Lewis to Dan Buchanan, June 29, 2019.

15. Timmins, Matt, "Drawing treasure from the deep," *The Pioneer*, November 25, 2006, private collection of Ed Burtt.

16. Timmins, "Drawing treasure from the deep."

17. Letter from Mrs. Roshan D. Jussawalla, Archaeological Licence Administrator, Ministry of Culture, Tourism and Recreation to Ed Burtt, H.M.S. Speedy Foundation, regarding 1995 licence and plans to catch up on reports, March 14, 1995, 02 Blue Box, 20 Licences and Forms, page 3, private collection of Ed Burtt.

18. Burtt, E.V., Project Technical Director. *HMS Speedy Project Report 1997*, March 24, 2005, Front Cover, page 1 of 120, 02 Blue Box, 17 Project Report 1997, private collection of Ed Burtt.

19. Burtt, Report 1997, page 23 of 120.

20. The Sophiasburgh Triangle is a geological phenomenon that is caused by iron deposits under the ground. There is a roughly triangular area underlying most of Prince Edward County that causes compass readings to swing wildly and changes radar readings spontaneously. Ed Burtt experienced the effect first-hand during survey work on Dobbs Bank and projected that effect onto the situation Captain Paxton faced with the *Speedy* in 1804. (Burtt, Ed, Project Report 1997, page 9 of 120, private collection of Ed Burtt.)

21. Burtt, Report 1997, page 9 of 120.

22. Isaac Maitland Wellington (1821–1897), genealogy website of Dan Buchanan, http://www.treesbydan.com.

23. Wellington, Isaac M. *The Tobey Book*, Chapter II, "1801–1810," page 41.

24. Burtt, E.V., Project Technical Director. *HMS Speedy Project Report 1997*, March 24, 2005, Front Cover, page 9 of 120, 02 Blue Box, 17 Project Report 1997, private collection of Ed Burtt.

25. Burtt, Report 1997, page 10 of 120.

26. Burtt, Report 1997, page 44 of 120.

27. Burtt, Report 1997, page 29 of 120.

28. Burtt, Report 1997, pages 35–37 of 120.

29. Burtt, Report 1997, page 61 of 120.

30. Burtt, Report 1997, page 84 of 120.

31. Burtt, Report 1997, page 33 of 120.

32. Burtt, Report 1997, page 10 of 120.

33. Letter from William H.P. Procter, Solicitor for the H.M.S. Speedy Foundation to Tom Mates, Park Superintendent, Presqu'ile Provincial Park, warning of search for other museums to use for *Speedy* project, June 3, 2004, 02 Blue Box, 23 Blue Folder, page 1, private collection of Ed Burtt.

34. Letter from Elizabeth Hunter, Manager of Museums, The Corporation of the County of Prince Edward, Community Services, to H.M.S. Speedy Foundation, regarding supporting the *Speedy* project, February 18, 2004, *HMS Speedy Project Report – 1997*, page 120, private collection of Ed Burtt.

35. Kuglin, Ernst, "Marine Heritage Museum proposed to house artifacts from HMS Speedy," *The Brighton Independent*, November 17, 1998, 02 Blue Box, 28 File Folder 04, pages 1–3, private collection of Ed Burtt.

36. Email from Michael Johnson of the Ministry of Culture, Ontario, to Ed Burtt regarding the policy of his ministry for the handling of marine artifacts, Friday, April 8, 2005, 02 Blue Box, 30 Folder 06, page 6, private collection of Ed Burtt.

37. Email from Clifford Cook, Senior Conservator with Canadian Conservation Society, to Phil Spencer, with comments and recommendations regarding finding a home for artifacts, October, 2012, copy provided by Phil Spencer.

38. Evans, Jack, "Belleville man excited that wreck could be Speedy," *Belleville Intelligencer*, August 23, 2004, 02 Blue Box, 05 Green Binder, 01 Ed with Cannonball Intelligencer 2004 08 23, page 1, *Ed Burtt, Collection*.

39. Letter from William P.H. Procter, barrister and solicitor for H.M.S. Speedy Foundation, to Michael Johnson, Ministry of Culture, regarding accusations of removal of items from *Speedy* site, February 25, 2006, 02 Blue Box, 21 Loose Misc., page 25, private collection of Ed Burtt.

40. Strobel, Mike, "This ship changed history," *The Toronto Sun*, Thursday, October 7, 2004, 02 Blue Box, 23 Blue Folder, page 8, private collection of Ed Burtt.

41. "Notice of Change," Ministry of Government Services, H.M.S. Speedy Foundation, 02 Blue Box, 24 Speedy Foundation, page 7, private collection of Ed Burtt.

42. "Notice of Change."

43. Picture of Ed Burtt and Dan Buchanan at the PROBUS Club of Brighton, March 13, 2014, sent to the author via email by program director of PROBUS Club.

44. "Speedy Storyboard," Lighthouse Interpretive Centre, Presqu'ile Provincial Park, in the author's collection. Content for the storyboard was produced by the author, and the physical board was constructed by Phil Spencer, who also did the installation, assisted by the author.

45. "The Loss of the Speedy," Historical Plaque, Presqu'ile Point, Ontario's Historical Plaques, http://ontarioplaques.com/Plaques/Plaque_Northumberland16.html.

46. "Obituary of Ed Burtt," *The Intelligencer*, https://intelligencer.remembering.ca/obituary/edward-ed-vernon-burtt-1074701377.

BIBLIOGRAPHY

Arculus, Paul. *Steamboats on Scugog*, Observer Publishing of Port Perry and the Port Perry Star Co., Limited. Port Perry, Ont. 2000.

Askin, John. *The John Askin Papers*. Edited by Milo M. Quaife, Secretary-Editor, The Burton Historical Collection. Published by the Detroit Library Commission. 1931. Downloaded PDF from the Southwestern Ontario Digital Archive, University of Windsor. https://archive.org/details/JohnAskinPapersVolume2/page/n4.

Berchem, F.R. *The Yonge Street Story 1793-1860: An Account from Letters, Diaries and Newspapers*. Natural Heritage Inc. Toronto. 1977. Kindle Edition from Amazon.ca.

British Military and Naval Records. Archives of Canada. RG.8, C Series. http://www. bac-lac.gc.ca/eng/discover/mass-digitized-archives/british-military-naval-records-documents/Pages/british-military-naval-records-documents.aspx.

Buchanan, Dan. *38 Hours to Montreal: William Weller and the Governor General's Race of 1840*. Published by Author. Produced by FriesenPress, Victoria, BC, 2018.

Butts, Edward. *Line of Fire: Heroism, Tragedy, and Canada's Police*. Dundurn Press. Toronto. 2009. Transcribed from Google Books Preview.

Canadian County Atlas Digital Project. https://digital.library.mcgill.ca/countyatlas/search.htm.

Canniff, William. *History of the Settlement of Upper Canada, (Ontario), with special Reference to the Bay of Quinte*. Dudley & Burns, Printers, Victoria Hall, Toronto. 1869. Downloaded from https://archive.org/details/historyofsettlem00cann/page/n6.

Combs, General Leslie. *General Leslie Combs: Incidents in the Early History of the Northwestern Territory*. Printed by J.T. and Lem Towers. Washington. 1855. Library of Congress. Downloaded PDF from https://archive.org/stream/narrativeoflifeo02wash#page/n4/mode/2up.

Dictionary of Canadian Biography. http://www.biographi.ca/en/.

Digital Kingston. Kingston Frontenac Public Library. https://www.digitalkingston.ca/.

Fairbairn, M. Jane. *Along the Shore: Rediscovering Toronto's Waterfront Heritage*. ECW Press. 2013. Kindle. Amazon Digital Services LLC.

Firth, Edith G. (Editor). *The Town of York 1793-1815: A Collection of Documents of Early Toronto*. The Champlain Society for the Government of Ontario, University of Toronto Press. Toronto. 1962. PDF purchased and downloaded from UTP.

Gilmore, James. *The St. Lawrence River Canals Vessel*, "The Canals." Maritime History of the Great Lakes. http://www.maritimehistoryofthegreatlakes.ca/Documents/gilmore/default.asp?ID = s003.

Guillet, Edwin C. *Cobourg 1797-1948*. Goodfellow Printing Company Limited, Oshawa. 1948.

Guillet, Edwin C. *Early Life in Upper Canada*. University of Toronto Press. Toronto. 1933.

Hamilton, James Cleland. *Osgoode Hall Reminiscences of the Bench and Bar*. The Carswell Company, Limited. Toronto. 1904. Downloaded from https://archive.org/details/osgoodehallremin00hami/page/n8.

Hunter, Peter. *Peter Hunter Papers, Copies of the civil and military letterbooks of Upper Canada, 1799-1805.* Library and Archives Canada. (M.G. 24, A 6, C-4581, 98646). Heritage Canadiana website http://heritage.canadiana.ca/view/oocihm.lac_reel_c4581/189?r = 0&s = 4.

Hvidsten, J. Peter. *Scugog Exposed.* Observer Publishing. Port Perry. 2004. Downloaded from https://scugogheritage.com/online_pdfs/exposed.pdf.

Jones, Rev. Peter. *History of the Ojebway Indians*, A.W. Bennett, London. 1861. Downloaded from https://archive.org/details/historyofojebway00jone/page/n8.

Jones, Rev. Peter. *Life and Journals of KAH-KE-WA-QUO-NA-BY (Rev. Peter Jones), Wesleyan Missionary.* Published under the direction of the Missionary Committee, Canada Conference. Published by Anson Green at the Wesleyan Printing Establishment, King Street East, Toronto. Toronto. 1860. Downloaded from https://archive.org/details/lifejournalsofke00jone/page/n7.

Journals of the Legislative Assembly of Upper Canada, Volume Two, Archives of Ontario, 1911, Microfilm B97, Reel 124, 1805–1808, 1810, 1811.

Kaiser, T.E. *Historic Sketches of Oshawa.* The Reformer Printing and Publishing Co. Ltd. Oshawa. 1921. Downloaded from http://localhistory.oshawalibrary.ca/pdfportal/pdfskins/kaiser/kaiser.pdf.

Karcich, Grant. *The Legacy of Vanished Trails.* Self-published by author. Printed by Red Handprint Publishing. 2017.

Karcich, Grant. *Scugog Carrying Place: A Frontier Pathway.* Dundurn Press. Toronto. 2013.

Langley, John G. *Canadian Confederate Cruiser.* Nimbus Publishing. Halifax. 2018.

Merz, John. "The Sinking of the Speedy," *The Hessians,* 2005, http://freepages.rootsweb.com/ ~ amrevhessians/military/speedy.htm.

Miller, J.R. *Skyscrapers Hide the Heavens: A History of Native-Newcomer Relations in Canada.* Fourth Edition, University of Toronto Press. Toronto. 2018.

Mohr, Tom. "Was Duffin Really Up the Creek?" *Pathmaster*, Autumn Edition. Pickering Township Historical Society. Pickering. 2014.

O'Brien, Brendan. *Speedy Justice: The Tragic Last Voyage of His Majesty's Vessel Speedy.* Dundurn Press. Toronto, 1992.

The Parish Register of Kingston, Upper Canada, 1785–1811, Published by The British Whig Publishing Company Limited, Kingston, 1921. Part 1: (http://my.tbaytel.net/bmartin/kingstn1.htm), Part 2 (http://my.tbaytel.net/bmartin/kingstn2.htm).

Pedlar, Samuel. "Samuel Pedlar Manuscript." Oshawa Public Library. Compilation of Samuel Pedlars Oshawa area history research collection. Downloaded from http://images.ourontario.ca/Partners/oshawa/OshPL0035787871T.PDF.

Pringle, J.F. *Lunenburg or the Old Eastern District.* Standard Printing House, Cornwall. 1890. Downloaded from https://archive.org/details/cihm_12272/page/n5.

Robertson, J. Ross. *Landmarks of Toronto*, Volume 1. *Toronto Evening Telegram.* Toronto. 1894. Downloaded from https://archive.org/details/landmarkstoronto01robeuoft/page/n10.

Robertson, J. Ross. *Landmarks of Toronto*, Volume 2. *Toronto Evening Telegram*. Toronto. 1896. Downloaded from https://ia800301.us.archive.org/30/items/ landmarkstoronto02robeuoft/landmarkstoronto02robeuoft.pdf.

Robertson, J. Ross. *Landmarks of Toronto*, Volume 3. *Toronto Evening Telegram*. Toronto. 1898. Downloaded from https://archive.org/details/landmarkstoronto03robeuoft/page/n6.

Robertson, J. Ross. *Landmarks of Toronto*, Volume 4. *Toronto Evening Telegram*. Toronto. 1904. Downloaded from https://archive.org/details/landmarkstoronto04robeuoft/page/n4.

Robertson, J. Ross. *Landmarks of Toronto*, Volume 5. *Toronto Evening Telegram*. Toronto. 1908. Downloaded from https://archive.org/details/landmarkstoronto05robeuoft/page/n6.

Robertson, J. Ross. *Landmarks of Toronto*, Volume 6. *Toronto Evening Telegram*. Toronto. 1914. Downloaded from https://archive.org/details/landmarkstoronto06robeuoft/page/n8.

Russell, Peter. *The Correspondence of the Honourable Peter Russell (The Russell Papers)*. Published by Ontario Historical Society. Toronto. 1932. Ref. 971.03 Rus V.1, V.2, V.3. Bracebridge Public Library, through interlibrary loan to Brighton Public Library.

Scadding, Dr. Henry. *Toronto of Old: Collections and Recollections*. Adam, Stevenson & Co. Toronto. 1873. Project Gutenberg. 2011. E-book #35225.

Schmalz, Peter S. *The Ojibwa of Southern Ontario*. University of Toronto Press. Toronto. 1991.

Seguin, Marc. *For Want of a Lighthouse*. Trafford Publishing. Bloomington, IN. 2015.

Simcoe, Mrs. John Graves. *The Diary of Mrs. John Graves Simcoe*. William Briggs. Toronto. 1911. Downloaded from https://archive.org/details/diaryofmrsjohngr00simcuoft/page/n12.

Smith, Donald B. *Sacred Feathers: The Reverend Peter Jones (Kahkewaquonaby) and the Mississauga Indians,* Second Edition. University of Toronto Press, Scholarly Publishing Division. Toronto. 2013. Kindle.

Surtees, R. *Indian Land Surrenders in Ontario 1763-1867*, Canadian and Northern Affairs Canada, Research Branch, Corporate Policy. Ottawa. February 1984. Downloaded from http://publications.gc.ca/collections/collection_2017/aanc-inac/R5-350-1983-eng.pdf.

Tobey, Wilmot Maxwell. *The Tobey Book*. Brighton Public Library. Brighton. PDF Version. Mr. Tobey's collection was edited and compiled into book form by Wilfred M. Sprung and Barbara Nyland in 1975. The book was digitized by Dan Buchanan in 2004, and PDF copies produced.

Tobin, Brian. *The Upper Canada Gazette and Its Printers*, Ontario Legislative Library, Toronto, 1993. http://www.ontla.on.ca/library/repository/mon/27002/159217.pdf.

TreesByDan. Genealogy website by Dan Buchanan, containing massive database of interconnected family trees. http://www.treesbydan.com.

Upper Canada Gazette, Legislative Library of Ontario, Toronto. Preston Microfilming Services Ltd. (1986). (Call number: FLM UPCG). Microfilm obtained by Brighton Public Library through interlibrary loan.

Villemaire, Tom. "Local History: Long road, long history." *Orillia Packet and Times*. August 19, 2016.
https://www.simcoe.com/living-story/8479759-local-history-long-road-long-history/.

Walker, Glenn. *The Changing Face of the Kawarthas: Land Use and Environment in Nineteenth Century Ontario.* A thesis submitted to McGill University in partial fulfillment of the degree of Doctor of Philosophy, 2012, downloaded from http://www.maryboro.ca/ChangingFaceKawarthas.pdf.

Watson, Paul. *Ice Ghosts: The Epic Hunt for the Lost Franklin Expedition*, McClelland & Stewart, 2017, Chronology, 1964 – Walter Zacharchuk, page 2, Kindle e-book.

Weld, Isaac. *Travels Through the States of North America, and the Provinces of Upper and Lower Canada, during the years 1795, 1796, and 1797,* Fourth Edition. Printed for John Stockdale, Piccadilly, London. London. 1807.
Downloaded from https://archive.org/details/travelsthroughst01weld/page/n8.

ILLUSTRATION CREDITS

Page xii   **Map of *Speedy* Places 1804:** Base sketch from the private collection of Ed Burtt, modified by the author.

Page 22   **York Harbour 1802:** Drawn by William Chewett. Plan of 916¼ acres, in the Township of York in Upper Canada; the property of the Honourable D.W. Smith Esquire, Surveyor General. *Historical Maps of Toronto.* (http://oldtorontomaps.blogspot.com/2013/02/1802-chewett-plan-of-916-14-acres-in.html)

Page 23   **York Shore 1803:** Toronto, in 1803, looking east along Front St. E. from northeast corner Jarvis St. by Owen Staples (1866–1949), 1909, Toronto Public Library. (https://www.torontopubliclibrary.ca/detail. jsp?Entt = RDMDC-JRR310&R = DC-JRR310)

Page 27   **Map of York 1813:** *Historical Maps of Toronto*, sketch of the ground in advance of and including York Upper Canada, by Geo. Williams, 1813. Image courtesy Library and Archives Canada: NMC 22819. Winearls, MUC no. 2035. (http://oldtorontomaps.blogspot.com/2013/01/1813-williams-sketch-of-ground-in.html)

Page 29   **Parliament House:** First Parliament House 1797–1813, *Landmarks of Toronto*, R. Ross Robertson, Volume 1, Chapter CXIV, "Houses of Parliament," page 351.

Page 50   **Allcock Note to Self:** Archives of Ontario, Microfilm Collection, RG1, E3, Reel C-1203, Part 100, page 182.

Page 56   **Survey Notes:** Archives of Ontario, Microfilm Collection, MS 924, Box 15, page 128

Page 58   **Survey Map:** Plan for John Stegmann's Survey of Border of Home/Newcastle Districts in 1804. Digital copy provided by Paul Arculus, President, Lake Scugog Historical Society, Port Perry, Ontario.

Page 89   **Presqu'ile Bay Entrance:** Lake Ontario, western part of the Bay of Quinte and Presqu'ile Bay, Deseronto to Presqu'ile (snipped to show only Presqu'ile Bay), Library and Archives of Canada, Cartographic Material, Survey of W.P. Anderson, 1893, Ref.: R11630-2427-2-E.

Page 102   ***Speedy* by Snider:** Snider Fonds F 1194, Archives of Ontario

Page 123   **Loss of the *Speedy*:** Robertson, J. Ross, *Landmarks of Toronto*, Volume 6, Toronto, 1914, Chapter XXXIV, "Gazettes of Upper Canada," Vol. XIV, The Oracle, Saturday, November 3, 1804, No. 28 Total No. 704, Loss of the Speedy, page 318.

Page 154   **Piece of Eight:** Pictures of the coin provided to the author by Ed Burtt's friend Kirsten Musclow of Belleville.

Page 155   **Clay Pipe and Spectacles:** Private collection of Ed Burtt.

Page 156   **Glen Rover:** Private collection of Ed Burtt.

Page 157   **Ed with Sea Otter:** Private collection of Ed Burtt.

Page 159   **Cannonball:** Private collection of Ed Burtt.

Page 162 **The Masts:** Private collection of Ed Burtt.

Page 163 **The Chest:** Private collection of Ed Burtt.

Page 169 *Explorad'oro*: Private collection of Ed Burtt.

Page 171 **Route of *Speedy*:** Private collection of Ed Burtt.

Page 175 *Speedy* **Historical Plaque:** By the author.

Page 215 *Statutes of Upper Canada*: Downloaded from HathiTrust (https://babel. hathitrust.org/cgi/pt?id = aeu.ark:/13960/t42r4wr64&view = 1up&seq = 197).

INDEX

A

abolitionists, 62
Allcock, Chief Justice Henry, 32-36, 40, 43, 44, 48-50, 54, 55, 57, 61, 65, 134
American, 26, 29, 30, 31, 33, 35, 48, 72, 75, 81, 122, 124, 125, 131, 143
Amherst, Upper Canada, 138
Amherstburg, 72, 78, 131
anchor, 100, 159, 172, 187, 188
Anderson, John, 44, 62, 98
Anderson, W.P., 89
Annis, Charles, 4, 10-13
Annis, Sarah (wife of Charles), 4,
Annis Creek, 4, 8, 9, 11-13, 17, 18, 108, 137, 145
archives, 27, 29, 167
Archives of Canada. *See* Library and Archives Canada
Archives of Ontario, 49, 56, 57
Arculus, Paul, 57
Ashbridge's Bay, 22
Askin, John, 120
assizes, 61, 64, 70, 87, 88, 116
Atocha, 154, 168, 192
Avon, 156
Avro Arrow models, 165, 190, 192, 193

B

Baagwating Community Association, 148
Bahamas, 170, 193
Baird, Nicol Hugh, 147
Baker, Dorine, 63
Baker, John, 47, 63, 103, 137
Baker, Simon, 63, 98, 106, 137
Baldwin, Alice, 81
Baldwin, Mary Warren, 81
Baldwin, Robert, 81, 82

Balmy Beach, 22
Balsam Lake, 147, 148
Barrie St., Kingston, 128
bateau, 36, 38, 94, 96
Bay of Quinte, 19
Bay Street, Toronto, 27
Beach, The, 22
Beaches, The, 21
Belden County Atlas, 22
Belize, 45
    see also British Honduras
Belleville, 154, 170, 174, 187, 192, 193
Belleville General Hospital, 175
Belleville Intelligencer, 169, 174
Bennett, John, 96, 122-125
Bermuda, 141
binnacle, 103, 105, 106, 109, 112, 118, 177
Black Watch, 43
Blackburn Shark, 165, 190
Blackstock, 12
blockhouse, 24, 28, 30, 36
blossom moon, 18
blue flag, 93, 94, 104
Boards of Survey, 73
Boston, 83, 161
Bouchette, Jean-Baptiste, 75, 76
Brant, Joseph, 19
brass buttons, 105, 161, 188, 189
Breckenridge, Maria, 81, 82
Brighton, 115, 139, 172, 174, 175, 193
Brighton Independent, 189, 191
British, 7, 19, 25, 29, 32, 35, 44, 51, 73, 83, 84, 87, 97, 125, 134, 143. 144, 162, 192
British Army, 4, 31, 71, 73, 124
British common law, 62

British Empire, 62
British government, 83
British gunboats, 19, 71, 87, 162, 167
British Honduras, 45
    see also Belize
British Military and Naval Records, 31, 72, 181
British Navy, 70, 71, 73, 74, 105, 107
British North American colonies, 70
British regulars, 33, 125, 131, 143
British Virgin Islands, 170, 193
Brock, Lt.-Col. Isaac, 72, 140
Buchanan, Dan (the author), 174, 175, 193
Burgoyne, General, 31
Burlington, 143
Burlington Bay, 65
Burnham, Asa, 138
Burnham Street, Cobourg, 138
Burtt, Ed, 153-175, 177-179, 185-193

C

Caesarea, 10, 12
Cameron, John, (merchant), 135
Cameron, John (ship's mate), 99, 128
Canadian Coast Guard, 186
Canadian Constellation, 46, 88
cannon, 19, 140, 161, 188
cannonball, 159, 161, 172, 174, 186, 188, 192
Caribbean, 45, 125, 192
cariole, 44
Carleton, Guy, 75
    see also Lord Dorchester
Carlton, New York, 118
Caroline, Princess of Wales, 26, 27
    see also Queen Caroline
Caroline Street, York, 27, 38
Cartwright Township, 138
Cassavoy, Ken, 155, 156, 159, 160, 185, 186-188
Cataraqui, 85, 128
Chemong Lake (Mud Lake), 147
chest, 96, 163, 164, 172
Chewett, William, 22, 54, 64

Chief Justice of Upper Canada, 32-34, 36, 43, 48-50, 53, 54, 59, 61, 64, 65, 120, 134, 136
Chippewa, 66
Church Street, 39
City Park, Kingston, 128
Clarington, 12
Clarke Township, 6, 81
Claus, Sup. William, 34, 35
Clay, General, 131
clay pipe, 155, 160, 161, 172, 188
CN Tower, 21
Cobourg, 138
Cochran, Justice Thomas, 61, 62, 97, 98, 119, 120, 141
Coldwater, 147
Collins, John, 25
colonies, 21, 32, 44-46, 70, 73, 75, 133, 134, 141,
Connecticut, 35, 87
Cook, Louis E., 161
Coombs, Leslie, 131
Coons, Terry, 157, 158, 161, 163-165, 187, 193
Cooper, William, 39
Cornwall, 43, 44, 51, 62, 141
Court of King's Bench, 61, 133
Court of Probate, 137
Cowan, George, 65, 66, 94, 95, 96, 106, 107
Cozens, Daniel, 81
Cozens, Samuel D., 6, 81-83
Craigie, John, 122, 128, 130
Cramahe Township, 114
Crane, Chief Jacob, 147, 148
Credit River, 18, 80
Crown Land Office, 18, 41

D

Danforth Road, 17, 20, 107
Darlington Township, 12, 57, 144
dead eye, 161, 162, 188, 189
Dean, Levine (wife of John Fist), 64
Dean's Creek, 110

debris field, 157, 159, 160-162, 164, 165, 170, 171, 173, 174, 178, 188
Deserontyon, Chief John, 19
Detroit, 34, 35, 120
Detroit River, 78
Devil's horse block, 171, 172, 191
Devil's Nose, 88, 124
divers, 186, 187, 189
Dobbs Bank, 153, 154, 164, 165, 170-172, 174, 178, 179, 185, 186
Don River, 22
drag marks, 172
Duchess of York, 87, 88
duel, 135, 136
Duffin, William, 18
Duffin's Creek, 18
Duke of Cambridge, 26
Duke of Clarence, 26
Duke of Kent, 26, 45
Duke of Kent, 20
Duke of Portland, 74
Duke of La Rochefoucauld, 71
Duke of Sussex, 26
Duke of York, 26
Durham County, 135
Durham Region, 149

E

Earle (or Earl), Lt. Hugh, 72, 75, 134
East Riding of York, 135
Eastern District, 43
Ecuador, 168, 191
Edwards, Capt. D. W., 76
Elegy, 141
Elgin Street, Cobourg, 138
Elmsley, Chief Justice, 136
Elmsley Township, 52, 53
emancipation, 62
England, 21, 28, 31, 44-46, 48, 50, 54, 61, 62, 118, 120, 121, 133, 134, 140, 143, 172
English, 11, 13, 15, 23, 37, 48, 66, 85, 95, 108, 134, 135, 141, 143, 153, 154
English farmers, 144
English settlers, 14, 15

English soldiers, 38
English traders, 66, 83, 84
Englishman, 13, 44
Etobicoke Township, 41
European immigrants, 11, 33
executive council, 30, 46, 47, 53, 140
Explorad'oro, 169

F

Farewell brothers, 4, 7, 8, 9, 11, 12, 54, 84, 85
Farewell, Elizabeth (wife of Moody), 4,
Farewell, Moody, 3-7, 10-13, 16-20, 22, 23, 28, 30-32, 35-38, 40, 41, 53, 54, 59, 80, 108-110, 114, 115, 116, 137, 143, 177
Farewell trading post, 55, 57-59, 85
Farewell, William, 5, 6, 11-13
Fighting Island, 78
Fishers, JW. *See* JW Fishers
Fisher, Mel, 154, 157, 168, 192
fishing weirs, 18, 145
Fisk, John, 33-40, 64, 65, 79, 94-97
Florida, 154, 157, 192
Forman, Norm, 193
Fort Frontenac, 25
Fort George, 71, 72, 117, 118, 177
Fort Haldimand, 125
Fort Niagara, 18, 45, 46, 125
Fort Pitt, 65, 84
Fortie, Lt., 75
Forty-first Regiment, 69
Forty-ninth Regiment, 23, 69, 79, 95
Frederick Street, York, 27, 39
French, 20, 25, 48, 65, 81, 83
Frenchman's Bay, 20
Frenchtown, Battle of, 131
Frenchtown, Michigan, 131
fur trade, 4, 7, 10, 25, 35, 65, 85, 137

G

Gages Creek, 110
Ganaraska, 14
Garrison, York, 36, 40, 44, 69, 70, 79, 94, 95, 96, 103. 104, 135
Genesee River, 125

George III, King, 26
George IV, King, 27
George Street, York, 27, 39
Georgian Bay, 65, 80
Gerrard, the Boatswain, 99, 103, 119
Gibraltar Point, 23, 33, 34, 36, 44, 48, 79, 80, 95, 108
Gibson, Elizabeth. *See* Elizabeth Selleck
Gibson, George, 87, 88, 90, 111-116, 139
Gibson, Joseph, 112, 113, 115
Givins, Col. James, 34-38, 40
Givins Homestead, 35
Glen Rover, 156
Globe and Mail, The, 191, 192
Golden Plough Lodge, Cobourg, 138
Gore, Sir Francis, 141
Gosport, 173, 191
GPS, 158, 171
Grafton, 114
Grand Isle, Vermont, 35
Grand River, 19
Grant, Alexander, 140, 141
Grass, Michael, 128
Gray, James, 43, 44
Gray, Solicitor General Robert Dey, 43, 44, 47, 62, 63, 98, 99, 106, 120, 135-137, 141
Great Blue Heron Casino, 148
Great Britain, 143
Great Lakes, 70, 74, 83, 84, 113, 162, 167
Green, Lt. Col. James, 30-32, 62, 69, 70, 71, 73, 76, 78, 80, 102, 112
green sward, 29, 38, 70, 80
grid layout, 158, 159, 186

H

Haldimand Township, 138
Halifax, 45, 55, 61
Halifax currency, 55
Hamilton, Robert, 120
Hamilton Township, 138
Harmony Creek, 9, 12
Harrison, General, 131
Hastings County, 136, 144
Havana harbour, 168
Henry, John, Sr., 145
Henry, John, Jr., 145

Herkimer, Jacob, 4, 84, 99, 120, 137
Herkimer, John Jost, 85
Herkimer, Lawrence, 4, 84, 137
Herkimer, Margaret (wife of Jacob), 137
Hessian(s), 51, 107
High Bluff Island, 114
High Constable of Home District, 33-35, 64, 65, 77, 79
Highland Creek, 20
Highlander, 43
Hinkson, Daniel, 145
His Majesty's Armed Vessels, 19, 70, 129
His Majesty's Forces, 31, 45, 46, 140
His Majesty's Marine Department, 87
Historic Sketches of Oshawa, 81
historical plaque, 175
HMS *Ontario,* 125
HMS *Speedy,* 19, 46, 70-73, 75-78, 88, 90, 93, 96, 97-119, 122, 125, 133-136, 138, 139, 141, 143, 149, 154, 155, 159, 160, 164-167, 169-172, 174, 175, 177-179, 186-193
HMS *Speedy* Project, 155, 156, 160, 164, 165, 167, 168, 174, 185, 186, 188, 189
HMS Speedy Project Report, 159, 170, 172, 178, 188-192
H.M.S. Speedy Foundation, 156, 157, 174, 175, 186, 187, 192, 193
HMS *Swift,* 19, 71, 76, 121
Home District, 33, 34, 39-51, 53, 54, 57-59, 64, 79, 99, 144
Home District Jail, 38-41, 44, 48, 95
House of Assembly, 43, 44, 64, 69, 133, 135, 136
Humber River, 18
Hunter, Lt-Gov. Peter, 20, 30-33, 35, 43, 44-49, 53, 55, 63, 66, 69-73, 76-78, 93, 94, 97, 102, 104, 117, 121, 122, 124, 128, 133-136, 139-141

I

inconvenient, 138
Indian Department, 34, 35, 133
Ireland, 18, 35
Irish Rebellion of 1798, 45
Iroquois, 25

J

Jones, Augustus, 18, 143
Jones, Rev. Peter, 143, 144
JW Fishers, 157, 190

K

Kaiser, T.E., 81, 82
Karcich, Grant, 17
Keeler's Creek, 114
King, John, 46
King Street, Cobourg, 138
King Street, York, 26, 34, 38, 39, 40, 41,
    95
King Township, 35, 64
Kingston, 3, 17, 19, 20, 31, 44, 71-74, 76,
    90, 93, 94, 99, 104, 106, 112, 117, 119,
    121, 127-130, 134, 167, 169
Kingston Chronicle, 130
Kingston Gazette, 130, 141
Kingston Road, 20, 139
Kirkland Lake, 154, 192
Knott, William, 39, 40, 79, 80, 94

L

La Capitana, 168, 191
Labard, Francis, 119, 128
Lady Murray, 88, 90, 115, 116
Lady Washington, 124
Lake Beobescugog, 57
Lake Erie, 131
Lake Ontario, 3, 4, 9, 10, 13, 16-20, 26,
    62, 70, 73, 77, 88, 93, 99, 102, 104,
    105, 107, 118, 125, 134, 139, 153, 154,
    157, 165, 169, 175, 177, 178
Lake Scugog, 3-5, 8, 9, 13, 16, 37, 49, 84,
    85, 138, 143, 144-146, 147, 148, 182,
    183, 138, 143-147
Lake Simcoe, 144, 147
Lakeport, 114
LaMagnifique, 161
Lanark County, 52
landing place, 24, 29, 30, 36, 38, 93, 94,
    96, 98, 99, 137
Landmarks of Toronto, 28
Legislative Assembly of Upper Canada,
    69, 138
Lewis, Doug, 192

Library and Archives Canada, 31, 72, 129
Lieutenant-governor of Upper Canada,
    45, 129, 136, 140
lighthouse, 89, 90
Lighthouse Interpretive Centre, 173, 175
Lindsay, 145, 146
Lockwood, Eleazer, 12, 13, 16-20, 22, 28,
    30-32, 35-38, 40, 41, 80, 108, 109, 114-
    116, 143, 177
LORAN, 188
Lord Camden, 133, 134
Lord Dorchester, 31, 75
London, England, 33, 46, 49, 50, 133, 134
London, Upper Canada, 26
Lot Street, York, 137
Lower Canada, 31, 44-47, 97, 122, 134
Loyalist, 34, 81, 85, 136
Lynde Creek, 18

M

MacDonald, Gary, 187
Macdonell, Alexander, 44, 64
Macdonell, Angus, 64, 80, 98, 135, 137
marine archaeologist, 155, 159-161, 168,
    178, 185, 191, 192
marine archaeology, 173, 185, 192
Mariners Park Museum, 154, 173
Markham Township, 65
Massachusetts, 34, 65, 161
mast(s), 19, 71, 96, 105, 107, 118, 158,
    161, 162, 172, 187, 188
Matchedash, 65, 107
Mexico, 154
McGill, John, 48
McQuest Marine, 189
Michilimackinac, 65
Middle Ground shoals, 89
Miller, J.R., 83
Minnie Slausson, 158, 165, 187, 190
Minorca, 45, 139
Mississauga camp(s), 6, 8, 17, 20, 36, 79
Mississauga people, 7, 9, 10, 11, 13-20,
    23, 32-35, 37, 38, 44, 48, 66, 79, 80-85,
    108, 143, 144-148, 183
Mississauga Point, Kingston, 130
Mississaugas of Scugog First Nation, 148
Mississippi Valley, 48

Mohawks, 18, 19, 48, 66
Moira River, 18
Monroe, Michigan, 131
Montreal, 4, 47, 99, 121, 131, 144
Morgan, Ian, 167
Muddy Little York, 18, 25, 28
Murney, Henry, 128
Murney Point, 128, 130
Murney Tower, 128
Murray Canal, 189, 190
Murray, Capt., 124
Musclow, Kirsten, 193

N
Napoleonic Wars, 70
nautical chart, 170, 171
New Jersey, 81
New Street, York, 27, 39
New World, 33
New York, 28, 107
Newark, 3, 26, 39, 74, 87, 88
Newcastle, 54, 55, 61, 62, 64, 65-67, 70,
    71, 76, 78, 87, 88, 90, 93, 94, 96, 97,
    98, 100, 103, 105, 107-111, 114-118, 127,
    135, 136, 138, 139, 171, 175, 177
Newcastle District, 49-51, 53, 54, 55, 57-
    59, 61, 97, 138, 139, 144
Newcastle District Courthouse and Jail,
    61, 64, 87, 88, 90, 91, 115, 138, 139,
    144
newcomers, 4, 11, 13, 14, 73, 144
Niagara District, 120
Niagara River, 3, 117, 124
nor'easter, 113, 114, 118, 125, 171, 172,
    177
North America, 51, 65
North West Company, 4,
Northumberland County, 136, 138
Nova Scotia, 34, 107

O
Oak Orchard Creek, 118
Ocean Scan Systems, 154, 156, 165, 168,
    191, 192
Ogetonicut, 6, 13, 15, 16, 32, 33, 34, 37,
    38, 40, 43, 44, 50, 61, 64, 70, 79, 80-82,
    85, 90, 94-96, 106-109, 142, 143, 149

Ojibwa, 15, 25, 35, 48, 66, 82, 84
Ontario Archaeological Report, 159
Ontario Heritage Foundation, 166, 190
Ontario Ministry of Culture and Commu-
    nications, 155, 160, 170, 173, 174, 178,
    186, 191, 192
Ontario Provincial Police (OPP), 153, 154
Ops Township, 145
Oracle, The, 123, 124, 136, 140
Orleans County, New York, 118
Oshawa, 3, 49, 137, 145
Oshawa Creek, 4
    see also Annis Creek
Osnabruck Township, 51
Oswego, New York, 124, 125
Our Lady of Assumption Cemetery,
    Windsor, 131

P
Parish Register of Kingston, 129
park lots, York, 137
Parliament House, 24, 29, 30, 31, 33-35,
    41, 43, 69, 76, 78, 94, 102, 104
Patriots, 51, 107
Paxton, Henry, 131
Paxton, Jane (wife of Lt. Thos. Paxton),
    119, 122, 127-131
Paxton, John, 131
Paxton, Lt. Thomas, 72-78, 88, 90, 93, 94,
    96-100, 102-106, 109, 111-115, 118, 119,
    121, 122, 127-130, 138, 139, 171, 177
Paxton, Thomas, Jr., 78, 130
Peak, William, 14, 15
Pedlar, Samuel, 145
Penetanguishene, 66
Perry's Corners, 18
Perthshire, Scotland, 45
Pickering Village, 20
piece of eight, 153, 154, 185
Pine Grove, 64
pinnacle rock, 172
Plains of Abraham, 83
Plymouth, Massachusetts, 161
Point Frederick, Kingston, 3, 19, 75, 76,
    128
Point Petre, 165
Port Hope, 4, 14, 110, 177

Port Perry, 57
Prescott, Robert, 73, 74, 75
Presqu'ile Bay, 88, 90, 105, 111-113, 115, 116, 139, 158, 171, 177, 187
Presqu'ile Point, 49, 61, 88-90, 112, 114, 115, 118, 139, 153, 154, 158, 170, 172, 173, 175, 177, 185, 189
Presqu'ile Point Lighthouse, 89, 90
Presqu'ile Provincial Park, 115, 173, 175
Prince Edward County, 118, 154, 165, 173
Prince Edward Island, 61
Princes Street, York, 26, 38
Princess Street, Toronto, 29
Printer to the King, 96
privilege, 134
PROBUS Club of Brighton, 175, 193
Procter, William P. H., 187
proton magnetometer, 187, 190
Provincial Marine, 70-75, 78, 88, 93, 97, 105, 119, 121-124, 128, 134, 161
Purdy, William, 145, 146, 147

Q

Quebec, 25, 31, 33, 35, 43, 45, 46, 47, 51, 75, 113
see also Lower Canada
Quebec City, 31, 45-47, 71, 74, 122, 139, 140
Queen Caroline, 27
Queen Street, Toronto, 35, 137
Queen's Park, Toronto, 57
Queen's Rangers, 35, 39, 40
Queenston, 120
Queenston Heights, 72

R

Raisin River, Michigan, 131
Rawdon Township, 144
Reach Township, 57
Reckoner, 141
Regional Road, 57, 12
Republican tendencies, 134
residential schools, 148
Rice Lake, 4
Rice Lake Treaty No. 20, 144
Ridout family, 27
Ridout, Thomas, 54, 64

Ritson Road North, Oshawa, 137
Robinson, John Beverley, 103
Rochester, New York, 88, 125
Rogers, David McGregor, 136
Ross, William, 117
Rouge River, 18, 20
Ruggles, James, 34, 65, 79, 94-97
Ruggles, Brig. Gen. Timothy, 34
Russell County, 43, 135
Russell, Peter, 46, 47, 63, 66, 74, 75, 85, 118

S

Sandwich, Upper Canada, 120
Salmon Creek, 18
Salt Point, 89, 90, 105, 112-114
Scadding, Henry, 26
Scarborough Bluffs, 21
Scarborough Highlands, 21, 105
Scarborough Township, 20, 21
schooner, 18, 24, 94, 103, 118, 124, 136
Schooner Days, 102
Scotch Bonnet, 189
Scotland, 65
Scott, Larry, 190
Scugog Carrying Place, 9-12
Scugog Island, 57, 58, 148
Scugog River, 3, 145, 146
Scugog Township, 149
Sea Otter ROV video camera, 157, 185-187, 190
Search Team News, 190
Secretary of State for War and the Colonies, 133
Selleck, Charles, 61, 87, 88, 90, 111-116, 138, 172
Selleck, Elizabeth (wife of Charles), 61, 87, 90, 91, 115, 172
SGO. See Surveyor General's Office
Sharp, John, 4-8, 10, 13, 15, 36, 37, 48, 49, 54, 57, 58, 81, 82, 109
shako, 95
Sherbourne Street, Toronto, 27, 29
Sherwood, Samuel, 53
ship's bell, 97, 100, 164
ship's hull, 77, 104, 105, 156, 164, 165, 167, 172, 188, 190

side scan sonar, 172, 189
Simcoe County, 135
Simcoe, Lt.-Gov. John Graves, 21, 26, 35, 40, 43, 44, 46, 62, 65
Simcoe, Lady, 21
Simcoe Street North, Oshawa, 137
'60s Scoop, 148
Slave Trade Act (1807), 62
slaves, 62, 63
Smith, David William, 48, 121
Smith's Creek, 4, 110, 114
Smoking Circle, 11
Snider, C.H.J., 102
Solicitor General of Upper Canada, 43, 44, 77, 80, 96, 133, 136
Somerset decision, 62
Sophiasburgh Triangle, 171, 191
spectacles, 155, 160, 161, 172
Spencer, Phil, 193
St. George's Anglican Church, Kingston, 127, 128
St. Lawrence River, 36, 62
Stamford, Connecticut, 87
Staples, Owen, 23, 102
Staten Island, New York, 51
Statutes of Upper Canada, 96, 97, 136, 163, 164
Steel, Capt., 76, 112
Steel, Commodore J.W., 119
Stegmann, John, 51-59, 63, 64, 98, 107, 137, 138
Stony Point, 89
Stormont County, 43, 51, 135
storyboard, 175
Strachan, Rev. John, 141
Stuart, Rev. George Okill, 103, 119, 120, 130
Stuart, Rev. John, 119, 128
sucker moon, 18
sugar-making moon, 17
survey, 5, 18, 21, 49-52, 54-59, 66, 89, 101, 137-139, 156-158, 160-162, 164, 165, 167, 170, 178, 179, 185-187, 189, 190-193
surveyor, 21, 25, 51-54, 56, 57, 77, 98, 101, 137, 138, 143

survey licence, 156, 160, 161, 170, 186, 189, 190-193
survey sheets, 177, 185, 186
Surveyor General of Upper Canada, 52, 54, 121
Surveyor General's Office, 51, 52, 53, 55-57, 63, 133, 137

T

Thames River, 26
Thayendanega, 19
   see also Joseph Brant
Toronto, 3, 20, 21, 23, 25, 26, 35, 57, 101, 102, 137, 186
Toronto Carrying Place, 20
Toronto Harbour, 25
   see also York Harbour
Toronto Islands, 22, 104
Toronto of Old, 26
Toronto Star, 168, 191
Toronto Sun, 174
Toronto Telegram, 102
Toronto Township, 138
Toronto Yacht, 20, 71, 121, 134
Tortola, British Virgin Islands, 193
tow video camera, 155, 157, 158, 186-188, 190
Trent River, 18, 49, 88, 144
Trenton, 154
Trentonian, 186
Two Chimneys, 65, 107

U

Underwater Observation Services, 161
underwater survey clause, 160
United States, 28, 85, 134, 144
University of Ottawa, 154
Upper Canada, 3, 19, 21, 26, 30-33, 35, 45-49, 52, 54, 61-63, 65-67, 69, 74, 81, 85, 87, 97, 99, 104, 105, 118, 120, 122-125, 127-129, 131, 134, 136, 139, 140, 141, 143, 144, 146, 147
Upper Canada Gazette, 28, 39, 63, 96, 103, 122-124, 127, 136
US Navy, 157
Uxbridge Township, 137

V

Vaughan Township, 52, 64, 98
Victoria Hall, Cobourg, 138
video of 1989, 155, 156, 158-161, 174, 178, 185,
Vincent, Lt.-Col. John, 117, 118
Visa Gold Explorations, 191, 192
visibility, 161, 163, 164, 178, 187-190

W

Wabakinine, 85
Wabbekisheco, Chief, 13-15, 33, 34, 36, 37, 79, 143, 145
Walsh, Edward, 23, 69, 70
wampum belt, 15
War of 1812, 30, 33, 35, 72, 78, 131, 139, 143
War of Independence, 18, 19, 35, 43, 87
Weekes, William, 98, 107, 116, 135, 136
Wellers Bay, 105, 113, 114, 116, 164, 165, 171, 177
Wellington, Isaac M., 172
Wesleyan Methodist Church, 143
West Indies, 45, 139
Western District of Quebec, 45
Whistling Duck, 6, 15, 80, 81, 82
Whitby, 18
Whitby Township, 4, 12, 14, 22, 41, 57, 116, 137
wigwam, 10, 11, 12, 36, 37, 145
Willcocks, Joseph, 98, 99
Williams, George, 27
Wilmot, Samuel Street, 137, 138
Wilson, Benjamin, 10, 12, 14, 15
Windsor, Upper Canada, 131
Windsor Harbour, 18
Wright, Phil, 160
Wyatt, Charles Burton, 54
Wyatt, James, 54

Y

Yonge Street, Toronto, 27
York, 124

York, Upper Canada, 3, 7, 8, 10, 11, 13, 16-18, 20, 22-24, 26-36, 38-41, 44, 46-49, 51-57, 59, 61, 62, 64, 65, 69, 70-72, 74, 76, 79, 80-82, 85, 87, 88, 90, 93, 94, 96, 100, 101, 103, 107, 111, 117-121, 123, 127, 129, 133-138, 146
York County, 52, 65
York Harbour, 22, 23, 25-27, 101, 102, 105, 108
York, England, 28
Youngstown, New York, 45

Z

Zacharchuk, Walter, 168, 191

ABOUT THE AUTHOR

Dan Buchanan is the author of two history books, *Murder in the Family: The Dr. King Story* and *38 Hours to Montreal: William Weller and the Governor General's Race of 1840*, as well as the proprietor of a large genealogy web site, www.treesbydan.com. Well known as "The History Guy," he is an engaging storyteller with a special interest in early Ontario history, in particular the crucial but forgotten roles played by individuals in the development of Canadian society. As a historian, public speaker and author, he uses extensive research and keen objectivity, combined with a generally positive attitude about human nature, to tell lively stories that make history come alive.

Dan grew up on a farm near the village of Codrington, north of Brighton, Ontario, and spent several decades working in technical support in Kitchener, Calgary and Toronto before moving back to his home area in 2010. Retirement in 2016 allowed lots of time for a wide variety of activities, including the research, writing and publication of history books.

Dan supports many local history projects around Brighton, including the development of the Brighton Digital Archives and preservation of the Presqu'ile Point Lighthouse. He is co-founder of the popular annual Brighton History Week, which features public presentations and displays about Brighton-area history.

As "The History Guy," Dan regularly receives questions about local or family history. For more information about his work and activities, please visit www.danbuchananhistoryguy.com.